For Natalie

Hotel California

The True-Life Adventures
of Crosby, Stills, Nash,
Young, Mitchell, Taylor,
Browne, Ronstadt,
Geffen, the Eagles, and
Their Many Friends

BARNEY HOSKYNS

BICENTENNIAL
1807
WILEY
2007
BICENTENNIAL

John Wiley & Sons, Inc.

Copyright © 2006 by Barney Hoskyns. All rights reserved

Published by John Wiley & Sons, Inc., Hoboken, New Jersey
Published simultaneously in Canada

First published in different form in Great Britain in 2005 by Fourth Estate, an imprint of HarperCollins, as *Hotel California: Singer-songwriters and Cocaine Cowboys in the LA Canyons 1967–1976*.

Credits appear on page 307 and constitute an extension of this copyright page.

Wiley Bicentennial Logo: Richard J. Pacifico

Design and composition by Navta Associates, Inc.

For general information about our other products and services, please contact our Customer Care Department within the United States at (800) 762-2974, outside the United States at (317) 572-3993 or fax (317) 572-4002.

Wiley also publishes its books in a variety of electronic formats. Some content that appears in print may not be available in electronic books. For more information about Wiley products, visit our web site at www.wiley.com.

Library of Congress Cataloging-in-Publication Data:

Hoskyns, Barney, date.
   Hotel California : the true-life adventures of Crosby, Stills, Nash, Young, Mitchell, Taylor, Browne, Ronstadt, Geffen, the Eagles, and their many friends / Barney Hoskyns.
     p. cm.
   Includes bibliographical references (p.   ) and index.
   ISBN 978-0-471-73273-0 (cloth : alk. paper)
   ISBN 978-0-470-12777-3 (paper : alk. paper)
   1. Rock music—California, Southern—History and criticism. 2. Rock musicians—California, Southern. 3. Music trade—California, Southern—History. I. Title.
ML3534.3.H67 2006
781.66092'2794—dc22

                                               2005031918

Printed in the United States of America

10 9 8 7 6 5 4 3 2 1

I warn ya,
I'm coming back to California.
Lend me a shack
And I'll perform ya
All kinds of happy songs to ease your pain.
Think of all we will gain.

—David Ackles, "Oh, California!"

Contents

Photographs follow page 158

Preface

On a baking day in August 1971, five naked young men sit in a sauna in Laurel Canyon, Los Angeles. Four are musicians, three of them on the cusp of unimaginable success. Two are out-of-towners come to sunny Southern California to find fame, glory, girls. All are lean, rangy, good-looking—"like Jesus Christ after a month in Palm Springs," in the words of their friend Eve Babitz.

The fifth naked man in the sauna is the one who owns it: a short, skinny agent who's moved to L.A. from New York and established himself as a talent broker of fearsome repute. Among his clients are Joni Mitchell and Crosby, Stills, Nash, and Young. As the sweat pours off their suntanned limbs, David Geffen tells the four musicians—Glenn Frey, Don Henley, Jackson Browne, and Ned Doheny—about his plans for his record label. "I want to keep Asylum very small," he avers. "I'll never have more artists than I can fit in this sauna."

Twenty years later, Geffen will sell his second label—one he named after himself—for a cool $550 million. At the same time, the first *Greatest Hits* album by the Eagles—the group formed by Glenn Frey and Don Henley—will officially be pronounced the biggest-selling album of all time. "David took the crème de la crème from that scene," says Eve Babitz, "and signed them on the basis of their cuteness." Not bad work for an afternoon's Nordic ogling.

Hotel California traces the amazing journey from the dawn of the singer-songwriter era in the mid-1960s to the peak of the Eagles' success in the late '70s. It is the story of an unparalleled time and place, the first in-depth account of the scene—"the mythically tangled genealogy," in the words of writer John Rockwell—that swirled around the denim navel-gazers and cheesecloth millionaires of the Los Angeles canyons.

At a time when the influences of Crosby, Stills, Nash, and Young, Joni Mitchell, James Taylor, Jackson Browne, and the Eagles have never been more pervasive, the moment has come to reappraise this remarkable group of artists. It is also time to reevaluate the powerful movers and shakers who shaped their careers: men such as Geffen, the agent-turned-mogul who established an unparalleled power base of L.A. talent; his partner Elliot Roberts, manager of Young and Mitchell; and Irving Azoff, who made multimillionaires of the Eagles.

This is an epic tale of songs and sunshine, drugs and denim, genius and greed. The setting is the longhair Olympus of Laurel and adjacent canyons. It's about the flighty genius of Joni Mitchell, the about-faces of Neil Young, the drugged disintegration of David Crosby, Gram Parsons, Judee Sill, and others. It's about the myriad relationships, professional and personal, between these artists and the songs they wrote; about the love affairs between Joni and Graham Nash, Joni and James Taylor, Joni and Jackson Browne, Stephen Stills and Judy Collins, Linda Ronstadt and J. D. Souther. More than anything, it's a narrative of rise and fall—from "Take It Easy" to "Take It to the Limit," from the hootenanny innocence of boys and girls with acoustic guitars to the coked-out stadium-rock superstardom of the mid-1970s.

Inevitably the recollections of the story's characters are colored by their sometimes selective memories, not to mention their own agendas. As Tom Waits, who began his career on Geffen's Asylum label, puts it: "The trouble with history is that the people who really know what happened aren't talking and the people who don't . . . well, you can't shut 'em up."

Whatever the ultimate truth, I have over the past decade elicited invaluable reminiscences from the following artists, managers, executives, producers, session musicians, writers, photographers, and scenesters: Lou Adler, David Anderle, Peter Asher, Eve Babitz, Walter Becker, Joel Bernstein, Rodney Bingenheimer, Dan Bourgoise, Joe Boyd, Jackson Browne, Denny Bruce, Allison Caine, Gretchen Carpenter, Cher, Ry Cooder, Stan Cornyn, Chester Crill, Chris Darrow, John Delgatto, Pamela Des Barres, Henry Diltz, Dave DiMartino, Tony Dimitriades, Craig Doerge, Ned Doheny, Denny Doherty, Mickey Dolenz, Donald Fagen, Danny Fields, Bill Flanagan, Ben Fong-Torres, Kim Fowley, David Gates, David Geffen, Fred Goodman, Carl Gottlieb, Barry Hansen, Richie Hayward, Jan Henderson, Judy Henske, Chris Hillman, Suzi Jane Hokom, Jac Holzman, Bones Howe, Danny Hutton, Jonh Ingham, David Jackson, Billy James, Judy James, Rickie Lee Jones, Phil Kaufman, Nick Kent, Martin Kibbee, Sneaky Pete Kleinow, Russ Kunkel, Bruce Langhorne, Bernie Leadon, Arthur Lee, Steve Lester, Mark Leviton, Nils Lofgren, Roger McGuinn, Robert Marchese, Ted Markland, Frank Mazzola, Bob Merlis, Joni Mitchell, Essra Mohawk, Frazier Mohawk, Graham Nash, Randy Newman, Tom Nolan, Michael Ochs, Anita Pallenberg, Van Dyke Parks, Billy Payne, Robert Plant, Mel Posner, Neal Preston, Domenic Priore, Nancy Retchin, Keith Richards, Perry Richardson, Elliot Roberts, Jill Robinson, Linda Ronstadt, Ed Sanders, Bud Scoppa, the late Greg Shaw, Joe Smith, J. D. Souther, Ron Stone, Bill Straw, Matthew Sweet, the late Derek Taylor, Ted Templeman, Russ Titelman, the late Nik Venet, Joe Vitale, Mark Volman, Waddy Wachtel, Kurt Wagner, Tom Waits, June Walters, Lenny Waronker, Jimmy Webb, Jerry Wexler, Ian Whitcomb, Nurit Wilde, Tom Wilkes, Jerry Yester, and John York. My thanks to all for their time and their willingness to revisit the (sometimes painful) past.

A major debt is owed to two people in particular: my U.K. editor Matthew Hamilton, and Hannah Griffiths, briefly my agent before she switched horses to become an editor herself. They conceived the book in the first place and were dual sources of inspiration and encouragement. My gratitude also to Nicholas Pearson at Fourth Estate, and to Nick Davies, who shepherded the project through key later stages. Also to Merlin Cox for an exemplary U.K. copy edit.

Tom Miller of John Wiley & Sons in the United States had much to do with the shaping of this edition of the book. My thanks to Euan Thorneycroft at Curtis Brown, who seamlessly succeeded Hannah Griffiths, and to Sarah Lazin and Paula Balzer at Sarah Lazin Books in New York.

For assistance and facilitation, often beyond any possible call of duty, thanks to the following: the indefatigable Harvey Kubernik; Henry Diltz and Nurit Wilde for their timelessly evocative images; Debbie Kruger for trawling through Henry's considerable archives and unearthing unseen treasures; to Eve Kakassy for getting those and other images to me; Jim McCrary; Dede at Redfern's Picture Agency; Johnny Black, esteemed keeper of the Rocksource Archive; Billy James, who corrected factual errors and made many helpful comments; Roger Burrows, who generously burned CDs for me; Eddi Fiegel, Barry Miles, Matthew Greenwald, John Einarson, Richard Bosworth, Paul Scanlon, Kevin Kennedy, Richard Cromelin, Steven Rosen, Marc Weingarten, Susan Compo, Carrie Steers, Jonh Ingham, Neil Scaplehorn, Richard Wootton, Rob Partridge, Val Brown, Oscar Thompson, Annene Kaye, Diedre Duewel, Tony Keys, Mark Pringle, Martin Colyer, William Higham, Paul Lester, Allan Jones, Ted Alvy, Dale Carter, Rod Tootell, Mick Houghton, Davitt Sigerson, Brendan Mullen, Andy Schwartz, Mick Brown, Nic de Grunwald, Erik James, Catherine Heaney, Silvia Crompton, Julian Humphries, Michelle Kort, Jon Savage, Johnny Marr, Ian MacArthur, John Tobler, and Pete Frame. And a special thank you to Simon McGuire, the heppest cat in all of Glendale.

1

Expecting to Fly

The businessmen crowded around
They came to hear the golden sound

—Neil Young

Impossible Dreamers

For decades Los Angeles was synonymous with Hollywood—the silver screen and its attendant deities. L.A. meant palm trees and the Pacific Ocean, despotic directors and casting couches, a factory of illusion. L.A. was "the coast," cut off by hundreds of miles of desert and mountain ranges. In those years Los Angeles wasn't acknowledged as a music town, despite producing some of the best jazz and rhythm and blues of the '40s and '50s. In 1960 the music business was still centered in New York, whose denizens regarded L.A. as kooky and provincial at best.

Between the years 1960 and 1965 a remarkable shift occurred. The sound and image of Southern California began to take over, replacing Manhattan as the hub of American pop music. Producer Phil Spector took the hit-factory ethos of New York's Brill Building

1

songwriting stable to L.A. and blew up the teen-pop sound to epic proportions. Entranced by Spector, local suburban misfit Brian Wilson wrote honeyed hymns to beach and car culture that reinvented the Golden State as a teenage paradise. Other L.A. producers followed suit. In 1965, singles recorded in Los Angeles occupied the No. 1 spot for an impressive twenty weeks, compared to just one for New York.

On and around Sunset, west of old Hollywood before one reached the manicured pomp of Beverly Hills, clubs and coffee-houses began to proliferate. Although L.A. had always been geared to the automobile, the Strip now became a living neighborhood—and a mecca for dissident youth. Epicenter for L.A.'s dawning folk scene was Doug Weston's Troubadour club, south of the Strip at 9081 Santa Monica Boulevard. Weston had opened his original Troubadour on nearby La Cienega Boulevard, but had jumped across to Santa Monica east of Doheny Drive in 1961. The more commercial-minded members of the folkie crowd went with him. Typical of the tribe was a cocky kid from Santa Barbara called David Crosby. A lecherous teddy bear with a playful brain, David warbled plangent protest songs in emulation of Woody Guthrie.

For all the lip service it paid to folk protest, the Troubadour always had one beady eye on success. The clubhouse for the more commercial folk music epitomized by the Kingston Trio, it rapidly became a hootenanny (small gathering of folk singers) hotbed of vaunting ambition. Pointedly different was Ed Pearl's club, the Ash Grove, which had opened at 8162 Melrose Avenue in July 1958. L.A.'s self-appointed bastion of tradition, the Ash Grove held fast to notions of not selling out. It was where you went to hear Doc Watson and Sleepy John Estes—blues and bluegrass veterans rescued from oblivion by earnest revivalists. "The Ash Grove was where you heard the roots, traditional stuff," says Jackson Browne, then an Orange County teenager. "Lots of people went to both clubs, but you didn't stand much of a chance of getting hired at the Ash Grove."

Another Ash Grove regular was Linda Ronstadt, who had deep, soulful eyes and a big, gutsy voice. She'd grown up in Arizona dreaming of freewheelin' Bob Dylan. During the Easter break of

1964 Linda followed Tucson beatnik Bob Kimmel out to the coast, moving into a small Victorian house on the beach at Santa Monica. "The whole scene was still very sweet and innocent," Ronstadt recalls. "It was all about sitting around in little embroidered dresses and listening to Elizabethan folk ballads, and that's how I thought it was always going to be." Among Ronstadt's contemporaries were obsessive young folk-blues apprentices: kids such as Ryland Cooder, John Fahey, Al Wilson. Some of them got so good that they were even allowed to *play* at the club. Cooder, sixteen years old in 1963, backed folk-pop singers Pamela Polland and Jackie DeShannon. The nascent Canned Heat—a blues band formed by Wilson after Fahey had introduced him to man-mountain singer Bob Hite—played at the club.

"The scene was just tiny," Ry Cooder reflects. "It was by and for people who were players, not for the general public. Ed Pearl was some sort of socialist, whereas Doug Weston was just an opportunist clubowner. We'd go down in the evening, mostly on the weekends. At that point Ed must have had a supply line, because he had Sonny Terry and Brownie McGhee and he had Lightnin' Hopkins and Mississippi John Hurt and then Skip James. Sleepy John Estes was the one I was waiting to see. He seemed the most remote and peculiar—and I'd assumed dead."

It was no coincidence, perhaps, that record companies in New York were waking up to what snobs called the "Left Coast." Paul Rothchild, a hip Artists and Repertoire (A&R) man with Jac Holzman's classy and eclectic Elektra label, flew out to L.A. to scout the 1964 Folk Festival at UCLA. Smitten with what he found, Rothchild began to commute regularly between the East and West coasts. "L.A. was less the promised land than the untilled field," says Holzman, himself entranced by Southern California. "We'd picked over the East Coast pretty well."

Columbia Records, a far bigger entity than Elektra, was also casting a wider net from its Manhattan headquarters. If its meat-and-potatoes income came from such pop and middle-of-the-road (MOR) acts as Patti Page and Andy Williams, the label also was home to Bob Dylan and Miles Davis. On New Year's Day 1964, Columbia publicist Billy James flew to Los Angeles to begin work as the company's Manager of Information Services on the West Coast. Already in his late twenties, Billy was pure beat generation, his sensibility shaped by Kerouac and Ginsberg. Thrilled at the way pop music was becoming a vibrant force in American culture, he plunged into the scene at the Troubadour and the Ash Grove. "Billy was a wonderful guy," says record producer Barry Friedman. "He was a charming, well-read, interesting fellow. In some ways I think he played the corporate game very well."

James also felt the seismic impact of the Beatles' first visit to America. The Liverpool group had done something no Americans were able to do: legitimize pop stardom for hipsters who despised idols such as Fabian and Frankie Avalon. All of a sudden young folkies such as David Crosby saw that you could write your own songs, draw on rock and roll, rhythm and blues, and country music and *still* be stampeded by girls. "The Beatles validated rock and roll," says Lou Adler, then an L.A. producer and label owner. "People could listen to them knowing that these guys were really writing their songs."

"What started happening was that these young, talented kids would band together," says Henry (Tad) Diltz of the Modern Folk Quartet (MFQ). "It was like double or triple the excitement." At the Troubadour and the Unicorn coffeehouse, opened by local promoter Herb Cohen in 1957 on Sunset Boulevard, David Crosby hung around the MFQ, envious of their ganglike camaraderie. Soon he was fraternizing with other folkies who'd gravitated to California in search of something they couldn't find elsewhere. Jim McGuinn, a slim and cerebral graduate of Chad Mitchell's Trio—and of a stint in the employ of Bobby Darin—was slipping Beatles songs into his hoot sets at the Troubadour. Gene Clark, a handsome, haunted-looking balladeer from Missouri, finished up his apprenticeship in the L.A.-based New Christy Minstrels. Shy and slightly bewildered, Clark approached McGuinn after one of his Beatle-friendly sets and told him he dug what he was trying to do. "You wanna start a duo?" Clark asked.

McGuinn had crossed David Crosby's path before and was wary of him. Clark, however, figured Crosby's velvety tenor was just the additional harmonic element they needed. One night at the Trouba-dour, Crosby took Tad Diltz over to meet McGuinn and Clark. With a smug grin Crosby announced they were going to form a group. "Crosby and McGuinn and Clark were in the lobby of the Troub every night in 1964," says folk singer Jerry Yester. "They'd sit there with a twelve-string guitar, just writing songs." Taken up by manager Jim Dickson, a worldly and well-connected veteran of the folk and jazz scene in Hollywood, Crosby, Clark, and McGuinn rounded out the lineup with drummer Michael Clarke and bluegrass-bred bassist Chris Hillman. From the outset the band was conceived as an elec-tric rock and roll group. "At some point the groups started plugging in their instruments," says Henry Diltz. "Doug Weston saw the MFQ rehearsing at the Troub with amps and was horrified."

"It was kinda like a tadpole growing legs," says Jerry Yester, briefly a member of the Lovin' Spoonful. "We just got closer and closer to being a rock band. Everybody else was doing the same thing—raiding the pawnshops for electric guitars. Inside of a year, the whole face of West L.A. changed." Secretly, Chris Hillman was horrified by the electrification of folk. "Chris told me he'd joined this rock and roll band," says bassist David Jackson. "He said it with this real sheepish look on his face, like he was betraying the cause."

After one single on Elektra as the Beefeaters, the group became the Byrds, complete with quaint Olde English spelling. Signed to Columbia, the band cut Bob Dylan's druggy "Mr. Tambourine Man" with producer Terry Melcher and a bunch of sessionmen. Released in April 1965, after the group had established themselves at gone-to-seed Sunset Strip club Ciro's, the single went to No. 1 in June and instantly enshrined the new electric folk sound. "You mainly just went to parties and to hear people play," says Jackson Browne. "But then the Byrds happened, and you heard them on the radio and they had a *huge* pop hit."

"We all came over and went, 'Ahhh! They got record contracts!'" said Linda Ronstadt. "I mean, as far as we were concerned they had made it, just because they had a record contract. David Crosby had a new suede jacket; that was affluence beyond description."

Pop life in L.A. would never be the same again.

Claims to Fame

Paying close attention to the Byrds' ascent were local industry figures, many of them caught off-guard. Lou Adler, the canny and highly focused L.A. entrepreneur who'd turned nightclub guitarist Johnny Rivers into a million-selling star, watched as "folk-rock" caught fire in California.

"The influx of the Greenwich Village folkies in 1964 and 1965 was very important," Adler reflects. "Music changed drastically. When Dylan plugged in his guitar he took a lot of people from the folk field to the rock and roll field. Folk-rock swept out the teen idols, and it gave pop a hip political edge." With his new Dunhill label, Adler homed in on folk-rock. Former surf-pop tunesmith P. F. Sloan was given a hat, a pair of Chelsea boots, and a copy of *Bringing It All Back Home* and instructed to write some protest songs. He returned a few days later with "Eve of Destruction," duly recorded by ex–New Christy Minstrel Barry McGuire. "Folk + Rock + Protest = Dollars," noted *Billboard* after the song topped the charts.

One afternoon, Barry McGuire brought a new folk group along to an Adler recording session at Hollywood's Western Recorders studio. John Phillips, their leader, had tried his luck in L.A. some years before, but his timing hadn't been right. He'd even married Michelle Gilliam, a beautiful California blonde who sang with him alongside Denny Doherty and Cass Elliott, former members of Greenwich Village group the Mugwumps. Now here they were in L.A., chancing everything on a move to the new promised land. The Mamas and the Papas' moment eventually came. Breaking into the pealing harmonies of Phillips's "Monday, Monday," they followed up with "I've Got a Feeling," "Once Was a Time," and "Go Where You Wanna Go." Shrewdly, they left the best for last: the soaring anthem "California Dreamin'." Adler was duly blown away. Released late in 1965, "Dreamin'" summed up what the rest of the nation was already feeling about the Golden State, except that this time it wasn't the clichéd California of surfing and blondes and hot rods that was being hymned—it was the blossoming hippie milieu of the Sunset Strip and its bucolic annex Laurel Canyon.

After "California Dreamin'," John and Michelle Phillips did what all self-respecting musicians were doing in Los Angeles: they moved from a decaying dump in the West Hollywood flatlands to a funky pad on Lookout Mountain Avenue, up in the canyon, high above it all. Cass Elliott, born Naomi Cohen in Baltimore, followed in their wake. A rotund earth mama, she began to hold court in the canyon in what was a kind of folk-pop salon. Among her close friends was David Crosby, with whom she'd bonded on a folk tour two years before.

Observing the success of both the Byrds and the Mamas and the Papas were the savvy executives at Warner-Reprise Records in Burbank, north of Hollywood. It was a testament to their acumen that the conjoined labels were still in business at all. Warner Brothers Records, launched merely because the rancorous Jack Warner thought his movie studio should have a music division, had nearly gone under just three years earlier. Nor had Reprise, bought from Frank Sinatra in a deal that was laughably generous to the singer, launched promisingly. But Morris "Mo" Ostin, who'd come into the Warner fold as Sinatra's accountant, turned out to have instincts and ears. "The company had learned some good lessons coming out of the Dean Martin era," says Stan Cornyn, who became head of creative services at the company. Warner-Reprise had missed the Byrds and the Mamas and the Papas but was swift to sign the Kinks and Petula Clark to North America. "We got on the London express, because we weren't getting fed artists here," says Joe Smith, who joined Warner in 1961. "We had to go dig out our own and sign them for North America."

Mo and Joe were determined not to let the next Byrds pass them by. Helping them was a young A&R man named Lenny Waronker. "It's amazing how little I paid attention to the Byrds," Lenny says today. "I'm embarrassed to even talk about it, but we were so focused in our own world." Waronker was the son of Si Waronker, founder of L.A. label Liberty Records. He'd got his grounding at Metric Music, Liberty's publishing arm, overseeing a stable of songwriting talent that was the closest California came to New York's Brill Building. Among Metric's writers—Jackie DeShannon, David Gates, P. J. Proby, Glen Campbell—was Lenny's boyhood friend Randy, nephew of movie composers Alfred and Lionel Newman. "We were a kind of poor man's Carole King and Barry Mann and Neil Sedaka,"

Newman recalls of his Metric days. "I was trying to do the same things as Carole and I knew I wasn't doing them as well."

"We used to crank out songs for singers like Dean Martin," says David Gates, who packed his wife and kids into a battered Cadillac in 1962 and drove from Oklahoma to California. "Seeing some nice songs go down the drain, you started to think, maybe I ought to do them myself."

"Dylan exploded the universe of folk songwriting," says Jackson Browne. "Suddenly there was a whole wealth of ideas out there, and you could discuss *anything* in a song. You also had Jackie DeShannon on pop TV shows talking about songs she'd written herself. Normally you wouldn't even wonder where the songs had come from, so it was really something to learn that Jackie had written them."

When an opening at Warner Brothers came in April 1966, Waronker jumped on it, exploiting the fact that Joe Smith had done business with his father. Ostin and Smith became a formidable duo: Mo the reclusive mastermind, Joe the more gregarious public face of the company. Lenny, shy like Mo, fitted in perfectly behind the scenes.

There were others, too. Ostin's greatest gift was delegating taste, cultivating an inner circle of trusted talent-spotters. More often than not these men were mavericks. Bernard Alfred "Jack" Nitzsche, who'd come from Michigan on a bus in 1955 and had arranged the early '60s hits of Phil Spector, was a difficult and belligerent man but a typical Ostin confidant. He had given Reprise one of its earliest hits, the 1963 instrumental "The Lonely Surfer."

Another man who had Mo's ear was Derek Taylor, a suave Liverpudlian who'd moved to L.A. after working as the Beatles' press officer back home in England. Dapper and witty, Taylor was a conduit to British talent, but he also was doing press for the Byrds and the Beach Boys. "I had 2½ percent of the Byrds and no fee," Taylor remembered. "That became quite a lot of money. I didn't really have to do a lot for them except express what I wanted to. Billy James had really done all the work, but he was such a generous soul he just said, 'Over to you.'"

By the spring of 1966, Warner-Reprise was poised to strike—to become a true power on the West Coast. "New York itself was going through enormous financial problems and became very hostile to the music business," says Joe Smith, who'd moved to L.A. in 1960 to work for a local record distributor. "So a lot of it shifted out here. California was now regarded by people as the place to go."

Among the freewheeling folkies who pitched up in Los Angeles in the late summer of 1965 was Stephen Stills. A tenacious Texan with thinning blond hair, Stills had spent time in a military academy and brought the discipline of the place to bear on his musical career. He quickly found the Troubadour more receptive to his talent than Greenwich Village. Hooking up with folk scenester Dickie Davis, he began networking, befriending several key people. Among them was Van Dyke Parks, a diminutive genius who looked like a child and spoke in a camp Mississippi drawl.

Parks and Stills knocked about together, sharing a love of Latin and Caribbean music. Parks was fascinated by calypso; Stills had spent part of his adolescence in Costa Rica. But it was Barry Friedman, former carny and fire-eater, who started making waves for Stephen. A native Angeleno, Friedman had done publicity for the Troubadour. When the Beatles played the Hollywood Bowl in August 1964, he was the publicist for the show. "Stephen ended up at my place," Friedman says. "I guess the floor was softer or something. He was pretty focused. He said he wanted to put a band together, and I thought that would be fun to do. So we just started finding people and phoning around."

Van Dyke Parks himself passed on the opportunity, as did a young Warren Zevon, then eking out a living as one half of folk duo lyme & cybelle. Stills's abrasive personality may have had something to do with their reluctance. "Stephen was definitely talented," says Nurit Wilde, a photographer and Sunset Strip scenester of the time, "but he was not a nice guy then and he continued being a jerk as long as I knew him." Drawing blanks in L.A., Stills summoned Richie Furay from New York, lying to him that he had a recording deal in place. Furay, a friendlier soul who conformed closer to the archetype of the optimistic folk singer, arrived in California in late 1965.

Parks remained pals with Stills but made his basic living from sessions and arrangements. His work with Brian Wilson on the Beach Boys' *Dumb Angel/Smile*—the unfinished psychedelic masterpiece that could have been America's *Sgt. Pepper*—had everybody in L.A. talking. Elbowed out of the Beach Boys picture in April 1967 by the play-it-safe Mike Love, Parks was devastated. Then a call from Lenny Waronker got his attention. Parks knew Lenny was a rich kid like Terry Melcher, son of actress Doris Day, but it was obvious he was as determined as Mo Ostin and Joe Smith to make Warner-Reprise a home of credible and innovative artists.

Not long after Waronker joined the company, Joe Smith took him up to San Francisco to evaluate the catalog of Autumn Records, a label Warner was proposing to buy. Cofounded by larger-than-life deejay Tom Donahue, Autumn had a roster of promising pop groups that Smith fancied: the Beau Brummels, the Tikis, the Mojo Men, and more. For Waronker this was an instant opportunity to experiment with ready-made pop groups. Along with Parks he brought in Randy Newman and Leon Russell, an Oklahoma writer and arranger who'd worked on hits by Gary Lewis & the Playboys. The records they wrote and produced at Warner—particularly those by the newly created Harper's Bizarre—were interesting and significant. They pointed backward to the Brill Building and early Beach Boys pop era, but were also in synch with the complex orchestral psychedelia of the Beach Boys' lost *Smile*. "We wanted hits," Waronker told writer Gene Sculatti, "but we wanted them on our own terms."

Hit versions of Stills's "Sit Down, I Think I Love You" (by the Mojo Men) and Paul Simon's "59th Street Bridge Song" (by Harper's Bizarre) helped build a creative nucleus around Waronker. Following Mo Ostin's lead in making A&R the primary focus at Warner, Lenny gradually introduced—and blended together—the company's backroom talent: Newman, Parks, Russell, Templeman, Ron Elliott, and guitarists Ry Cooder and Russ Titelman. "We never made profit the thrust," says Joe Smith. "It sounds very self-serving, but that was the reputation we wanted. Van Dyke we were in awe of. This little drug-ridden crazy kid from the South was so talented."

Yet Waronker also could sense that the days of pop groups such as Harper's Bizarre, in their matching suits and ties, were all but done. The new template for bands was the Rolling Stones, who looked and sounded more threatening than the Beatles ever did. Here was the ultimate gang of rebels, openly flaunting their sexuality and drug use.

Meanwhile, Mo Ostin, who'd already signed the Kinks for North America, was checking out another U.K. export, a flamboyant guitarist born and bred in the United States. Jimi Hendrix wasn't Waronker's personal style, but he rightly identified him as the avatar of a new sensibility in pop—or rock, as it was increasingly being called.

A native Angeleno, Waronker was himself more intrigued by a new strain in the L.A. sound: a countryish, back-to-the-roots feel heard in songs by the Byrds and other groups. "My goal was very simple," he says. "It was to find a rock band that sounded like the Everly Brothers."

So You Want to Be a Rock and Roll Star

"I'm sitting in Barney's Beanery," says Denny Doherty of the Mamas and the Papas, "and in walks Stephen Stills. He looks kinda down, so I ask him what he's doing. He says, 'Fuck all, man, I ain't doin' nothin'.' Two or three weeks later I walk into the Whisky and *Bam!*— there he is onstage with a band. I said to him, 'What the fuck? Did you add water and get an instant band?'"

Early in April 1966, Stills and Richie Furay were stuck in a Sunset Strip traffic jam in Barry Friedman's Bentley. As they sat in the car, Stephen spotted a 1953 Pontiac hearse with Ontario plates on the other side of the street. "I'll be damned if that ain't Neil Young," Stills said. Friedman executed an illegal U-turn and pulled up behind the hearse. One of rock's great serendipities had just occurred.

Young, a lanky Canadian, had just driven all the way from Detroit in the company of bassist Bruce Palmer. They'd caught the bug that was drawing hundreds of other pop wannabes to the West Coast. "I didn't know what . . . I was doing," Young said. "We were just going like lemmings." A week later Stills had the band he'd fantasized about for months. With drummer Dewey Martin recruited from bluegrass group the Dillards, the lineup was complete: three singer-guitarists (Stills, Furay, Young) and a better rhythm section than the Byrds. Van Dyke Parks spotted a steamroller with the name "Buffalo Springfield," and everyone loved it. It was perfect, conjuring a sense of American history and landscape that interested all of them—Neil Young in particular.

Young was skinny and quiet and more than a little freaked out by the bright automotive sprawl of Los Angeles. His intense dark eyes in a face framed by long sideburns mesmerized women. "Neil was a very sweet fellow," says Nurit Wilde, who'd known him in Toronto. "He was sick and he was vulnerable. Women wanted to feed him and take care of him." At least Young and Palmer didn't have to sleep in the hearse anymore. When Stephen and Richie took them over to Barry Friedman's house on Fountain Avenue, a floor and mattresses were proffered. "The whole thing was . . . a tremendous relief," Young told his father, Scott. "Barry gave us a dollar a day each for food. All we had to do was keep practicing."

"People thought Neil was moody, but he didn't seem moody to *me*," says Friedman. "He seemed like just another guy with good songs, though he did have a funny voice." To Young, the affable Richie Furay was "the easiest to like" of the Springfield members, though he told *World Countdown News* that Richie's "hair should be longer." Furay had a small room in a Laurel Canyon pad belonging to Mark Volman of successful L.A. pop group the Turtles. "Our living room was the frequent meeting place for Stephen, Neil, and Richie," Volman recalls. "Dickie Davis was always coming by. With the Springfield, a lot of it was created around the energy of Dickie."

Between Davis and Friedman, the Springfield's career took off with a flying start. Their first performance was at the Troubadour on April 11, barely a week after their formation. Little more than a public rehearsal, the set was the prelude to a minitour in support of the Byrds, whose Chris Hillman was an early and ardent champion. To the other Byrds, the Springfield came as a galvanizing shock. Within weeks the group had developed a fearsome live sound that was rooted in the twin-engine guitar blitz of Stills and Young. "The Springfield live was very obviously a guitar duel," says Henry Diltz, who took the group's first publicity shots on Venice Beach. "They'd talk back and forth to each other with their guitars and it would escalate from there."

Friedman wanted to sign the Springfield to Elektra, but Jac Holzman wasn't the only record executive interested in the band. Nor was Friedman the only person keen to manage them. When the Springfield returned from their tour, Dickie Davis introduced them to a pair of Hollywood hustlers named Charlie Greene and Brian Stone. The duo had hit town five years before, ambitious publicists who set up a phony office on a studio lot. With Greene as the front-man schmoozer, Stone hovered in the background and controlled the cash flow. Inspired by flamboyant svengalis such as Phil Spector, Charlie and Brian rode around in limos and played pop tycoons.

For Van Dyke Parks, schemers such as Greene and Stone changed L.A.'s innocent folk-rock vibe. "There was a severe competitive atmosphere in this scene," Parks recalled. "The Beatles had exploded and the youth market had defined itself." Greene and Stone set about wowing the Springfield, fueling Stephen Stills's fantasies of stardom. And they were ruthless in cutting Barry Friedman out of the picture. Taking him for a limo ride, the duo sat Friedman between them. Minutes into the journey, Greene quietly placed a pistol on Friedman's thigh. By the end of the trip Barry had signed over his rights to Buffalo Springfield on a hot dog napkin. "People like that do what they do," Friedman says. "I don't, though I'm still waiting for a check. I read in Neil's book that he owes me money, but he must have lost my address."

When Lenny Waronker saw the Springfield live they were wearing cowboy hats, with Neil Young positioned to one side in a fringed Comanche shirt. He went berserk: "I thought, 'Oh, my God, this is *it!*'" Waronker got Jack Nitzsche interested early on: "I needed weight behind me, and Jack had that weight. I talked to him about coproducing the group." Nitzsche instantly bonded with Neil Young, intuitively recognizing a fellow square peg in L.A.'s round hole. "Jack really loved Neil," says Judy Henske. "He told me Neil was the greatest artist that had ever been in Hollywood." Young, aware of Jack's pedigree, reciprocated. Nitzsche's approval wasn't enough, however, to land the Buffalo Springfield in Burbank. Greene and Stone turned to Atlantic's Ahmet Ertegun in New York. Upping Warners' offer of $10,000 to $22,000, Ertegun was only too delighted to whisk the group from under Mo Ostin's nose, assigning them to Atlantic's affiliated Atco label.

By the time Greene and Stone were in the studio with the Springfield, having imposed themselves as producers of the band's Atlantic debut, it was too late. The group's career was obviously in the hands of charlatans. For the naive Neil Young especially, the sense of scales falling from the eyes was almost too much to take. "There were a lot of problems with the Springfield," he later said. "Groupies, drugs, shit. I'd never seen people like that before. I remember being haunted suddenly by this whole obsession with 'How do I fit in here? Do I like this?'" Compounding Neil's unease was the growing competitiveness between him and Stills—the band wasn't big enough for both of them. Neil acknowledged and respected Stephen's drive and versatility, but the guy's ego—the presumption that Buffalo Springfield was *his* group—began to grate. Although Buffalo Springfield's first Atco single was Young's fey and slightly pretentious "Nowadays Clancy Can't Even Sing," Stills was soon coming down hard on Young's material. To the consternation of the hippie women who nursed Neil's emotional wounds, Stephen undermined Neil at every turn.

Robin Lane, briefly Neil's girlfriend, recalled Stills storming into the small apartment his bandmate had rented. Irate because Neil had missed a rehearsal, Stephen picked up Lane's guitar and only just restrained himself from smashing it over Neil's head. "You're ruining my career!" Stills screamed at the cowering Canadian. Dickie Davis thought it no coincidence that Young had the first of several epileptic fits just a month after the Springfield formed. During the band's residency at the Whisky in the groovy summer of 1966, the sight of Young thrashing around onstage in a seizure was not uncommon. The real truth was that Stills and Young were both driven and egomaniacal—Stills's pigheadedness was merely more overt. Neil, a classic passive aggressive, stifled his resentments and licked his wounds in private. "We know each other," Stills would later say of his relationship with Young. "There was always a kind of alienation to the people around us. They are old things that no amount of analyzing and psychotherapy and all of that stuff can wash away."

For all the conflicts, Buffalo Springfield represented a new chapter in the unfolding narrative of L.A. pop. They were hip and genre-splicing, angry young men with talent and attitude. Last of the folk-pop groups, they also were one of the new electric rock bands. Now they even had a hit record. After Stills watched the LAPD break up a demonstration march on the Sunset Strip on November 12, 1966, he wrote "For What It's Worth (Stop, Hey What's That Sound)." With its lines about paranoia striking deep and "the man" taking you away, it was as cheesy as Barry McGuire's "Eve of Destruction." But unlike Neil's singles, it cracked the Top 10.

Like the Springfield, the Byrds were riven by internal feuds and resentments. The enmity between David Crosby and Jim (now Roger) McGuinn was plain to see. McGuinn, lean and aloof, was the antithesis of the chubby, hedonistic Crosby in his hat and cape. McGuinn's cerebral voice and glinting guitar runs had defined the Byrds' sound, but Crosby was determined to insert his more rambling and flowery ballads into the mix. "David was a bit of a brat," says Billy James. "There was this contentiousness about him. His hackles got up very quickly." The Byrds' best writer, meanwhile, was sandwiched between Crosby and McGuinn. The group's tambourine-rustling front man, Gene Clark was paradoxically its most introspective member. He had supplied the B side of "Mr. Tambourine Man" and written the most songs on the first album. As a result—to the envious indignation of his bandmates—publishing royalty checks were pouring into his mailbox. Soon he was running around town in a maroon Ferrari.

Alcoholic from an early age, Clark was a troubled soul. In contrast to McGuinn's and Crosby's songs, his folk-throwback ballads sounded grave and timeless, closer to the soulful grandeur of a Roy Orbison than to the amphetamine poetics of a Bob Dylan. The bittersweet "Set You Free This Time," a failed single from *Turn! Turn! Turn!*, was the template for several folk-country masterpieces Clark would record. Crosby recognized that Gene was "an emotional projector on a huge and powerful level," but it didn't stop him and McGuinn from preying on his insecurities. "In the beginning, David was very musically intimidated, so he tried to intimidate others," said Jim Dickson. "He shook [Gene's] sense of time by telling him he was off." Early in 1966, Clark decided he'd had enough—enough of the sudden fame, enough of the tensions.

"After 'Eight Miles High' I felt we had a direction to go in that might have been absolutely incredible," Clark said in 1977. "We could have taken it from there, but I felt because of the confusion and egos—the young, successful egos—we were headed in a direction that wouldn't have that importance or impact." One afternoon in March 1966, Barry Friedman and drummer friend Denny Bruce went to score some pot from a friend named Jeannie "Butchie" Cho. Sitting in her Laurel Canyon living room was none other than Clark. He had black bags under his eyes and looked ravaged.

Clark was in crisis, pouring out his heart to Butchie, saying he was due to go on tour with the Byrds the next day. "I can't do it," he kept repeating. "I can't see myself on that airplane tomorrow." Butchie said that nobody left a successful group. "I don't give a shit," Gene insisted. "I don't like what it's doing to my head." Clark did make it to LAX but started screaming as the plane taxied to the runway. The Byrds flew to New York as a quartet. The official announcement of Clark's exit came in July.

The departure only increased the tension between McGuinn and Crosby, even as the Byrds propelled folk-rock into a new psychedelic realm with *Fifth Dimension*. By the summer of 1967, relations between the two were severely strained. McGuinn approached the Byrds' music with what Derek Taylor described as "a fussy schoolmarm attitude." Crosby, enamored of the wild new scene up in San Francisco, felt the Byrds had become square. He wanted to be in a dynamic band like the Buffalo Springfield or the Jefferson Airplane. He was seeing an increasing amount of Stephen Stills, whose sheer appetite for playing and jamming thrilled him. "I remember hearing all these horror stories about what an arrogant asshole David was," said Stills, often accused of the same trait. "But when I met him I found he was basically just as shy as I was and making up for it with a lot of aggressive behavior."

Crosby had interests besides music. One was hanging out with scenesters such as Cass Elliott. The other, despite the shame he felt about his roly-poly physique, was sleeping with any woman who offered herself to him. "David was charming around chicks," says Nurit Wilde, who lived around the corner from Crosby in Laurel Canyon. "But there was a revolving door with him—one girl in, one girl out. And if a girl got pregnant, he was mean to her and dumped her." By the summer of 1967 Crosby had become so obnoxious that McGuinn and Hillman could take no more of him. After he used the

Byrds' appearance at the Monterey Pop Festival to launch into a tirade about the Warren Report on the Kennedy assassination—and then compounded that by appearing onstage with the Buffalo Springfield—the decision was made to ax him.

In October, McGuinn and Hillman drove in their Porsches to Crosby's new place on Lisbon Lane in Beverly Glen. "They drove up," Crosby said in a 1971 radio interview, "and said that I was terrible and crazy and unsociable and a bad writer and a terrible singer and I made horrible records and that they would do much better without me." Shaken as he was, the firing came as a relief. Accepting a $10,000 payoff from the Byrds, he was ready to cut loose and take time out. An obsession with sailing got him thinking about boats. He hung with Mama Cass, now holding court in a funky new abode on Summit Ridge off Mulholland Drive. A bold, narcotic adventuress, Cass was even dabbling in heroin and pharmaceutical opiates—a major no-no in the LSD and marijuana community of that time. "[Smack] was always the bad drug," Crosby would write. "It got a little more open around the time that Cass and I were doing it, but it wasn't something you told people."

Crosby was the nexus of a nascent scene, the supercool spider at the center of a web of new relationships. "He was the main cultural luminary to me," says Jackson Browne, then struggling on the scene. "He had this legendary VW bus with a Porsche engine in it, and that summed him up—*a hippie with power!*" For Bronx-born Ron Stone, owner of a hippie boutique on Santa Monica Boulevard that Crosby regularly frequented, the ex-Byrd *was* the scene. "The Byrds were *the* California band of the time," he says, "and there he was, the rebel within that group, tossed out on his ass. There was no question that it all spun around him and Cass."

If Crosby used the Monterey Pop festival to sabotage his position in the Byrds, he was nonetheless a key presence on that seminal weekend in June 1967. Bridging a sometimes insurmountable gulf between the Los Angeles faction behind the event and the Haight-Ashbury bands that dominated it, David hobnobbed with everyone from an edgy Paul Kantner to a diaphanous Brian Jones. Of all the L.A. stars he was the one who'd responded the quickest to what was happening in the Bay Area.

The brainchild of Lou Adler and John Phillips—whose Mamas and the Papas hits had made both men rich—Monterey Pop was effectively a rock and roll trade show masquerading as a love-in. Wresting control of the festival away from L.A.-based paper fortune heir Alan Pariser, Adler and Phillips transformed it into a seismic event starring as many of their superstar friends and contacts as they could cram into one long weekend. Also present at the event were the key rock executives of the day: Clive Davis of Columbia, Ahmet Ertegun of Atlantic, Mo Ostin and Joe Smith of Warner-Reprise. Following Mo's acquisition of Jimi Hendrix, Joe had signed the Grateful Dead, the quintessential Haight-Ashbury band. Clive Davis now picked up Big Brother & the Holding Company, featuring Janis Joplin.

Country Joe McDonald described Monterey as "a total ethical sellout of everything that we'd dreamed of." Perhaps it was. But it was also the inevitable, unavoidable moment when the underground went mainstream. "The San Francisco groups had a very bad taste in their mouths about L.A. commercialism," Adler admitted decades later. "And it's true that we were a business-minded industry. It wasn't a hobby."

It was the very tension between L.A. and S.F. that made Monterey so fascinating. "I saw everything change there," Judy James, wife of Billy James, says. "It was as if everyone went, 'Wow! We're no longer preaching to the converted.' They walked into this candy store of drugs and sex and saw that people would buy the music as the sound track to that."

"The industry totally changed after Monterey," says Tom Wilkes, who designed the famous poster for the festival. "The festival was basically a peaceful protest against the Vietnam war, against racism and all those things that were going on. Afterward, everything opened up."

2

Back to the Garden

Light the lamp and fire mellow cabin essence
Timely hello welcomes the time for a change
—Van Dyke Parks

Little Village

A warren of winding, precipitous lanes, Laurel Canyon drew rock and roll people in the same way it had attracted artists of all types for half a century. Rising between the flatlands of Los Angeles to the south and the San Fernando Valley to the north, the canyon was above it all—a funky Shangri-la for the laid-back and long-haired, who perched in cabins with awesome views of L.A.'s sprawling basin. Pine and oak grew alongside palm and eucalyptus trees. Yucca and chaparral covered the sheer hillsides and hung over the wedged-in homes. Rabbits and coyotes lurked in the vegetation. "The canyon was old and woodsy and strange and interesting," says Lenny Waronker, who grew up in posh Bel Air but occasionally visited his canyon-dwelling artists. "It was interesting because of the geography as it related to the rest of Hollywood."

"You'd go up Laurel Canyon Boulevard from the Sunset Strip, and then you'd hit the Country Store on your right," says Henry Diltz, who moved into the canyon in 1964. "You'd then make a left on Kirkwood Drive, which was one big spur that went up. Lots of musicians lived up there, and they'd all come down to gather around the Canyon Store." A second spur was Lookout Mountain Avenue, off which Frank Zappa dwelled with family and entourage. A little way up the street lived Joni Mitchell. "About a quarter of a mile after Joni's place you came to the Wonderland school," Diltz continues. "Then you'd either go left and carry on up the hill on Lookout or you'd go straight past the school and on to Wonderland Avenue. There were lots of little veins and arteries and capillaries, and lots of musicians lived on those winding streets."

For Diltz and his fellow musicians, Laurel Canyon was the perfect antidote to urban stress and pollution. "That you can actually tuck yourself away in a canyon in the middle of Los Angeles is extraordinary," said Lisa Cholodenko, director of the 2003 film *Laurel Canyon*. "[There's a] kind of irreverent, *Land of the Lost* thing that people get into up there in the middle of a high-pressure, functioning city." Cholodenko set her rock movie in Laurel Canyon because—despite the steady influx of lawyers and other professionals into the area—the place still seemed to her "kind of lazy and kind of dirty and kind of earthy and sort of reckless."

The mountainous geography of the Los Angeles basin means that there are numerous canyons running north to south most of the way from the desert to the ocean. Laurel Canyon, being the closest to Hollywood, is merely the most populated. "There are canyons every twenty or thirty miles at least," says Chris Darrow. "They've always tended to be havens for artists and musicians and people who had alternative lifestyles."

In the 1950s, the canyon housed a motley community of artists and radicals, many seeking refuge from the climate of Joseph McCarthy's Red scare. *Caine Mutiny* director Edward Dmytryk, one of the Hollywood Ten, lived in the canyon. The hippest young actors (Marlon Brando, James Dean, James Coburn, Dennis Hopper) and artists (Ed Ruscha, Ed Kienholz, Billy Al Bengston, Frank Stella, Larry Bell, Bob Cottingham) gravitated to the area. "It was more like the Village, or like the bohemian parts of Paris or London," says June Walters, an Englishwoman who moved into the canyon in the late '50s. "All the artistic, radical people had come up here. It wasn't a chic place to live."

"Laurel Canyon was darker and denser than the other canyons," says Jill Robinson, daughter of movie producer Dore Schary. "It was inherently the outsiders' community, and it was more political because it was closer to Hollywood. There were lots of Communists living in Laurel Canyon. You could hide there and have meetings and gatherings. We felt that L.A. was becoming something quite different from what it had been. We were redefining what the city was."

A singular advantage of Laurel Canyon was that a car got you down to the clubs and coffeehouses on the Sunset Strip in minutes. "The first espresso machines came on to the Strip, so the coffeehouses became like bars," Walters recalls. "People would read poetry and there was so much activity. I'd have breakfast with Lenny Bruce and Mort Sahl." Another magnet was the strip of avant-garde art galleries along La Cienega Boulevard. "Every Monday night," says Jill Robinson, "you could see a circle of the cars going down Lookout Mountain and Wonderland and Laurel Canyon Boulevard toward La Cienega. We'd wander around the galleries, talking to each other, drinking coffee at Cyrano's on the Strip."

Folkies, too, liked the proximity to the Strip when they began moving into Laurel Canyon in the mid-1960s. "You could always hear a couple of banjo tunes coming around the hills, echoing and stuff," Roger McGuinn recalled. Up in the clouds one minute, they could be at the Whisky a Go Go club ten minutes later, usually after a slalom down Laurel Canyon Boulevard in a dented sports car. "People would swoop down from the canyon to the Strip and then retreat back to the mountains," says Barry Friedman. "The canyon had great roads to drive Porsches fast on, which was definitely another attraction."

"The canyon was part summer camp and part everybody's first apartment," says screenwriter Carl Gottlieb. "Except the apartment turned out to be a little house with trees and bucolic surroundings." More than anything, the canyon represented escape. "It was so exciting just to be there and to get out of Burbank, where I grew up," says

Jerry Yester, who moved to the canyon cul-de-sac of Rosilla Place in early 1962. "Laurel Canyon meant freedom. It meant being able to *go somewhere*."

With money from the success of *The Monkees*, former child actor Mickey Dolenz bought a house on Horseshoe Canyon Road. TV idol he may have been, but native Angeleno Dolenz nonetheless exemplified the cool canyon lifestyle. "When I was a kid growing up in the Valley, the canyon was obviously very rustic," he says. "I'd heard stories about how it was a hunting retreat and a place where people went camping at weekends. But when I moved in, there were already lots of actors and musicians and artists living up there." Dolenz's house became one of the key canyon hangouts of the late '60s. June Walters, who lived opposite, remembers endless actors and musicians swimming naked in Mickey's pool. Jack Nicholson, who wrote the satirical Monkees film *Head*, was a fixture. So were *Head*'s director Bob Rafelson and Jack's pals Dennis Hopper and Harry Dean Stanton. After Dolenz married model Samantha Just, his new mother-in-law asked Jack and his cronies to show some consideration and wear swimming trunks. "It was a tough adjust-ment for Samantha," Dolenz says with a smile. "On one of her first days in the house, she went down into the basement to do some washing and stepped on one of my friends who was sleeping in the laundry. But that's very much how the canyon was."

If Dolenz was typical of the musicians moving up into the canyon from the Hollywood "flats" below, the exodus from city to country had begun with the arrival of Love's Arthur Lee and singer Danny Hutton, along with producers Paul Rothchild and Barry Friedman. Lee was a canyon maverick, a law unto himself. A black man fronting a psychedelic, Byrds-ish, garage-folk-rock band, Arthur hid away in various places—on Briar, Kirkwood, Sunset Plaza Drive. In awe of Arthur was the young Jim Morrison, a fellow Elektra artist. "Jim Morrison used to sit outside my door when I lived in Laurel Canyon," Lee recalls. "He wanted to hang out with me. But I didn't want to hang out with *anybody*." Morrison himself became a canyon dweller, living on Rothdell Trail across the street from the Country Store—"the store where the creatures meet," as he sang on the Doors' "Love Street"—with his feisty redhead girlfriend Pamela

Courson. "I remember Jim showing up at the Fillmore with Pamela and she just looked like someone had been dancing on her jaw," says Linda Ronstadt. "I asked her what had happened and she said, no pun intended, 'I ran into a door!'"

Paul Rothchild, who produced both Love and the Doors for Jac Holzman, was already established as one of the canyon's leading lights. The house on Ridpath that Rothchild shared with engineer Fritz Richmond became a de rigueur drop-in for anyone interested in sex, drugs, and music. "Paul really believed in the canyon," says Carl Gottlieb. "He had a real hippie house, and the more money he made the more he expanded it. That was the quintessential canyon house." Like Rothchild, Barry Friedman was a wild man running riot in the nascent rock industry. "People like Paul and Barry contributed a huge amount," says Jac Holzman, "mostly as *sous-chefs* who stuck very large spoons into the pot of Laurel Canyon and stirred it up."

"It was *always* open house at Paul Rothchild's and Barry Friedman's," says Jackson Browne, a protégé of both men. "People were constantly dropping in." Among them was a gaggle of girls who mainly lived at Monkee Peter Tork's house. "They kept coming over with these big bowls of fruit and dope and shit. They'd fuck us in the pool." In his pad at 8524 Ridpath, Friedman pushed a bunch of beds together and staged semi-orgiastic groupings involving Browne and other good-looking corruptibles. A Kesey-esque ringmaster of depravity, Friedman could often be seen around town in a King Kong suit bequeathed to him by a hooker in Las Vegas. "Barry was off the scale of craziness," says Jac Holzman, "but always there was a kernel of something worthwhile to what he did."

Holzman himself dipped the occasional toe into the canyon craziness but remained wary of fully letting go. "Jac would make his royal visits," remembered Elektra engineer John Haeny. "We all gave him denim points." Former MGM A&R man David Anderle competed with Paul Rothchild to see who could roll the best joints for Holzman. Anderle himself made another interesting addition to the Elektra family. "L.A. was all about hanging in those days," he reminisces. "It was the constant hanging at other people's houses, which was the magic of the hills and canyons. All you had to do was drive up into Laurel Canyon and so much would happen en route."

Back Porch Majority

In 1965, Billy James moved from Beverly Hills to a funky house on Ridpath Drive. Uninterested in playing the corporate game at Columbia, he wanted an alternative lifestyle, and Laurel Canyon seemed to offer it. "Billy got very heavily into the Bob Dylan mentality, which was anticorporate," says David Anderle. "He was never somebody I would have picked to make that step into the corporate world and sit behind a desk."

James had played a key role in the success of the Byrds but wasn't sufficiently empowered to build on the group's success. Weary of heading the publicity division, he asked Byrds' comanager Eddie Tickner if there might be a job for him within Jim Dickson's management stable. Tickner instead urged him to "get his piece" from Columbia. The upshot was that James switched from publicity to "artist development" at the label.

As much as Columbia wanted new acts, James was frustrated in his attempts to sign such talent as Tim Hardin, Lenny Bruce, Frank Zappa, the Doors, and the Jefferson Airplane. The one act he did get signed in the wake of the Byrds—the blues-rock band the Rising Sons—never got the backing they deserved. "Columbia never gave people like Billy and me the control we needed," says Michael Ochs, who worked under James in 1966 and was the brother of folk singer Phil. "I couldn't stand the New York bureaucracy, which was why I was fired."

"At the time the industry was as risky and guess-filled as anything is," says Judy James, then Billy's wife. "It was Billy's job to say 'Listen, listen, listen' and Columbia's job to resist. He went nuts trying to sign Lenny Bruce." Judy saw how unhappy Billy was at Columbia and suggested they form a management company together. Working out of their home, the couple made 8504 Ridpath a de facto headquarters for the coalescing canyon community. "I wasn't the first to move into the canyon, but there weren't too many here then," James told *Rolling Stone* in 1968. "Arthur Lee lived nearby, and that was about it. It's all happened in the last year or so. If creative artists need to live apart from the community at large, they also have a desire to live among their own kind, and so an artistic community develops."

"Billy's house was a gathering place for musicians, some of whom became his clients and some of whom were sort of *budding* clients," says L.A. writer Tom Nolan. "You could go up there for social conversation and a meal." In addition to her role as stepmom to Billy's son Mark, Judy became den mother to a number of musical strays and protégés. Many hailed from the unlikely climes of suburban Orange County. "We would go to hoot nights at the Golden Bear down in Huntington Beach and Billy would roam around the back of that room watching these kids," Judy remembers. "They were sixteen and seventeen."

For a year, 8504 Ridpath was home to young Jackson Browne, who hailed from a middle-class Orange County background. Almost old enough to be his father, Billy was determined to get the teenage troubadour a deal. "Billy was sort of a hipster cat, something like a dancer," Browne remembered. "And he was very funny, very smart, somewhere in between a James Dean and a Mort Sahl." An artlessly handsome boy with a repertoire of pure and prescient songs, Browne slept in the Jameses' laundry room. One of a precocious group of strumming youngsters who included Jimmy Spheeris, Pamela Polland, and Greg Copeland, he had already received press attention as one of "the Orange County Three," a label Tom Nolan bestowed on him, Steve Noonan, and Tim Buckley in the pages of *Cheetah*. "Jackson was very talented and a class act," Judy James says. "He had this perspective and wisdom that were extraordinary for a boy of that age."

As much as he enjoyed his new freedom, Billy James jumped when Jac Holzman asked him to head Elektra's West Coast office in the fall of 1966. "Billy was extremely bright," says Holzman. "He was sort of a pleasant Iago, always moving around in the root system of what was going on." It was no surprise that Jackson Browne was one of the first artists James brought to Holzman. Yet Jac was unsure of Browne's voice. "Jackson was not a terribly good singer at that point," says Barry Friedman. "He came close to the notes, some of the time." Early in 1967, Browne demoed no fewer than thirty songs for Elektra, among them "Shadow Dream Song," "These Days," and "Colors of the Sun." The demos weren't enough to bag him a record deal with Elektra, but they did attract the attention of East Coast folkie Tom Rush, who cut "Shadow Dream Song" on his 1968 album *The Circle Game*.

Frustrated at the lack of a recording deal, Browne decided to split for New York with his friend Greg Copeland. The pair drove across America in a station wagon in the vibrant spring of 1967. In New York they joined Steve Noonan, who was already ensconced on the Lower East Side. Although he was there for only six weeks, Manhattan was a crash course in harsh, cynical glamour for Browne. Fresh from the womb of Judy James's laundry room, suddenly Jackson was deep in the world of Andy Warhol—"not a place for somebody with a tender heart," as he later remarked. Fixing the cute California boy in her steely sights was German-born model and part-time Velvet Underground chanteuse Nico. A brief affair with this valkyrie of pop left him stunned and slightly numb, but it also brought him the opportunity to accompany her in live performances and to contribute to her solo album *Chelsea Girl*. "For those who were listening," Richard Meltzer later wrote in *Rolling Stone*, "Jackson was where the action was. Here was the prototype singer-songwriter years before it had a context." To Browne's displeasure Meltzer also recorded the evening that Nico abused her seventeen-year-old lover as he performed at the Dom, causing him to leave the stage virtually in tears. Nor did Meltzer omit the attraction that Jackson held for many of the gay men in Warhol's circle.

Returning to Los Angeles older and slightly less innocent, Jackson idled away the late summer until he was adopted by Barry Friedman. Ironically, Friedman garnered fresh interest from Elektra, who advanced money for an album. But once again Jac Holzman was unconvinced. Friedman persevered. His new idea was to build a band around Browne, to which end he auditioned a number of young musicians at 8524 Ridpath. One was guitarist Ned Doheny, scion of a wealthy L.A. oil family whose history had been scarred by the 1929 murder of son and heir Edward L. Doheny Jr. (Though married with a child, Doheny was killed by his male lover. For decades his homosexuality was covered up by his powerful family.) Browne and Doheny hit it off instantly. Talented and good-looking, they smoked pot, skinny-dipped in Friedman's pool, and took their pick of pulchritudinous females. "Jackson and I were sort of friendly adversaries," Ned says. "He was a much more deliberate songwriter than I was, and he'd made his choice about his path long before me. He was an old soul."

A particular influence on Browne and Doheny were the songs from the "basement" sessions Bob Dylan and the Hawks were recording at the Big Pink house near Woodstock, New York. Some of them—"The Mighty Quinn," "You Ain't Goin' Nowhere," and others—were already making the rounds on tapes from Dylan's publishing company, to be covered in due course by the Byrds, Manfred Mann, and more. For Jackson and Ned, the fact that Dylan and his sidekicks were pulling back from rock's psychedelic circus was significant. It was as though people needed to come down from 1967's summer of love and evolve into something more rooted and rustic. Browne, whose acoustic, inward-looking songs had fallen on deafened ears in the age of Hendrix and the Who, felt a kinship with this back-to-the-roots trend.

On the Sunday morning of the Monterey Pop Festival, Barry Friedman took Jac Holzman aside and proposed that Elektra fund a kind of West Coast Big Pink—a "music ranch" in the remote Plumas National Forest in northern California. "In those days you could actually get people to bankroll fantasies and immense fictions," says Ned Doheny. "Barry was just crazy enough to be able to convince Jac to part with that kind of money." Friedman's Big Pink was a place called Paxton Lodge.

"We persuaded Jac Holzman to send us there to make a record, citing the fact that we didn't want to work under constraints in a studio," Browne recalls. "It was an attempt to create a small musical community out of this circle of friends. Holzman was a real pioneer, an adventurous guy." Rather than taking a specific act to Paxton, Friedman assembled a motley crew of singer-songwriters and technicians, many fueled by drugs of various descriptions. Holzman dubbed it Operation Brown Rice. "Paxton was a kind of *Star Search* for emerging folkie singer-songwriters," says Chris Darrow. "It was an extension of the canyon thing." Along with drummer Sandy Konikoff and guitar-toting warblers Browne, Doheny, Rolf Kempf, Jack Wilce, and Peter Hodgson came engineer John Haeny. Later a group of women showed up at the lodge: Janice Kenner, Connie Di Nardo,

Annie the Junkie, Nurit Wilde, and several others. For Jackson it was "kind of like bringing in the dance hall girls for the miners."

"In terms of girls, Ned and Jackson pretty well had it all under control there," remembers Friedman. "Ned wore a smoking jacket and was quite the gentleman at all times. He came from a long line of old money and he had that dignified demeanor about him." In the midst of all this, Friedman himself metamorphosed into "Frazier Mohawk" shortly before Christmas 1967. Like some demented movie director, he orchestrated scenes of sexual and narcotic depravity that soon spun out of control. "It was certainly dysfunctional," he admits. "To call it bizarre might be to compliment it. It was a very strange place, and the people were a bit crazed. Plus there were a lot of very evil drugs around." The drugs included heroin, with which Mohawk was flirting—and in which even Jackson Browne dabbled at Paxton.

When Jac Holzman finally came to see what fruit his $50,000 investment had borne, panic set in. The troupe went into overdrive, preparing a massive dinner of Cornish game hens. A wonderful and unrepeatable evening of music was staged in the lodge's main living room but never captured on tape. Afterward, as stoned as everybody else, Holzman was bathed in a tub by various lissom creatures, one of whom just may have been Friedman in drag.

Holzman flew out the next morning, thereby avoiding Paxton's subsequent spiral into near-madness. David Anderle, who'd succeeded Billy James as Elektra's head of A&R, wasn't so fortunate. "By the time *I* got up there it was Wackoville," he recalls. The snow, which some of these Southern Californians had never seen before, didn't help. Come December, cabin fever set in. Jackson Browne split for L.A. and then scuttled back to the lodge. Undercurrents of resentment began to be felt by everyone. Threatened by Ned Doheny's refusal to accept his mind games, Friedman manipulated Jackson into giving his friend his marching orders. "I refused to be corrupted by Barry and so was asked to leave that group of people," Doheny says. "Jackson was chosen to deliver the note, but the beast was already dead by then." This 1960s experiment was going nastily wrong.

Slowly, Friedman abnegated his paternal role in the proceedings. On New Year's Eve he had a nervous breakdown, retreating to his upstairs bedroom and refusing to answer questions about the recording sessions going on below. John Haeny, struggling to mask his homosexuality, freaked out and flew back to Los Angeles, where he collapsed, sobbing, into the arms of a waiting David Anderle. As spring neared, Holzman pulled the plug on Paxton. Mentally and emotionally bruised, as if they'd witnessed some unspeakable trauma, the company straggled back to Southern California.

"They came back from Paxton ragged but never said why," says Judy James. "I never really did find out what happened there. I just knew they needed healing. I had the sense that our living room was where they could come back to and feel safe and secure."

Young Girls Are Coming to the Canyon

For Jackson Browne if not for everyone, Paxton proved a sobering experience. On a microlevel it suggested there were limits to how far you could really "let it all hang out." "My stopping smoking dope had a lot to do with my becoming serious as a musician," Browne reflected later. "After two or three years of walking barefoot around Laurel Canyon and sleeping in people's living rooms and smoking the best dope on the planet . . . I had this huge self-conscious flash."

For Judy James, Laurel Canyon became as much a sanctuary as a creative seedbed. It was as though California's flower children had flown too close to the sun: victims of LSD were already being identified within the culture. "You cannot discount the incredible effect that drugs had," Judy says. "All these people who were so young they weren't yet formed, who did or didn't have talent, who did or didn't believe they were geniuses, who were or were not con men. And it was all wrapped up in one big thing." Early 1968 was about retrenching, putting down roots to counter the lysergic disorientation—not to mention the general political unrest in America. "Slowly but surely," says Judy, "people poured into the canyon. Bill Brogan at the Country Store supported us all in our hard times. He'd been there twenty years already when I moved to the canyon."

Still holding court in the canyon were "Butchie" Cho, Lotus Weinstock, and Tim Hardin, along with a new group called International Submarine Band, who lived on Ridpath Drive and revolved around a lanky trust-fund kid named Ingram "Gram" Parsons. "Laurel Canyon just seemed to be the place," says former Bob Dylan sideman Bruce Langhorne, who moved into a house on Lookout Mountain Avenue in 1968. "The winters really drove people out of New York."

Still in the canyon, too, were the Mamas and the Papas, whose John Phillips captured the essence of the place in his song "12:30 (Young Girls Are Coming to the Canyon)." "John began that song in New York," says fellow Papa Denny Doherty, "but he didn't know what to do with it. When we moved out here, the canyon fit the bill perfectly. Everybody was up there, and all the young girls were looking for all the rock stars. They'd wander the hills calling out names. *'We have a cake for you, Denny!!'* You'd hide and peek out the windows hoping they didn't see you."

Cass Elliott, now living in Natalie Wood's old house on Woodrow Wilson Drive, best defined the canyon's spirit. "Cass was Elsa Maxwell meets Sophie Tucker," says Doherty. "She was a big broad who knew what she looked like to others, and there was no facade. It was 'Hi there, come on in, let's get right to real.'"

"Cass was a major catalyst," says Henry Diltz. "You could drop in at her place anytime. She wanted to feed everybody. She would always meet these English lads on a TV show and she'd bring them back to the house because they didn't know anybody in town." Attracting what John Phillips later characterized as "a band of stoned hippie-worshipers," Cass kept permanent open house—even after giving birth to her daughter Owen. "I don't have the psychology of the fat person," Elliott told writer Richard Goldstein, who described her as "Tinkerbelle, sprinkling magic dust over a grooving generation." But deep down Cass was unhappy. In the company of David Crosby—footloose and fancy-free after his ejection from the Byrds—she pursued her love of opiates, including heroin. "There were a couple of good-looking guys that were *schtupping* Cass," says Denny Bruce. "They were basically there for her drugs. She got her little taste of sex and they got their dope."

All was not well in the Mamas and the Papas' world. The group had closed out the Monterey Pop festival but now were in disarray. Not for nothing did they release a greatest-hits collection titled

Farewell to the First Golden Era. "They were under a tremendous amount of pressure," says John York, who played bass at the group's final show in 1968. "They'd gone from being great friends to tolerating each other. There were moments where there was camaraderie, but they also maintained their own camps."

"By this time we were all burned out completely," admits Lou Adler. "We were on such a high for those three or four years. Everything we touched turned to gold, and the lifestyle was incredible. We were so high there was no place to go." John Phillips was exhibiting early signs of the arrogance that would eventually destroy his life. Intoxicated by success, he and Michelle moved out of Laurel Canyon and into the late Jeanette MacDonald's mock-Tudor mansion on Bel Air Road, cramming the place with Lalique crystal, Limoges china, and other appurtenances of celebrity living. "The public relates very strongly to the music and to the lifestyle," Phillips announced. "It's all one thing. There's an aristocracy of lifestyle. It's a pop star's life that counts; that's what involves you, not his performance."

"America always re-creates an aristocracy, usually drawing on sports, politics, the arts and show business," wrote Carl Gottlieb. "The new princes and princesses of rock 'n' roll lost no time in exploring a way of life that had led Old World nobility to ruin and revolution."

Human Highway

Phillips's hubris was all too clear once the Mamas and the Papas' success waned. His fatal error was his failure to notice the new mood Laurel Canyon represented. For the new back-to-the-earth minstrels—chilling out in split-level cabins with their cats and patched-denim jeans, penning soul-searching songs about themselves and each other—living in Bel Air and driving a Rolls-Royce simply wasn't hip. "A lot of the music hearkened back to a simpler time and place," says Chris Darrow. "The style of clothing went back to the Victorian era. We all wanted it to be the way we thought it was in the '20s or '30s. We wanted to be cowboys."

If Laurel Canyon was organic, Topanga Canyon—ten miles west and abutting the Pacific Ocean—was a veritable wilderness. In Laurel Canyon you rode motorcycles; in Topanga you rode horses.

This was where you came to get distance from Hollywood. The sound of Topanga was acoustic, laid-back. Weary of amplified bombast, songwriters were reconnecting with their folk roots and dabbling in newly hip country music. "One of the reasons people slipped out to Topanga was because you could pretend you were in Kentucky or Tennessee," says Dan Bourgoise, then an A&R man at Liberty Records. "Everything was getting more woodsy and rustic, and the music got very country."

Mark Volman of the Turtles, who'd tasted almost as much success as the Monkees and the Mamas and the Papas, was quicker than John Phillips to perceive the general shift in sensibility. "What came in at that time was really the foundation for the music of the 1970s," Volman reflects now. "The Turtles were not connected to that kind of hip counterculture that was beginning to flourish. We were really maybe holdovers from a different era—the last vestiges of that early 1960s Brill Building era."

The new ethos of singer-songwriters and self-contained bands spelled trouble for the likes of P. F. Sloan and Warren Zevon, who wrote minor hits for the Turtles. "I really think that record companies just *forgot* guys like Phil Sloan," says Volman. "Dunhill was a very pop record label that didn't really know how to deal with an artist like him." Another successful "backroom boy" in Los Angeles, pop/MOR writer Jimmy Webb, also sensed the wind changing direction. For his first album he penned a lament for Sloan that spoke of the pathos of the hired hand shunted aside by the new, hipper breed of singer-songwriter. "I genuinely felt that [Phil's] was the first—and a very heroic—attempt to break out of the box labeled 'pop songwriter,'" Webb says, "and that he should've gotten some credit for helping liberate a lot of us."

Songbird Jackie DeShannon, who'd started out at Metric Music, straddled the two worlds of writing and performing. She was also alert enough, in the fall of 1968, to release an album called *Laurel Canyon*, complete with a golden-throated paean to the Edenic place she now called home. "It was the right time and the right place," she stated. "All the elements I envisioned fell together."

Nowhere were the changes felt more keenly than at Warner-Reprise. "We just felt we were out on some limb," says Stan Cornyn.

"There was Capitol sitting there having trouble with the Beatles, not to mention Liberty, Dot, ABC, and those other floundering labels that didn't quite *get it*. We seemed to get it and we were having fun with it." Arguably the most catalytic figure at the company, however, was not Lenny Waronker but the svelte, sardonic, and very British Andy Wickham. Following the model of Billy James, Reprise head Mo Ostin wanted his own "house hippie" at Reprise, and Wickham fit the bill perfectly. "Mo had had the very astute realization that he needed an ambassador to the counterculture," says producer Joe Boyd, who first met Ostin and Wickham in late 1967. "Mo would hang with people and listen to people and take their cues," says Stan Cornyn. "Andy was worth listening to. He had real intelligence. What he came up with was generally unknowns."

Wickham had been a commercial artist in London before working at Immediate Records for Rolling Stones manager Andrew Loog Oldham. A fascination with American culture had brought him out to California—and a publicity job with Lou Adler's Dunhill label—in 1965. "In those days he already looked like a hippie," says singer Ian Whitcomb, a fellow Brit in Hollywood. "He was wearing beads and chains and long hair. He loved it in Los Angeles." Ostin put Wickham on a generous salary of $200 a week, though Andy's principal duty was to hang out with musicians in Laurel Canyon and keep his finger firmly on the pulse of the times. As a result, the canyon—in Stan Cornyn's words—became "a Reprise lode of gold."

"In my head, Andy took over Laurel Canyon for us," Cornyn says. "I can't think of who else really repped us in those narrow-laned hills. He hung there and he had long hair and he did not keep office hours." For Mo Ostin and Warner Brothers Records head Joe Smith, Wickham wasn't the easiest sell to their colleagues. But the Englishman's track record began to speak for itself. "Andy knew about things," says Smith. "He was our long-haired kid. We guided him through the hostile waters of the rest of the staff, which was a much more establishment group of people."

It was one of Wickham's hunches, a young Canadian folk singer, whose arrival in L.A. in early 1968 would mark the true onset of the Laurel Canyon era. Joni Mitchell's time had come.

3

New Kids in Town

The mountains and the canyons start to tremble and shake
The children of the sun begin to wake

—Led Zeppelin

A New Home in the Sun

Joni Mitchell was a stranger in a strange land—twice removed from her native Canada, new to California from America's East Coast. She was strange-looking, too, willowy but hip, with flaxen hair and big teeth and Cubist cheekbones. Men instinctively knew Joni as a peer. They also sensed a prickliness and a perfectionism.

In tow with Mitchell was Elliot Roberts, né Rabinowitz, a rock and roll Woody Allen with an endearing devotion to his single cause—Joni Mitchell. "Elliot pitched being my manager," she recalled of him. "I said, 'I don't *need* a manager, I'm doing quite nicely.' But he was a funny man. I enjoyed his humor." This odd couple had come out to Los Angeles from New York, where the Greenwich Village folk scene was petering out before their very eyes. Roberts, a Chartoff-Winkler agent, was a graduate of the legendary William Morris mailroom. He'd worked there with the even more ambitious agent, David

Geffen. Elliot decided to give up in the world of agenting after Buffy Sainte-Marie, a client, dragged him to see Joni perform in late October 1967.

Joni had already crammed a lot into her short life. She'd been married to a fellow Canadian singer, Chuck Mitchell, and had given up a daughter for adoption—an abandonment that ate at her like a wound. Songwriting served as therapy for her pain. "It was almost like she wanted to erase herself and just let the songs speak for her," reflected her friend the novelist Malka Marom. Joni's unusual open guitar tunings also set her songs apart from the folk balladry of the day. "I was really a folk singer up until 1965, but once I crossed the border I began to write," Mitchell says. "My songs began to be, like, playlets or soliloquies. My voice even changed—I no longer was imitative of the folk style, really. I was just a girl with a guitar that made it look that way."

"Elliot became wildly excited about Joni, and he introduced me to her and I became her agent," recalled David Geffen. "And it was the beginning of her career—it was the beginning of *our* careers. Everything was very small time." Established stars were lining up to cover songs from the Mitchell catalog. "When she first came out," said Roberts, "she had a backlog of twenty, twenty-five songs that most people would dream that they would do in their entire career . . . it was stunning." One artist to pay close attention was Judy Collins, folk's ethereal blue-eyed queen. For her 1967 album *Wildflowers* Collins chose "Both Sides, Now" and "Michael from Mountains." Tom Rush and Buffy Sainte-Marie both sang Mitchell's "The Circle Game."

Joe Boyd, who produced the English folk group Fairport Convention, met Mitchell at the 1967 Newport Folk Festival and brought her to London that summer to open for the Incredible String Band. Both in America and in England, people sat up and noticed the blonde with the piercing prairie soprano, the idiosyncratic guitar tunings, and the wise-beyond-her-years lyrics. When Roberts and Mitchell went to Florida to play the folk circuit there, David Crosby came to see her at a club called the Gaslight South. "Right away I thought I'd been hit by a hand grenade," he reported later. There was something about the way Mitchell combined naked purity with artful sophistication that shocked Crosby—the sense of a young woman who'd seen too much too soon. He set Joni in his sights, bedding her that week. The affair was never likely to last. "We went back to L.A. and tried to live together," Crosby said. "It doesn't work. She shouldn't have an old man. . . . She's about as modest as Mussolini."

"These were two very willful people," says Joel Bernstein. "Neither was going to cave in. I remember being at Joni's old apartment in Chelsea in New York and I heard this commotion on the street. And it was Crosby and Joni screaming at each other on the corner. It gave me a real sense of the volatility of their relationship." The volatility did not obscure David's deep admiration for Joni's talent, nor his awareness of the obstacles she and Elliot were encountering. "Everything about Joni was unique and original, but we couldn't get a deal," says Roberts, who took tapes to Columbia, RCA, and other majors. "The folk period had died, so she was totally against the grain. Everyone wanted a copy of the tape for, like, their wives, but no one would sign her."

Roberts touched down at LAX in late 1967, knowing few people in the city but using Crosby's endorsement as a calling card. Joni followed close behind. Immediately she was received with open arms. Epitomizing the hospitality of Laurel Canyon was B. Mitchel Reed, the KPPC-FM disc jockey whose radio show was the pipeline of all cool sounds in L.A. Reed put Roberts and Mitchell up in his rented house above the Sunset Strip on Sunset Plaza Drive.

Joni wasn't sure about Los Angeles. She was used to crowded sidewalks, teeming urban life—the bustle and commotion of Toronto and Manhattan. She didn't like it that people went everywhere in their big gas-guzzling cars. But once she and Elliot got into Laurel Canyon, up among the cypresses and eucalyptus trees that lined the bumpy, snaking roads, she started to see the City of the Angels as the new golden land that had seduced so many outsiders: the land of David Hockney's painting *A Bigger Splash*, of exotic palms and dry desert air and the omnipresent vault of blue sky. "Driving around up in the canyons there were no sidewalks and no regimented lines like the way I was used to cities being laid out," she recalls. "And then, having lived in New York, there was the ruralness of it, with trees in the yard and ducks floating around on my neighbors' pond. And the friendliness of it: no one locked their doors." As for Elliot Roberts, well, he'd grown up in the Bronx—how bad could this paved paradise be?

"Elliot would sleep on my couch at 8333 Lookout Mountain," says Ron Stone. "At the same time, Crosby had been tossed out of the Byrds and was mooching off me. We'd smoke a joint and play chess. We were both obnoxious brats. He was my entrée to all of this." Crosby urged Roberts to try Reprise Records. "Go see Andy Wickham," he counseled Elliot, who found David inspiring and radically different from anyone he'd known in New York. "Because Crosby 'hangs out' so much," Jerry Hopkins wrote in *Rolling Stone*, "there's a tendency to think he isn't producing much. In a sense this is true. Yet he is an integral part of the L.A. scene—thanks largely to his track record but also because he is so volatile and opinionated."

When Roberts officially left Chartoff-Winkler, he asked Ron Stone to work for him. To Stone it looked more exciting than selling used leather jackets to the socialites of Beverly Hills. Together they found an office farther down Santa Monica Boulevard, in a building with the fanciful name "Clear Thoughts." "Right away it was like Elliot and Ron could take a New York entrepreneurial viewpoint on the whole thing," says Joel Bernstein, who would soon be taking photographs of Joni for Elliot. "I think it was really eye-opening to these guys that you could come out here and live up in Laurel Canyon in little wooden houses where you didn't even need heating or air-conditioning . . . and you could still do *business*." With Ron Stone as his new aide-de-camp, Roberts duly trotted off to see Wickham. The young Englishman loved what he heard. "In his heart, Andy was a folkie," Roberts remembers. "His best friend during that whole period was Phil Ochs."

With Wickham as her first label champion, the twenty-three-year-old Joni had a demo session green-lighted by Mo Ostin on condition that Crosby produce it. "David was very enthusiastic about the music," says Mitchell. "He was *twinkly* about it. His instincts were correct: he was going to protect the music and pretend to produce me. I think perhaps without that the record company might have set some kind of producer on me who'd have tried to turn an apple into an orange." The sessions that eventually became *Joni Mitchell* could not have been more auspicious. Recording at Sunset Sound, Mitchell and Crosby kept things stripped and simple: in the main just Joni, her guitar, and such well-worked songs as "Marcie" and "I Had a King." The two of them had now officially split up. "They each described to me crying at the other through the glass in the studio," says Joel Bernstein. Sitting in on occasional guitar and bass was Stephen Stills, who was across the hall with his group Buffalo Springfield. His bandmate, the dark and brooding Neil Young, was known to Mitchell from her apprenticeship on the Canadian folk circuit. Sharing a uniquely dry Canadian humor, Young and Mitchell had always gotten along. Neil's coming-of-age song "Sugar Mountain" had indirectly inspired Joni's similarly themed "Circle Game." "You gotta meet Neil," she told Elliot. "He's the only guy who's funnier than *you* are."

Roberts wandered down the hall to meet Joni's enigmatic compatriot. Having heard stories about the ongoing friction within Buffalo Springfield and specifically about Young's moodiness, Elliot was pleasantly surprised when the singer turned out to be approachable and affable. Joni and Neil compared notes on their respective musical journeys. If Joni's tastes didn't stretch to the febrile rock the Springfield played, she could sense the electricity in the air— the vibrancy of the scene and the exploding of talent on and off the Sunset Strip.

Mitchell divided her debut album into two loosely autobiographical sections—a conceit easier to bring off in the days of vinyl LPs. The first side ("I Came to the City") commenced with "I Had a King," a song detailing—with more than a trace of self-protective bitterness—the breakup of Joni's marriage to Chuck Mitchell. Part Two ("Out of the City and down to the Seaside") found the heroine in the country, by the sea, settled in rustic Southern California. "The Dawntreader" was a gushing homage to Crosby and the boat he tethered at Marina Del Rey. "Song to a Seagull" summarized the theme of the album, with Joni recapping on her urban adventures and subsequent departure for the sea. The song played perfectly into the image of Mitchell as a kind of a fairy maiden striving to float free of human need. The final song, "Cactus Tree," pointed forward to deeper themes in the singer's subsequent work: themes of romantic love, of female autonomy, of commitment versus creative freedom. Describing three lovers—the first almost certainly Crosby—Joni "thinks she loves them all" but fears giving herself completely to any of them. These were important issues for liberated women in the 1960s, rejecting a society where women had tended to live somewhat vicariously as caretakers to men. A self-proclaimed "serial monogamist," Mitchell would struggle for years with the conflicts between her desire for love and her need for independence.

Listening to *Joni Mitchell* again decades later, it's difficult to ignore how earnest and worthy she sounds on it—yet the power of her swooping, pellucid vibrato and idiosyncratic, questioning chords is right there. "Joni invented everything about her music, including how to tune the guitar," said James Taylor. "From the beginning of the process of writing she's building the canvas as well as putting paint on it."

In March, with the album about to be released, David Crosby presented his protégée to his peer group. Crosby's favorite gambit was to host impromptu acoustic performances by Joni, usually at the Laurel Canyon homes of his friends. "David says, 'I want you to meet somebody,'" recalls Carl Gottlieb. "And he goes upstairs and comes back down with this ethereal blonde. And this is the first time that everybody heard 'Michael from Mountains' and 'Both Sides Now' and 'Chelsea Morning.' And then she goes back upstairs, and we all sit around and look at each other and say, 'What was *that*? Did we hallucinate it?'" Eric Clapton sat spellbound on Cass Elliott's lawn as Joni cooed "Urge for Going," a song inspired by the death of the folk movement. Crosby was at her side, a joint in his mouth and a Cheshire-cat smile of satisfaction on his face. "Cass had organized a little backyard barbecue," says Henry Diltz. "Because she'd met Cream she invited Clapton, who was very quiet and almost painfully shy. And Joni was there and doing her famous tunings, and Eric sat and stared at her hands to try and figure out what she was doing."

The following day Joni performed on B. Mitchel Reed's KPPC show in Pasadena and answered questions that whetted L.A.'s appetite for the new neofolk star. So much did Reed talk her up that her first live dates in town were all sellouts at the Troubadour. Not that the local attention made much difference to the commercial prospects of *Joni Mitchell*, which peaked on the *Billboard* chart at the lowly position of No. 189. As she often would in her career, Joni felt at odds with her record label, whose Stan Cornyn promoted the album with flip irreverence. "Joni Mitchell is 90% Virgin," Cornyn's copy read in the ads he furnished to the new underground press— *Crawdaddy!*, *Rolling Stone*, and company. Joni was irked by the line. "She got me on the phone and said it drove her crazy," says Joe Smith. "I said, 'Sleep on it and think about it tomorrow. Anybody who knows you or of you would never associate "virgin" in the same sentence with you.' And she laughed at that."

"Like Neil, Joni was quiet," says Henry Diltz, who photographed her soon after her move to L.A. "A *lot* of these people were quiet, which was why they became songwriters. It was the only way they could express themselves. It was very different from the Tin Pan Alley tradition, where guys would sit down and try to write a hit song and turn out these teen-romance songs about *other* people."

Joni found a perfect place of retreat in Laurel Canyon. In April 1968, with money from her modest Reprise advance, she made a down payment on a quaint A-frame cottage built into the side of the hill on Lookout Mountain Avenue. Soon she filled it with antiques and carvings and stained Tiffany windows—not to mention a nine-year-old tomcat named Hunter. Within a year her songs were setting the pace for the new introspection of the singer-songwriter school.

On July 5, 1968, Robert Shelton wrote a *New York Times* piece about Mitchell and Jerry Jeff Walker titled "Singer-Songwriters Are Making a Comeback." In it he noted that, while the return of solo acoustic performers had at least something to do with economics, "the high-frequency rock'n'roar may have reached its zenith." Nine months later, folk singer and *Sing Out!* editor Happy Traum came to a similar conclusion in *Rolling Stone*. "As if an aural backlash to psy-ky-delick acid rock and to the all-hell-has-broken-loose styles of Aretha Franklin and Janis Joplin," Traum wrote, "the music is gentle, sensitive, and graceful. Nowadays it's the personal and the poetic, rather than a message, that dominates." It was time to turn inward.

Outside of a Small Circle of Friends

The Los Angeles scene that Joni Mitchell and Elliot Roberts found in the early months of 1968 was in a state of transition. The departures of Gene Clark and David Crosby from the Byrds were symptomatic of a general fragmenting. "Groups had broken up over 1967–68," Ellen Sander wrote in her 1973 book *Trips*. "Everyone was wondering what was next, a little worried, but grooving nonetheless on the time between. Days were permeated with a gentle sense of waiting, summer blew up the hills, past the painted mailboxes and decorated VW buses, and musicians were floating about."

Crosby, outside whose Beverly Glen house Cass Elliott's dune buggy was often spotted, was struggling to land a solo deal. His new best friend, Stephen Stills, offered consolation. To Paul Rothchild, Crosby touted such new songs as the beautiful "Laughing" and the brooding "Long Time Gone." The Lovin' Spoonful's John Sebastian, killing time in L.A., helped Crosby demo tracks for Elektra. But, as with Jackson Browne, Jac Holzman couldn't make up his mind.

Now Stills's band, too, was unraveling. Neil Young's on-off membership of the Buffalo Springfield was perplexing to some but understandable to those who saw how Stills bullied him. "It would make me really angry, because Stephen pushed Neil back constantly," said Linda McCartney, who photographed the Springfield. "Neil was painfully shy. I thought, 'Well, he just doesn't stick up for himself.'" Jack Nitzsche, who'd worked closely with Young on the Springfield's "Expecting to Fly" and "Broken Arrow"— orchestral epics inspired by the Beatles' "Day in the Life"—was among several people encouraging Neil to go solo. Young was over at Nitzsche's house in Mandeville Canyon one night when they heard a hammering at the door. It was Stills, hunting for his errant bandmate.

According to Denny Bruce, Stills sneered when Nitzsche answered the door, "I know that baby is here and you're hiding him." Finding Neil in Nitzsche's living room, Stills seized him by the lapels and yelled, "Listen, you fuckin' pussy, this is a band!" He reiterated to Neil that Richie Furay was the lead singer, that he himself was "the second lead singer," and that Neil was merely "a guitar player and occasional vocalist" whose songs had already failed to crack the Top 40 three times. Then he stormed out of the house.

"The Springfield had started to dissolve," Elliot Roberts recalls. "By the time I was around them, Neil and Stephen were never in the studio at the same time." At a band meeting to discuss a motion to replace Charlie Greene and Brian Stone with Roberts—rooming with Young at the time—Young rose to his feet and left the room. Roberts was devastated, so shocked by Young's brusqueness that he moved out of the singer's Laurel Canyon pad and found his own place. Two weeks later, after the Springfield's final live performance, on May 5, 1968, Young showed up at Roberts's new place and asked if he would manage him as a solo artist. "Oh, he'd plotted it all out," Roberts reminisced years later. "I thought, Wow, cool—this guy is as devious as I am."

Young's decision to fly solo was a pivotal moment. In time he would become rock's ultimate loner, partnering with his peers only when it suited him. "Everyone thought of the group as the strongest unit for success," Dickie Davis said. "And Neil didn't. In the end, of course, he's right. The managers, the professionals—they know those groups aren't going to stay together. Jack [Nitzsche] knew. But we didn't."

"I think Neil always wanted to be a solo artist," said Richie Furay. "And I can't hold that against him. It just seems there may have been a different way to make that point clear, rather than just not show up." The tendency to avoid confrontation would be one of the themes of Young's long career. "I just had too much energy and so much creative flow coming out," Young told Cameron Crowe; "when I wanted to get something down, I just felt like, 'This is my fucking trip and I don't have to listen to anybody else's.' I just wasn't mature enough to deal with it."

Matters accelerated still faster for Roberts when Graham Nash came to Los Angeles at the start of July 1968. Struggling to make things work with Brit invaders the Hollies, Graham urgently needed to recharge his musical batteries. The first port of call was Casa Crosby and a big hang with Crosby, Mama Cass, John Sebastian, and—most significantly—Stephen Stills. Nash had gotten to know Crosby slightly during a Byrds tour of England. "I'd never met anybody like him," Nash said. "He was a total punk, a total asshole, totally delightful, totally funny, totally brilliant, a totally musical man."

Already intrigued by Los Angeles, where the Hollies had played several times, Nash also was the archetypal Cass Elliott pet. "Cass showed me many wonderful things in a very gentle way," he told writer Dave Zimmer. "She was the person who introduced me to grass. I'd always been curious." Cass wasn't alone in warming to this personable guy from Manchester, England. Five months before, Joni Mitchell had had a fling with the married Hollie when their touring schedules coincided in Canada. Now Mitchell accompanied Roberts and Steve Stills to see the Hollies play at the Whisky a Go Go. Afterward they took Nash back with them to Joni's new house on Lookout Mountain.*

"Joni's place was a little different from Cass's," says Mark Volman. "It was not so much maternal but about holding court in terms of songwriters who could find themselves there on any given night and would present their music to a kind of inner circle of people. If Joni did drugs it was pretty well hidden."

At the Mitchell gathering, Stephen started fooling around with a new, country-flavored song called "Helplessly Hoping." Crosby joined in with a tentative harmony vocal. As he listened, Nash heard a top-layer falsetto harmony in his head. When Stills and Crosby came back in with the second verse, Graham laid his high harmony over their voices. Everyone in the room beamed simultaneously: it was as though three angels had been reunited in space and time. "I was in there on top," Nash told B. Mitchel Reed, "and we all fell down laughing. It was really joyous."

Although he wouldn't officially leave the Hollies until November of that year, Nash was now deeply smitten with Laurel Canyon. For a man who'd grown up on the rainy streets of northwestern England,

---

*Over the years there has been much hazy dispute about the exact location of this impromptu gathering on the night of July 3, 1968. Stills thought it took place at Cass Elliott's house, Nash wasn't sure, and both Crosby and Roberts insist it was chez Joni.

Lookout Mountain was simply idyllic. "I can only liken it to Vienna at the turn of the century, or Paris in the 1930s," Nash reflected many years later. "Laurel Canyon was very similar, in that there was a freedom in the air, a sense that we could do anything."

"There really was an ethic of peace and love and art and poetry among that crowd," says Elliot Roberts. "Poetry, even more than musicality, was revered, and Joni was the best poet at the time. She had a lot to say, and everybody wanted to hear it." Nash, in particular, was all ears: he and Joni were falling in love. When he got back to England he made plans to leave his old life—and wife—behind. "England was boring me," he told author Ritchie Yorke the following year. "I decided to leave everything there, every single thing, every penny I earned is still there, and I brought $500 with me and my suitcase to start a complete new life."

Both Sides, Then

With Joni Mitchell established at Reprise, Elliot Roberts now capitalized on his relationship with Andy Wickham and Mo Ostin to bring them Neil Young. "It's hard to define that period," Roberts says. "It wasn't a money market yet—everyone was just shooting craps. Warners got more of the folk/writer-oriented end of it: the James Taylors and Van Morrisons and Van Dyke Parkses. All these people reflected Andy Wickham's taste in particular." But it was really Jack Nitzsche, one of Mo's most trusted ears, who got Young in the door at Reprise. Young, for his part, felt immediate trust in Ostin. "Warner Brothers," he later told his biographer Jimmy McDonough, "was making music for adults rather than children."

"Warners was a big standard-bearer for the hip Hollywood fraternity," said Bob Merlis, later the company's head of publicity. "It said that you didn't have to be in the Village to be hip, and I think that was one of the reasons a person like Joni Mitchell was prepared to risk leaving New York for Hollywood Babylon." For Lenny Waronker, the fact that sensitive, introspective artists such as Mitchell and Young were signing to Warner-Reprise was vindication of the label's artist-friendly approach to the music business. "Neil and Joni were coming at it from a less trained place than Randy Newman or Van

Dyke Parks," Waronker says, "but it was basically the same. There was a line that connected everybody."

Newman claims, affectionately, that Waronker exploited their boyhood friendship to get him cheap. Lenny's father and Randy's uncle had worked together in the 20th Century-Fox orchestra, and the two boys—Lenny was two years older than Randy—played together constantly. "I told Lenny that A&M were offering me $10,000," Randy says. "He said, 'How can you do this to me? Don't you understand that money isn't important now?' But Warners matched A&M's offer and I went with them."

Artists such as Newman and Parks posed problems for Reprise. Scholarly, almost nerdish writers, they weren't part of the counter-culture in the way that Young, Mitchell, or the Grateful Dead were. But then neither were they Top 40 hacks. "Randy and some others weren't joiners," says Waronker. "Their goals were a little different. It was almost self-consciously trying not to join the game. But everybody wanted to be the best. That was a big deal—'Who's the best?'" Newman did not aspire to rock credibility. One glance at his hopelessly square, polo-necked appearance on the cover of his 1968 debut album makes that clear. Nor did Randy hang out with the Laurel Canyon crowd: by now he was married, with a son. "There was marijuana but I never liked it that much," he says. "I'd see Harry Nilsson sometimes. But I wasn't part of anything. If they had a club I wasn't in it."

"Randy was sadder than I was," says Van Dyke Parks. "He'd seen the dark side of the moon, for some reason that I couldn't figure out. He got more nervous and upset about it all." *Randy Newman*, coproduced in 1968 by Parks and Waronker, was an astounding debut. The jump from the attractive but insubstantial material Randy had written at Metric to the wry satire of "Laughing Boy" and the bleak self-pity of "I Think It's Going to Rain Today" was clear to anyone paying attention. Sadly, just as Joni's debut had done, the album struggled to find an audience. More specialized still was Parks's own *Song Cycle*, a highbrow concept album about Southern California that included the track "Laurel Canyon Boulevard" ("the seat of the beat"). "I was trying to ask questions like, 'What was this place? What does it mean to be here?'" Parks claimed. "I wanted to capture the sense of California as a Garden of Eden, a land of opportunity."

"Warners was comfortable," says Russ Titelman, a guitarist/producer whom Waronker brought into the Burbank fold. "It was people who knew about music and had a lot of fun making it. The signings were incredibly hip. Lenny turned Arlo Guthrie into a pop act, which wasn't easy, and he made hit records with Gordon Lightfoot. It created a certain vibe and a certain perception. In a way—a good way—it was all things to all people." One Warner-Reprise insider who could not have been described as comfortable was Jack Nitzsche. If his unhappy adolescence had been alleviated by a worship of James Dean, his mind now wandered to darker places of comfort: alcohol, cocaine, the occult. "Jack's mother was a medium and Jack believed in all that stuff," says Judy Henske, who often visited him in George Raft's old house in Mandeville Canyon. "If you went around with Jack for long enough, *you* believed in it, too. One time, Jack and I were playing with a ouija board and his mother came in and snatched it away, saying, 'That's a pipeline to the devil!'"

It was no coincidence that Nitzsche was so infatuated with the Rolling Stones, on many of whose mid-1960s albums he had played. In the summer of 1968 the English band was flirting heavily with Satanism and the occult, as "Sympathy for the Devil"—lead track on that year's *Beggars Banquet*—made only too clear. At the same time they were delving deep into their love of the root American music forms—blues and country—and spending a lot of time in Los Angeles. The song "Sister Morphine," which derived from a lyric by Mick Jagger's girlfriend Marianne Faithfull, was written at Nitzsche's house. "That was quite a summer," Denny Bruce recalls. "Everyone was listening to *Music from Big Pink*, and Marianne and Anita Pallenberg were swimming nude in Jack's pool."

When Jagger agreed to play Turner, the debauched rock star in Donald Cammell's and Nic Roeg's *Performance*, Nitzsche was asked to create the film's sound track. That he did so with the help of Lenny Waronker's Burbank "team"—Ry Cooder, Russ Titelman, and Randy Newman—didn't change the fact that the *Performance* sound track was sonically the antithesis of the cozy Laurel Canyon vibe of 1968. Indeed, one would have to say that, like *Beggars Banquet*, the

Performance music was a lot closer to the zeitgeist than the debut album by Joni Mitchell. Acoustic introspection was less a response to race riots, protest marches, and assassinations than a retreat from them.

Composed in a witch's cottage in the canyon, with Donald Cammell—godson of infamous occultist Aleister Crowley—plying Nitzsche with cocaine, *Performance* remains one of the scariest collections of music ever: a brilliantly creepy mix of malevolent Moogs, graveyard gospel vocals, and voodoo blues guitar that fit Cammell's dark vision perfectly. "Death is always part of the music I make," Nitzsche once said. No wonder Warner Brothers shelved the film for two years after an executive's wife freaked out during an advance screening.

Neil Young, a Stones fan, loved the *Performance* music. The very things that alarmed others about Nitzsche were what fascinated Neil, who asked Jack to help him with his first solo album. In August 1968 he moved from Laurel to Topanga Canyon, putting more distance between him and the Hollywood scene in which Stephen Stills and David Crosby were so engrossed. Tellingly, the first vocal track on *Neil Young* was called "The Loner." "Neil wasn't as social as other people," says Henry Diltz. "He wasn't as out-there, getting buzzed and drunk. He wasn't partying. He was more serious about his life and music. Unlike Crosby, he never had a big entourage of people partying around him."

Young's flight to Topanga was in one sense a flight from the shock of the 1960s. Shy and still prone to epileptic fits, Neil was ill equipped to deal with the sexual and narcotic adventures of the time. According to Henry Diltz, he was also the victim of a shaming, invasive mother who'd profoundly affected his ability to relate to women. Neil tended to become passive in the presence of girls. He felt marginally safer living off the beaten track in Topanga. *Neil Young* was the logical extension of songs he had written in the Buffalo Springfield—songs such as "Mr. Soul," "On the Way Home," and "Out of My Mind," that spoke of his struggle and disorientation within the swirling Sunset Strip scene of 1966–1967. "Here We Are in the Years" was a statement about rejecting the smoggy city for "the slower things/That the country brings."

Assisting Young with the record was another Topanga outcast, producer David Briggs. Like Nitzsche, Briggs was a macho misfit—the kind of truculent outsider whom Young adored and fed off. Along with Elliot Roberts, a front man masquerading as a manager, Nitzsche and Briggs formed a human shield that protected and insulated Young from the outside world. Behind this shield he began to write from a deeper, more intuitive place. "When I was very young and first came in contact with these musicians, I thought that the ones whose lyrics I loved must be really smart," says Nurit Wilde. "And I found out that some of them really *weren't* smart, they just seemed to have some sort of instinctive feel for words. Neil was one of those."

Released in early 1969, *Neil Young* wasn't quite the album Young had intended to make. When he listened back to it, it was over-arranged and overproduced. But it was shot through with distinctive riffs and passages of spooked beauty that made it a minor landmark. "The beginnings of the singer-songwriter school were the first albums by Neil and Joni," says Jackson Browne. "After that you started to get songs that only the songwriter could have sung—that were part of the songwriter's personality."

An Elf on Roller Skates

With everything heating up around him, Elliot Roberts felt over-whelmed. When Graham Nash quit the Hollies and moved to L.A. in December 1968, Roberts couldn't see a way to free him or Crosby and Stills from their contractual obligations. He turned to the one man he knew who was sharp enough to find a solution: his old colleague from William Morris in New York.

David Geffen had already provided free advice on how to nego-tiate Neil Young's contract with Reprise; Roberts had gotten $15,000 out of Mo Ostin as a result. Now Elliot *really* needed David's formi-dable brainpower. "I knew he could get this done," Roberts says. "By now he was in television at the Ashley Famous agency, but he was making a lot of side deals for everyone. You could hire David to make deals without having the *involvement* of David. He preferred it that way, because it gave him a broad spectrum of people from movie stars to rock stars to producers."

Geffen had grown up in blue-collar Brooklyn, a skinny kid with dreams of mogulism. He was seventeen when his pattern-cutter father died and left him with an adoring mother who sold girdles and referred to her son as "King David." He first visited Los Angeles in 1961, staying with his brother Mitchell, a student at UCLA. "From the day I arrived," he says, "California seemed like an enchanted land."

Back in New York in 1964, David landed a mailroom job at William Morris. After lying about UCLA references of his own, he steamed open a letter from the university denying that he'd ever studied there. He regularly embellished his résumé to enhance his standing. Elliot Roberts was an agent who witnessed Geffen steaming open other letters to get jump starts on what was happening in the company. The guy's drive and ruthlessness, appalling to others, thrilled Roberts. It didn't take David long to rise from the mailroom.

As pop music became bigger business in the mid-1960s, William Morris opened its doors to long-haired musicians it might have disdained two years before. Geffen was perfectly placed to deal with this emerging talent. "Stay with people your own age," senior agent Jerry Brandt counseled him. "Go into the music business." In truth, Geffen knew little about music. When television director Steve Binder turned him on to a remarkable singer named Laura Nyro, he'd never heard of her. Nyro was a Gothic Cass Elliott, a boho Barbra Streisand in black. Her swooping voice and street-operatic songs were starting to be covered by successful pop/MOR acts. Geffen eagerly seized the opportunity to offer his services. Nyro was quickly won over by his infectious enthusiasm, especially after she bombed at the Monterey Pop Festival and he rushed to her side to comfort her.

"She was a very strange girl," Geffen told Joe Smith. "She had hair down to her thighs. She wore purple lipstick, Christmas balls for earrings, strange clothes. But very talented." David Crosby believed that Laura was "a window into something in [Geffen] that was not primarily about money." The fact that Nyro and Geffen were both primarily gay helped: those who weren't in the know even thought they'd become a couple. "People said, 'You know he's gay,'" says Judy Henske. "And I thought, 'Well, you don't get a really gay hit from him, but whatever.' In any case he was great, and the reason that he was so great was that he was so smart. He was really, really fun and really, really smart." Journalist Ellen Sander, who'd written about him in the New York press, also failed to get "a gay hit" from Geffen. She even seduced him one night in her apartment on East Twentieth Street. According to his biographer Tom King, "[David] credited Sander with helping him to conquer his fear of sex with women."

For at least two years, Geffen was jetting between New York and Los Angeles. A fast-rising star, he lived in a chic apartment on Central Park South and stayed at the Beverly Hills Hotel when he was in L.A. On one trip he pressed a demo of Laura's songs into the hands of Bones Howe, producer of the pop-soul group the Fifth Dimension. Subsequently they recorded several Nyro tunes, notably the smash hits "Stoned Soul Picnic" and "Wedding Bell Blues." To Geffen's delight, the value of Laura's catalog increased exponentially as a result. Brazenly disregarding rules governing conflict of interest, he worked as both her agent and her publisher, forming Tuna Fish Music in partnership with her. "David was an opportunist," says Joe Smith. "He was very quick and very smart."

Geffen's energy was formidable. "He never stopped," says Essra Mohawk, an aspiring singer-songwriter adopted by Nyro. "I called him the Elf on Roller Skates. He seemed gay to me, so I never bought that he and Laura were a couple. I liked him a lot. He was very friendly." In May 1968 he quit William Morris and joined Ted Ashley's agency. His responsibilities were now almost entirely musical. When he wasn't in California himself he would receive at least one phone call a day from Elliot Roberts. Usually it involved the careers of Joni Mitchell and Neil Young.

Before a year was up, Geffen was tiring of Ashley Famous. He began scheming to form not just his own agency but his own label and personal-management firm, too. With unprecedented audacity he suggested to Clive Davis that he leave his job as president of Columbia and partner him in a new label. Davis declined. In February 1969, turning twenty-six, Geffen resigned from Ashley Famous and launched David Geffen Enterprises. First, however, came a major challenge: the disentangling of Crosby, Stills, and Nash so they could form a new group.

Taking a break from L.A. in early 1969, Crosby, Stills, and Nash honed their new material in a house that Paul Rothchild kept on Long Island. While there they went into New York City to formalize their relationship with David Geffen. Elliot Roberts flew out from L.A. to be present. What CSN proposed in Geffen's Central Park South apartment was a straight no-paper handshake deal. Geffen hesitated for a split second, then agreed. Clive Davis, who thought highly of Geffen's talent, released David Crosby without a whimper; if anything, he was delighted to be rid of "the Bad Byrd." In exchange Davis would get the Buffalo Springfield's Richie Furay and his new group Poco. A tougher sell was producer Jerry Wexler, who fiercely resisted Geffen's request that Atlantic release Stephen Stills. When Geffen came to see him, the meeting sparked a decade of bad blood. Jerry, a well-read jazzophile who scorned agents as parasites, physically threw the smaller man out of his office.

"I knew [Jerry's] accomplishments and went to him with great respect," Geffen later protested. "I'm not saying I was completely in control of my emotions, because I wasn't. But Wexler wouldn't even listen to me. He treated me like dirt. He screamed and yelled and acted like I was looking to rob him." Altogether wilier was the response of Ahmet Ertegun. The legendary cofounder of Atlantic thought a few moves ahead of Wexler. What, he asked himself, can *I* get out of this arrogant kid? "I saw in him a potential genius entertainment executive or entrepreneur," Ertegun said in 1990. "He was very bright, very fast. He was younger than me and he had a keen sense of where youth was going in America."

Turning on all his Park Avenue charm, Ahmet seduced Geffen, who left thinking that the goateed Atlantic prez was "the most sophisticated, amusing, and encouraging man I had ever met in my life." Within weeks, Crosby, Stills, and Nash was an Atlantic act. "Later I saw [Geffen's] devotion to his artists," Jerry Wexler would concede. "His group of California rock poets worked for him without a contract—that's how deep their trust ran." But the two men were to clash even more unpleasantly.

With the CSN deal inked, Geffen decided to make Los Angeles his base. "There was so much going on in California that it was the only place to be," he says. With Elliot Roberts already based there and building a stable of talent, David knew it was the right time to strike. The two men cemented their partnership as they drove to Carl Gottlieb's house on Gardner Street one afternoon. "David stopped the car," says Roberts. "Then he turned to me and said, 'Listen, let's just *do* this.'" When Elliot faintly protested that he'd done most of the hard work himself, David told him to shut up. "You know you'll make twice as much money with me," he said.

Installed in a fancy new office at 9130 Sunset Boulevard, the two men plotted to shape the destinies of the canyon ladies and gentlemen. "The word got around that there were these music-industry guys who were also human beings," says Jackson Browne. "Crosby told me that Geffen was really brilliant but you could also trust him. And you could. David and Elliot would have done *anything* for their artists. In an industry full of cannibals, they were like the infantry coming over the hill."

"[David] had a description—he said these people were *significant artists*," Bones Howe recalls. "The significant artist is an artist who creates his own music, records it, and produces it. These people created and crafted themselves. And he was fascinated with that process." "By 'significant artists' I really meant singer-songwriters," Geffen says. "People who were self-contained."

Geffen-Roberts was a fearsome double act, like Charlie Greene and Brian Stone with credibility and Levi's. Elliot was the people person, emotional caretaker to the sensitive stars; Geffen was the financial wizard behind the scenes, outsmarting the industry's cleverest titans. "We were both very involved with the artists, but in different ways," Geffen says. "Elliot would go on the road with them but I would not. I did most of the business for the artists and Elliot did most of the hanging out with them."

"Elliot in some strange way was the vehicle for David to be so successful, because in some regard it was his musical taste that defined all of this," says Ron Stone, hired to help manage the Geffen-Roberts acts. "Elliot had this amazing sensitivity to this kind of music and made some incredibly insightful choices. I forgive him all his other foibles, because there was a touch of genius there."

"In the Laurel Canyon and Topanga areas, Elliot was the rare manager who actually *lived* there rather than Beverly Hills," says photographer and architect Joel Bernstein. "The whole vibe of Elliot's office, with a rolltop desk, told you they'd got into the whole canyon vibe—this whole updated Western fantasy." Geffen-Roberts's clients were under no illusions about the duo's master plan, however. "Elliot Roberts is a good dude," David Crosby told writer Ben Fong-Torres. "However, he is, in his managerial capacity, capable of lying straight-faced to anyone, anytime, ever." And if Roberts didn't rob you blind, the grinning Crosby continued, "we'll send Dave Geffen over: he'll take your whole company. And sell it while you're out to lunch, you know."

But it wasn't *all* about money for Geffen. There was a part of David that fed off the egos and insecurities of his stars, compulsively trying to make everything perfect for them. David stayed sober and focused while the talent indulged.

"David may have wanted to have a successful business," said Jackson Browne, "but he also wanted to be part of a community of friends. He became our champion, and years later—after a lot of therapy—he finally got over his need to caretake people to the detriment of his own life." In the meantime there were plenty of fragile egos to caretake—and much remarkable talent to exploit.

4

Horses, Kids, and Forgotten Women

*We wanted to turn away from all the intensity and
social foment and just sort of go have a picnic.*

—Bernie Leadon

Hand Sown . . . Home Grown

The night of June 22, 1966, found an unusual-looking group taking
the stage of the Whisky a Go Go on the Sunset Strip. Four men in
buckskin jackets and cowboy boots ambled into the spotlight and
performed a short set of country and western songs. The response to
the ensemble, led by departed Byrd Gene Clark, was one of brow-
furrowing bafflement. Here was the Tambourine Man himself, the
Prince Valiant of folk-rock, rigged out like some cornpoke Opry veteran and singing *that* music—the songs of southern racists. Just how
unhip could you get?

For Clark, country songs were simply what you were reared on in
Tipton, Missouri. It was no small coincidence that he returned there

shortly after his Byrds meltdown. Connecting with his roots seemed to ground him in this dark passage of his fitful career. While the Byrds flew on into the *Fifth Dimension*, Clark lost interest in Roger McGuinn's "jet sound." His brief if heady trip as a mid-1960s pop star only confirmed his need to dig down into the original sources of the folk boom: bluegrass, Appalachian balladry, old-time string-band instrumentals.

Not that the trappings of L.A. stardom were a total turnoff for the Missouri Kid. Brooding and introverted he may have been, but Clark was as wowed by women and cars as most rock idols. At a party in Laurel Canyon, he met Michelle Phillips of the Mamas and the Papas and began his affair with folk-pop's überbabe. "John [Phillips] and Denny [Doherty] were having parties every night and they were screwing everybody," Michelle remembered. "And then very innocently this thing started with Gene."

The romance scandalized the little village of Laurel Canyon, filling Gene with guilt and leading to Michelle's departure from the Mamas and the Papas in early June. "He was an odd guy," says David Jackson, who played bass with Gene. "But he had his Ferrari and we went to Vegas one time. The guy was going at 150 mph. Now this is a guy who's quiet, sensitive, a little weird, so it was incongruous to me. There was a discrepancy between the Ferrari and the art."

Clark wasn't the only L.A. folk-rocker flirting with country music. Chris Hillman had sneaked Porter Wagoner's "Satisfied Mind" onto the second Byrds' album, *Turn! Turn! Turn!* As the group geared up to record the *Younger than Yesterday* album, Chris drew still deeper from the bluegrass well by penning two stone-country tunes, "Time Between" and "The Girl with No Name." He also brought in guitarist Clarence White and former Hillmen singer Vern Gosdin to play on them.

Hillman would be the first to acknowledge that country music was already an integral strand in California's musical fabric. The "western" part of the country and western classification did not denote California per se but it certainly encompassed the Golden State: western swing and cowboy songs were as big west of the Rockies as they were down in Texas. The roots of country rock lay in the music of migrants uprooted by the Depression—Okies and other southwesterners who'd drifted toward the Pacific from the drought-blighted dust bowls in the 1930s and 1940s. Many such migrants settled in the small city of Bakersfield, north of Los Angeles in the dry-baked San Joaquin Valley of California. By the early 1960s, Bakersfield had unofficially become a "Nashville West," spawning the gritty, unsentimental honky-tonk of Buck Owens and Merle Haggard. Los Angeles itself swarmed with displaced southwesterners: its thousand-and-one suburbs boasted hundreds of dance halls, havens of drinking and fighting. And Capitol Records, the city's biggest independent label, attracted the cream of country music talent, from Owens and Haggard to Wynn Stewart and Tommy Collins.

"Most of us that came out of bluegrass didn't like Nashville music," says Chris Darrow. "We liked country music, but we liked country music from California—from Bakersfield. We were really true to our school: we loved Buck Owens and Merle Haggard." For writer John Einarson, the sound of Buck Owens and his Buckaroos was "the first real electric country rock." Owens, a conventional man next to brooding ex-jailbird Haggard, had a profound influence not only on a generation of country rockers but also on such far-flung stars as the Beatles, who covered "Act Naturally," and Ray Charles, who hit with "Together Again."

Like Gene Clark, brothers Rodney and Douglas Dillard hailed from Missouri. In late 1962 they packed themselves into a beat-up 1955 Cadillac and brought their fiery little bluegrass combo to Los Angeles. In no time they were the talk of the folk underground, thrilling fans at the Ash Grove and the Troubadour. Their first album bore the title *Back Porch Bluegrass*. "Everybody went, 'Oh, my God, this is astonishing,'" says David Jackson. "Everybody else was kind of folkie and nice and genteel and white, and here come these guys just *plowing through*." Of the brothers, Rodney stayed the truer to his rural Christian upbringing. Douglas, on the other hand, took to Sin City immediately. Tall and rake-thin with a weasely Ozark Mountains face, Doug would play his relentless, bubbling banjo licks wearing an unearthly grin. The smile, more often than not, was the result of the substances he had ingested. "Doug became the focal point for anything anybody wanted to say or do," says David Jackson. "All the girls wanted to show him their tits and all the guys wanted to play him their new songs."

As galvanizing and irreverent as the Dillards were, the bluegrass craze that swept through Southern California was rooted more in nostalgia than in eclecticism. "The wave hit L.A., which was ripe for something like that," said sessionman Ry Cooder. "It . . . suggested that there might be a carefree, simple-minded world beyond all the stress and strain of Los Angeles, and that people could wear cowboy hats and boots and play banjos and be cowboys."

For all the success the Dillards enjoyed, brother Douglas was more interested in fun and frolics than in steady employment. He was also keen to move beyond traditional bluegrass. So were several other musicians. Clarence White, the hottest guitarist on the scene, was tiring of the acoustic, bluegrass-based music he played in the Kentucky Colonels. One of his chief accomplices was pedal steel player "Sneaky" Pete Kleinow, a veteran of California western swing bands. "We were fooling around there with country rock but we didn't know what to call it," Kleinow says. "Clarence was one of the ringleaders of all that, but there wasn't a label for it at the time."

Troubadour hootmaster Larry Murray led Hearts and Flowers, a trio playing an uncategorizable mix of folk, pop, and bluegrass that got them signed to Capitol Records subsidiary FolkWorld by A&R man Nik Venet. "[Hearts and Flowers] were probably the closest thing to what we were all flowing into," said Jimmy Messina, a new guitarist recruited by Richie Furay to help patch up the Buffalo Springfield. "They were the cutting edge of where the rest of us were going." Venet, who had been instrumental in the career of the Beach Boys, wasn't exactly hip to the new direction; he even fought Hearts and Flowers on their cover of Merle Haggard's "I'm a Lonesome Fugitive." Yet inadvertently FolkWorld became a creative petri dish for country rock, especially after Venet signed ex–Kingston Trio singer John Stewart and the Linda Ronstadt–fronted Stone Poneys to the label.

Venet figured he could sell the Stone Poneys as a kind of Sunset Strip version of Peter, Paul, and Mary. The young Ronstadt, puppy-ishly eager and grateful, was happy to go along with the plan. But when Venet added sweeping strings to "Different Drum," a song by her boyfriend Mike Nesmith, the barefoot chanteuse was appalled—especially when, in late 1967, the track became a hit. "I hated it," Ronstadt says. "I never set out to make it. If I was playing some pizza place in Westwood or the Insomniac in Hermosa Beach, I was happy."

With her dark skin and doe eyes, Ronstadt was already turning heads and breaking hearts. "Linda was young and she was very cute," says Nurit Wilde. "She was adorable. You could tell right away that she *was* the Stone Poneys." Flirtatious and precocious, Ronstadt seemed only semi-aware of her sexual power. When Judy Henske took the unhappy Phil Ochs to visit her in Topanga Canyon, he asked her out. "Linda says to me, *in front of Phil*, 'Phil just asked me out,'" Henske remembers. "She says, 'I told him no. I decided I didn't dig him.' And she started giggling."

Ronstadt, who recorded her debut solo album *Hand Sown . . . Home Grown* in the fall of 1968, was just one of the artists on the post-folk L.A. scene who sensed the move toward a new kind of country music. "Everybody's going to the country," she said in October 1970. "Everybody's trying to get some air. Obviously we screwed it up here pretty badly for human beings. They're trying to seek shelter in any way they can."

"I think it was unconsciously a reaction to the volatility of the times," agrees Bernie Leadon, a bluegrass-schooled picker who'd gigged with Chris Hillman back in the early folk days. "By 1967 we all already knew people we'd been to school with who'd been killed in Vietnam. And then in 1968, Bobby Kennedy *and* Martin Luther King got killed. So you had all this intense political stuff going on but at the same time you were struggling with questions like 'Am I going to have a family? Is that a wise thing to do?'"

When Bob Dylan's *John Wesley Harding* appeared early in 1968, its sparse Nashville sound and biblical imagery confirmed his apparent retreat from the exploding plastic counterculture. His former backing group the Hawks—or the Band, as they became known when their 1968 debut *Music from Big Pink* was released—had if anything more impact even than their mentor. While country music was only one of several rootsy ingredients in their Americana brew, the use of such old-timey instruments as fiddles and mandolins made them a key part of this retrogressive trend. When *Time* magazine put the group on the cover in 1970, the headline read "The New Sound of Country Rock." And when the Band came to record their second album in 1969, they chose to cut most of it in California in a pool house overlooking the Sunset Strip.

Nashville Skyline, released in the same year, took Dylan's retreat one step farther. Sung in a strangely plummy voice at several removes from the caustic timbre of *Highway 61* and *Blonde on Blonde*, *Skyline* was another rebuff to the politicos who'd looked to Dylan for militant leadership. It also changed the image of Nashville forever. "It broke the city open," says Lambchop's Kurt Wagner, who grew up in Nashville. "After that, things started to get interesting as far as other people coming to town to record on a fairly regular basis." In Nashville at the same time was John Stewart, working on an album called *California Bloodlines*. Employing the same Music Row session players Dylan used, producer Nik Venet wanted to cross the Nashville Sound with L.A. country rock. The resulting record—an Americana classic flecked with the influences of John Steinbeck and Andrew Wyeth—sounded like a missing link between Johnny Cash and Gene Clark. "I wanted to do a sort of modern folk thing, not L.A. country," Venet said. "By making this cross, John made it possible for Gram Parsons and the Burrito Brothers to happen. I wanted to define a new folk movement with Stewart and Ronstadt." The "new folk movement" was on its way, but it had little to do with folk as Nik Venet had known it.

Wheatstraw Sweet

In California, country music was now setting the pace for late 1960s rock. Even as the Buffalo Springfield unraveled in the sessions for the farewell album *Last Time Around*, country was clearly audible in the clipped rimshots of Neil Young's "I Am a Child"—and even more markedly in Richie Furay's song "Kind Woman," featuring a pedal steel guitar. "I think Neil Young and I were playing country rock before [The Band] ever got out of what they were playing with Ronnie Hawkins," Stephen Stills told *Circus* in 1970. "I mean, we were playing Chet Atkins guitar and stuff like that, which may sound like an ego trip."

If Stills and Young were barely speaking during the recording of *Last Time Around*, the sessions at Sunset Sound cemented the bond between Richie Furay and guitarist Jim Messina. As the two men worked on the Springfield's swan song, the seeds of their own country-rock band Poco were planted.

The Byrds themselves underwent the most radical of all stylistic changes when they made the bold decision to replace David Crosby with southern-born Gram Parsons, late of the International Submarine Band. Skinny and cute with a warm, boyish smile, what set Parsons apart from his country rock contemporaries was the $30,000 he received each year from a trust fund set up by his wealthy family. He suffered from rich kids' dilettantism, dropping out of bands and other projects when he tired of hard work. He'd also had an upbringing as dysfunctional as anything in a Tennessee Williams play. His father shot himself, and his mother died of alcoholism. "Gram was a good kid, with a good heart," says Chris Hillman, who brought Parsons into the Byrds. "If you delve into his background, though, it's pure southern Gothic."

Parsons had first come to Los Angeles in late 1966, in the company of actor Brandon De Wilde, a hyperactive screen rebel in the Dennis Hopper mold. Within a month De Wilde had introduced the lanky charmer to his circle of rock and roll friends. Just before Christmas the two men wound their way up to Beverly Glen to meet David Crosby. When Crosby's girlfriend, Nancy Lee Ross, returned from shopping, Gram's eyes locked with hers. That evening, Crosby split for a Byrds tour and Gram and Nancy fell in love. By early 1967 they'd moved into an apartment in West Hollywood, with the Submarine Band installed in a Laurel Canyon pad dubbed "the Burrito Manor." Gram's trust fund paid for everything. "Gram and Nancy lived on Sweetzer Avenue in a beautiful apartment with stained glass windows," says Eve Babitz. "He was like a kind of F. Scott Fitzgerald hero in a place where nobody had ever heard of F. Scott Fitzgerald."

A musical break of sorts came when De Wilde recommended the Submarine Band to Peter Fonda, another hip actor with rock aspirations. Fonda persuaded director Roger Corman to hire the band for his drugsploitation movie *The Trip*, a paean to LSD scripted by Jack Nicholson. Converted to country music by John Nuese, Parsons made the first of several visits to Nudie's Rodeo Tailors in North Hollywood, fitting himself out like a hippie Hank Williams. With Nuese he ventured out to redneck dives in distant satellite suburbs such as El Monte and City of Industry, soaking up the subculture of farmers and truckers and befriending a coterie of pickers who included Clarence White and Pete Kleinow. On Thursdays he'd play talent nights at the Palomino, north of Laurel Canyon in the San Fernando Valley. "It took me two years to win the talent contest," he said. "I would religiously drive out there and wait my turn. For two years I was beaten by yodeling grandmothers and the same guy who sang 'El Paso' every week."

In late June 1967 a new International Submarine Band auditioned for Suzi Jane Hokom, girlfriend of Lee Hazlewood. With her blessing they were signed to Hazlewood's LHI Records, recording the *Safe at Home* album in two sessions, in July and November 1967. "My main recollections are of the hours and hours of rehearsals Gram and John and I did at my house in Laurel Canyon," says Hokom. But there was immediate friction between Parsons and Hazlewood. "Lee was older and his ego just kind of got in the way," Suzi says. "I think he was jealous—he couldn't stand all this attention I was lavishing on these guys who were more of my generation."

There are those who dispute *Safe at Home*'s status as the first country rock album, along with Gram's posthumous standing as godfather to the genre. "There were probably twenty, thirty guys on the West Coast who were all basically trying to do the same thing," says Chris Darrow. "I don't think any of us thought of Gram as the Duke Ellington of our deal." This may sound like kvetching from an unsung hero who has watched Gram's star ascend in death, but it is a fact that the true roots of L.A. country rock have been persistently overlooked or discounted by rock historians. (Former teen idol Ricky Nelson, no less, recorded the *Bright Lights and Country Music* album as early as February 1966.) Yet the very fact that Gram—like Neil Young and Joni Mitchell—was an outsider was what gave his music its distinctive flavor.

Sadly the Submarine Band sank before *Safe at Home* was even released. By the spring of 1968 Parsons was once again a free musical agent. One day he ran into Chris Hillman in a Beverly

Hills bank. "I knew very little about Gram," Hillman says. "On first acquaintance he was very sweet, very naive in the sense of being in Hollywood." By Hillman's own admission the Byrds were in crisis. "We were in a state of limbo," he says. "We were looking at each other thinking, 'We're the last guys left and we don't know where this is going'—and now here comes Gram."

"We were simply looking for someone to replace Crosby," recalls Roger McGuinn. "It was only gradually that he started to play his Hank Williams things. And we thought, Wow, that's really cool." McGuinn would be the first to admit that he was less interested in country than Hillman. But when he heard Chris and Gram harmonizing on Buck Owens's "Under Your Spell Again" he was happy to let things take their natural course. The chemistry between the two country freaks led to a radical rethinking in Byrdland. In March 1968 a session was booked at Columbia's studio in Nashville.

When *Sweetheart of the Rodeo* was released in August, heads were scratched—and not just in Los Angeles. To hear the band that flew "Eight Miles High" now sporting short hair and warbling bluegrass classics "I Am a Pilgrim" and "The Christian Life" came as a shock. "Our fans were heartbroken that we'd sold out to the enemy," McGuinn says. "Politically, country music represented the right wing—redneck people who liked guns." McGuinn also felt upstaged by Parsons. "He was a rich kid, which meant that he was already a star," he reflects. "It was as though *Mick Jagger* had joined the band."

As with most of Gram's musical involvements, his stint as a Byrd wouldn't last long. And among those who played a part in his departure was Mick Jagger himself.

Rural Free Delivery

Gene Clark, the original ex-Byrd, finally released his first solo album in February 1967. He called it *Gene Clark and the Gosdin Brothers*, a selfless nod to harmonizing vocalists Vern and Rex Gosdin. The album, which also featured Glen Campbell and Van Dyke Parks, blended bluegrass soul ("Tried So Hard," "Keep on Pushin'") with baroque orchestral pop (the Leon Russell–arranged "Echoes"). Clark, a prolific writer, loved the Beatles' *Rubber Soul* and wanted to make a California version of that masterpiece. But he was as lacking in confidence as ever. "Gene was nervous about doing his first album," said the velvet-voiced Vern Gosdin. "He was a good fella but he was into drugs too much."

It was typical somehow that *Gene Clark and the Gosdin Brothers* was released the same week as the Byrds' *Younger than Yesterday*. If Columbia had intended to bury the album they couldn't have done a better job. Sessions for a second Clark album, in April 1967, were canned. Lost and disenchanted, Gene was coaxed back into the Byrds as David Crosby's replacement in October. Once again his fear of flying led to his departure. After just three weeks, Clark refused to board a flight from Minneapolis to New York, instead taking a long and ·lonely train ride back to California.

Back in L.A., Gene fell into the easy-rolling company of Doug Dillard, who'd played on *Gene Clark and the Gosdin Brothers*. The two Missourians shared a passion for the bluegrass and country music they'd been raised on. They also shared a passion for alcohol and chemicals. One of their favorite pastimes was to drop acid and then down rows of martinis at Dan Tana's, the Italian restaurant next door to the Troubadour. The combination of ersatz sophistication and lysergic fracturing delighted them. In April 1968 Clark drunkenly gate-crashed a farewell party for Derek Taylor, who was returning to England to rejoin his original employers, the Beatles, at the newly founded Apple Corporation. After stumbling onstage with the Byrds at Ciro's, Gene was very nearly ejected from the club. "He watched the show for a little while and then literally *crawled* across the dance floor to the stage," says former Byrds groupie Pamela Des Barres. "Finally he just wound up curled around a microphone on the floor, and they played the rest of the set with him like that."

Dillard accompanied the Byrds on a tour of Europe that summer, rooming with Gram Parsons and tagging along with Mick Jagger and Keith Richards on a nocturnal visit to Stonehenge. On his return to California, Clark asked Doug to play on a new solo album he was recording for A&M Records. Slowly the project evolved into a joint venture called *The Fantastic Expedition of Dillard & Clark*. The album came together at Dillard's place in Beechwood Canyon, east of

Laurel Canyon. Rooming and jamming with Doug was country/ bluegrass guitarist Bernie Leadon, then nearing the end of a stint with Hearts and Flowers. Living upstairs was Dillard's tenant—and Leadon's occasional squeeze—Linda Ronstadt. "Doug and I were just sitting around playing this bluegrass stuff," remembers Leadon. "Gene started turning up in this magnificent V-12 Ferrari, and then he'd come back the next day with a whole set of lyrics for the instrumentals. That's how a lot of the songs on the *Fantastic Expedition* album got written."

Also on board the *Expedition* was ever-reliable bass player David Jackson, shyly approached one night at the Troubadour by Gene Clark. To this day Jackson recalls the rehearsals as magical. The same epithet could be applied to *The Fantastic Expedition*, released in October 1967. As much an example of Gram Parsons' "soul-country-cosmic" hybrid as anything Parsons himself achieved, the album stands time's test as well as the Flying Burrito Brothers' *The Gilded Palace of Sin*, which it preceded. It's certainly a more satisfying record than *Sweetheart of the Rodeo*. From the Byrdsish "Out on the Side" to the wistfully jaunty Clark-Leadon song "Train Leaves Here This Mornin'" via the heartache melody of "The Radio Song," the *Expedition* is the missing link between *Back Porch Bluegrass* and the Grateful Dead's *American Beauty*: hippie country rock that's influenced everybody from R.E.M. to Teenage Fanclub. "Doug and Gene did some really good records that nobody paid attention to," Chris Hillman told John Einarson. "That first album was fabulous, way better than anything the rest of us were doing when you measure it song-per-song."

The fact that the *Expedition* bombed was partly the fault of A&M Records, formed as a pop label by trumpeter Herb Alpert and a company with scant understanding of Dillard and Clark's musical roots. A&M would expand its country-rock roster with the Flying Burritos' *Gilded Palace of Sin*, Phil Ochs's *Tape from California*, and Steve Young's *Rock, Salt, and Nails*, but if the label's instincts were right they lacked the underground marketing savvy of Warner-Reprise. "A&M wanted to become hip, so they brought me in and tried to attract some major talent," says Tom Wilkes, who became the label's art director in 1968. "It was all Boyce and Hart, Sergio Mendes, Herb Alpert, and now they were really trying to sign bands. They wanted to get into the mainstream of rock."

Dillard and Clark themselves hardly helped their own cause. On the cover of *The Fantastic Expedition* they posed as bikers and smirked like schoolboys as they shared a joint. "I was around during that Dillard and Clark period, and all they were doing was drinking and taking drugs," recalls Chris Darrow. "You'd go in there and hang out for four and a half hours and you wouldn't play a note." Gene and Doug couldn't even hold it together for their Troubadour debut. When David Jackson showed up for the gig, the club's doorman advised him to go next door, to Tana's. There the two men sat, olives bobbing in their martinis, stoned out of their skulls. David hauled them back into the club. When the lights came up on the band, Dillard stood stage-central with his banjo and grin. Jackson, Leadon, and mandolinist Don Beck flanked him. At the rear of the stage was Harold Eugene Clark, sitting on his amp and facing the back wall. Jackson somehow got Clark turned around for the second song, on which Doug Dillard was playing fiddle. At the end of it, still grinning, Doug placed the fiddle on the ground and jumped on it. "That was pretty much the end of that version of Dillard and Clark," says Leadon. "They didn't have the discipline or really the desire to be a performing act."

It wasn't all mayhem with Dillard and Clark. Some nights they set the Troubadour on fire, especially after going fully electric and bringing ex-Byrd Michael Clarke in on drums. "The Eagles will tell you that the Dillard and Clark shows were like revival meetings," says L.A. music historian Domenic Priore. "Pogo and Dillard and Clark and Linda Ronstadt were really the seminal events." If *Through the Morning, Through the Night*, the second Dillard and Clark album, was covers-heavy, it still included two Clark classics in the title track and the sublime "Polly." No one ever did waltz-time sadness as tenderly as the guy from Tipton.

"Gene always seemed unhappy, like there was a cloud over his head," said fiddler Byron Berline, who joined Dillard and Clark before the second album. "He'd be happy one day, and you'd see him the next day and he would be a bucket of gloom." The wonder is that

so many extraordinary songs poured out of this melancholy booze
hound. For John York, who briefly played bass with Gene before joining the Byrds in 1969, the man was "a hillbilly Shakespeare."

Clark's melancholia only deepened as he lost whatever grip he'd
had on his own group. After Dillard brought in his latest fling,
Donna Washburn, as a second singer, Gene quit. Significantly, he
also turned his back on Los Angeles. Heading north to the coastal
hippie town of Mendocino, Gene Clark would begin a career as one
of the greatest if most neglected singer-songwriters of the 1970s.

Up on the Strip, the live scene was hurting. Name bands were now
too big to play small clubs such as the Whisky: they'd be booked into
bigger venues, such as the Kaleidoscope or the Shrine Auditorium.
And the Strip itself was hardly the bustling beads-and-bells mecca it
had been in 1965 and 1966. It was a different story down on Santa
Monica Boulevard, where Doug Weston's Troubadour was now the
de facto clubhouse for L.A.'s denim in-crowd. "The Sunset Strip sort
of shut down after Monterey," says Domenic Priore. "Doug managed
to ride the storm out. He had the place, and the people that had
been involved with the folk-rock scene on the Strip gravitated to the
Troubadour."

"When the Troub came along, that was right up our alley," says
Linda Ronstadt. "It was small enough that you could really hear the
music well and get close to it. Of course, we were all so self-centered
that to us it was *already* the center of the universe." On any given
night one might see the angelic Jackson Browne emerging from the
kitchen with a bottle of Dos Equis. Arlo Guthrie, newly signed to
Reprise by Lenny Waronker, would flirt shamelessly with any girl
who worked at the club. In a corner would be comedian/banjo
player Steve Martin, who, in the recollection of Troubadour mainstay Eve Babitz, sat with "a single glass of white wine in the midst of
all that cigarette smoke," unwilling "to look on the bright side of
total debauchery." Janis Joplin or Jim Morrison might be holed up
with a small entourage and a bottle of Jim Beam. Later they would
be poured into a Red & White cab after becoming belligerent and
abusive.

"If you sold out the Troubadour, that was it," says Tom Waits, who played the club early in his career. "At the Troub they announced your name and picked you up with a spotlight at the cigarette machine, and then they'd walk you to the stage with the light. Then Doug would go out onstage naked and recite 'The Love Song of J. Alfred Prufrock.'" At the Troubadour the waitresses—Reina, Black Sylvia, Big Tit Sue—and the bartenders—Ray, Kevin, Gatt, Jim Maxwell, John Barrick—were almost as famous as the entertainers who hung out there. "There was Big Tit Sue and Bigger Tit Sue, and there was Black Sylvia behind the bar," recalls Robert Marchese, a tough-talking former football player from Pittsburgh who produced Richard Pryor's first album at the club in September 1968. "The Troub nearly brought the Whisky to its knees. Everybody started hanging out at the bar on Monday hoot night. They would all get together, get drunk, talk about how great they were, and go home."

Few went home alone. Drunk or wired, boys and girls fell into bed with each other and retained scant recollection of their couplings the next day. "It was such a sexual experience being in that place," says Michael Ochs. "You could fall asleep there and wake up in bed with some woman."

For fastidious executives such as Jac Holzman there was "too much posturing and moving around" at the club, but for good-time guys such as Doug Dillard the place was like heaven. On one deeply cherished occasion Doug broke into the opening lines of "Amazing Grace," joined moments later by a lustrous Linda Ronstadt harmony—and then by David Crosby, Gene Clark, Harry Dean Stanton, and Jackson Browne, all pitching in a cappella. Dillard also was the chief protagonist in umpteen extramusical legends. On one occasion a frenziedly jealous Suzi Jane Hokom—whom Doug had stolen away from Lee Hazlewood—attempted to run the banjo player over in the street, instead missing him and crashing into the karate studio next door.

Doug Weston still made artists sign contracts that obliged them to return to the Troubadour long after they'd made it big. Many resented it bitterly. "Weston would sign you for five years and pay the same amount for every performance—$1,000," Don McLean said. "Sure, in 1970 this was good money, but when I became No. 1 all over the world with "American Pie" I still had to play his goddamned lousy club because he had me under contract." At least as important as the stage at the Troubadour was the club's front bar, where everyone on the scene congregated. "The bar was the place where it all happened," says musician Judy James. "The Monday night hoot was fabulous and people just poured in."

"The Troub was the only place where you could go and showcase for record companies," remembered Jackson Browne. "If you were lucky you might get to sing three or four songs that night." Most importantly, the club was the crucible for L.A.'s burgeoning country rock sound—the headquarters for "the people who had grown their hair long but who still loved country music and wanted to play it," in the words of Texan pedal steel player Al Perkins.

"There *was* a sort of music community at that time," says Browne. "With the Byrds and the Burritos came a whole resurgence of interest in country music that led eventually to the Eagles." If any one event can be said to have ignited L.A.'s country rock scene it would have to be the debut show by Pogo at the Troubadour in November 1968. Formed out of the ashes of Buffalo Springfield, Pogo set the club on fire with a tight, ebullient set that was as good as any performance the Buffalo Springfield had given. (The group renamed itself Poco after *Pogo* cartoonist Walt Kelly threatened to sue.) Jim Messina's love of Bakersfield country was even more pronounced than Richie Furay's midwestern immersion in country pop. With drummer George Grantham, Rusty Young on pedal steel, and Nebraska-born bassist/harmony singer Randy Meisner on bass, Pogo/Poco was a group polished to perfection. And everyone was there at the Troubadour to witness them, from Rick Nelson to Linda Ronstadt.

"There'd been a long period of time where country music had not impacted on pop music or rock and roll," says Ronstadt. "There was pure country stuff, where someone like George Jones might have had a crossover hit or something, but people weren't mixing the two." For all that Poco presented a fresh and genial version of the Springfield's California-country amalgam, Furay's songs secreted bitter feelings toward his former bandmates. Quietly livid at the way he'd been squeezed out by the overbearing egos of Stephen Stills and Neil Young, Richie used Poco's debut album *Pickin' Up the Pieces* to attack them. It was ironic, therefore, that bassist Randy Meisner decided to leave Poco because he felt excluded by Furay and Jimmy Messina. With a seamlessness endemic to country rock, Meisner immediately transferred to Rick Nelson's Stone Canyon Band, named after the affluent Brentwood canyon where Nelson lived. Taken with Dylan's *Nashville Skyline*, Nelson made the Bakersfield connection explicit by hiring former Buckaroo Tom Brumley as his pedal steel player. When the Stone Canyon Band played six nights at the Troubadour at the start of April, it was another country rock landmark.

So much was happening at this time, and most of it centered on the Troubadour. The club's former hootmaster Mike Nesmith—Texan-born and country-steeped—quit the Monkees and formed his own back-to-the-roots group, the First National Band. The Frank Zappa of country rock, Nesmith was less interested in making country hip than in using the genre to paint his own singular portrait of America. The First National Band's trilogy of albums—*Magnetic South* (1970), *Loose Salute* (1971), and *Nevada Fighter* (1971)—was the result.

Like Rick Nelson, the Nitty Gritty Dirt Band were profoundly influenced by the Pogo shows at the Troubadour. They'd started out as a Long Beach jug band, with the young Jackson Browne briefly a member. When John McEuen replaced him in the summer of 1966 he steered them in a pointedly more country/bluegrass direction, culminating in the 1969 album *Uncle Charlie and His Dog Teddy*. The group was managed by McEuen's brother Bill. Another of Bill's stable of acts was Steve Martin. On at least one occasion, Steve had the entire audience exit the Troubadour, board a flatcar train that ran past its entrance up to La Cienega Boulevard, and walk back down to the club—singing and playing his banjo the whole way.

Sweetheart queen of the scene was Linda Ronstadt, whose latest backing band was the Corvettes, a group formed by Chris Darrow and ex–Dirt Band member Jeff Hanna. "In those days it was more about who you liked than what you could do," Ronstadt remembers. "I had gotten real into Cajun music, and Chris was the only other person on the scene who'd ever heard it."

"Linda was the most underrated of all the country rock people because she was female," Darrow says. "I think she was one of the

most naturally gifted singers I've met in my life, and she had impec-
cable taste." Toward the end of 1969 Ronstadt was living with her
producer, John Boylan, on King's Road above the Sunset Strip.
Boylan was a well-to-do East Coast preppie who'd worked with the
Lovin' Spoonful before moving west to work with Rick Nelson
and the Dillards. Galvanized by L.A.'s new country rock sound, he
was determined to make Linda more than the one-hit wonder of
"Different Drum."

Ronstadt herself had become fanatical about getting her music
right, especially given the lack of understanding from both her manager, Herb Cohen, and her label, Capitol. "Linda was relentless
about trying to find great songs because she didn't write herself,"
says Bernie Leadon, who replaced Jeff Hanna in her band. "If someone said he was a songwriter, she'd have them over in the corner with
a guitar and she'd say, 'Right, play me your songs.'" At the Troubadour Linda was at the heart of a clique of lean and hungry young-
bloods. Most were male, although two were Karla Bonoff and Wendy
Waldman, who'd sung in the group Bryndle with Kenny Edwards
and Andrew Gold. "It's like the musician pool and the sex pool, you
know?" Ronstadt said in 1974. "Like, if you needed a new player
there was this big tank full of whoever's not busy at that point, so you
just reach in . . . and get one. Or, 'Gee, I just broke up with my old
man, I need a new honey'—reach into the same tank."

Splashing around in the Troubadour "tank" were Jackson
Browne, David Ackles, David Blue, Jack Wilce, Ned Doheny, and a
lean and good-looking duo—Glenn Frey and John David Souther—
who performed under the folksy appellation Longbranch Pennywhistle. Souther was a reddish-headed Texan who'd drifted out to
California from Amarillo in the spring of 1967. "I think I knew
exactly what I would find there," he says. "I even knew what the air
would smell like. It was ozone and ocean and automobile exhaust
and eucalyptus." Frey hailed from Detroit, where he'd played guitar
with Bob Seger but secretly hankered for the fantasy land conjured
up in Beach Boys' records. "I saw copies of *Surfer* magazine," Glenn
reminisced. "I took acid and bought the first Buffalo Springfield
album and got goosebumps and had to lay on the floor and stuff. I
got into this whole 'California consciousness.'" In a sign of things to

come, the early California adventures of these denim desperadoes were entwined with women. "I came out here chasing my girlfriend [Joanie] from Detroit," Frey told *Rolling Stone*. "John David was going out with my girlfriend's sister [Alexandria] and I met him my first day in California."

Souther was already a country fan, obsessed with Hank Williams. Though he knew little about Bakersfield, moving to California broadened his musical education to encompass that hot, dusty city. Frey said that Souther taught him "to sing and play country." The two men combined forces as a neo–Everly Brothers folk/country duo and snagged a deal with Amos, an independent label launched by ex-Reprise A&R man Jimmy Bowen, himself a Texan. The following year they recorded their first and only album. Unfortunately, *Longbranch Pennywhistle*, released in September 1969, was lackluster, despite featuring such sessionmen as James Burton, Jim Gordon, and Ry Cooder. Even if it *had* been good, Amos lacked the clout to break the album out of the L.A. market. More to the point, Bowen couldn't really hear what Longbranch Pennywhistle were trying to do. When Frey and Souther came to him and suggested making a more stripped-down record with Neil Young's producer David Briggs, Bowen asked who Young was. It didn't bode well. When Amos refused to release a second album, Glenn and J. D. did what any other broke country rockers did in L.A. in 1969: hang around the Troubadour bar.

At a benefit concert down in Long Beach, Frey and Souther bonded with local hero Jackson Browne. When the two men split up with their girlfriends, Jackson stumbled on a two-apartment house in Echo Park, and the three amigos moved in together. 1020 Laguna Avenue was a long way from Laurel Canyon, but the rent was dirt-cheap, with Jackson occupying the downstairs studio apartment and the Pennywhistle boys holed up above him. The neighborhood was predominantly Mexican, dotted with funky eateries such as Barragan's, which served killer huevos rancheros and lethally strong coffee.

Depressed that so little was happening with Amos, Glenn and J. D. would knock around the apartment waiting for success to knock at the door. At night it got scarier, especially when the Fugs's Ed Sanders—researching a book on Charles Manson—stayed with them. "A couple of times," Jackson Browne remembered, "Glenn had to throw milk bottles through the window to discourage what Sanders called 'the sleazo inputs' who were after him." Unlike Frey and Souther, Jackson worked assiduously at his songs, repeating and reworking phrases on an old upright piano until he'd gotten them right. For the Longbranch boys it was a lesson in application. One of the songs floating through the floorboards was "Rock Me on the Water," inspired by mythologist Joseph Campbell. Another had a chorus about taking life easy: it caught Frey's ear and lodged in his subconscious. By night, more often than not, the trio would bundle themselves into a dilapidated car and head over to West Hollywood. Life at the Troubadour was mainly about posing. "J. D. once told me he spent his first six months in L.A. learning how to stand," says Eve Babitz with a laugh.

For those on the outside of its in-crowd, the Troubadour wasn't necessarily the friendliest place. On hoot nights, aspiring bards lined up along Santa Monica Boulevard like cattle, waiting for gatekeeper Roger Perry to give them the nod or send them on their way. "There is no room for compassion here, or pity," *L.A. Free Press* columnist Liza Williams wrote in 1970. "It's a voluntary slaughter, it is self-induced agony, and it rubs off and it corrupts." Williams reported that even when Troubadour hopefuls got their "big chance," a swinging door separated them from industry heavies too busy carousing and deal-making to keep ears open for undiscovered talent.

In a song about the club written almost a decade later by Glenn Frey's band the Eagles, the Troubadour "seemed like a holy place/protected by amazing grace." But the song was titled "The Sad Café," its clientele described as "a lonely crowd." "[It] was and always will be full of tragic fucking characters," Frey told Cameron Crowe. "Sure, it's brought a lot of music to people, but it's also infested with spiritual parasites who will rob you of your precious artistic energy."

"Glenn had very long hair and would always come sidling up and coming on to you," says Nurit Wilde. "But he didn't talk very much about what he was doing. He seemed to be kind of poor, a guy with no money and no prospects, and yet he was always at the Troub. Always." Souther, by contrast, played the role of mysterious stranger, an act that attracted girls in droves. Already acquiring a reputation as the Troubadour's No. 1 heartbreaker, he would—in Eve Babitz's words—"scorch the bar with his eyes, ignoring all the girls in case they thought their souls their own." Linda Ronstadt was among those who couldn't quite tear their eyes away.

Another cute Troubadour aspirant, Ned Doheny, became a fourth member of the Frey/Souther/Browne posse. Unlike them, however, he had few financial worries. Like Gram Parsons and Terry Melcher, he was a rare example of a trust-fund kid on the scene. "Southern California doesn't have much of a bar culture, and the Troub was the closest we got to that," he says. "It was really a social thing, an opportunity to rub elbows and see all our friends and get laid and all the rest of that."

Doheny was less impressed by Frey and Souther as musicians. "I didn't think about Longbranch Pennywhistle one way or another," he says. "Jackson seemed to come from a pretty deep place, but I didn't have much truck with J. D. or Glenn. I was always kind of an outsider with that group." Drinking and skirt-chasing by night, Frey and Souther now spent their days trying to free themselves from Amos Records.

There was another new face on the scene, and it belonged to a fellow Amos artist. Don Henley was the drummer with Shiloh, a band recommended to Jimmy Bowen by country-pop singer Kenny Rogers, whose wife managed them. Shiloh was a Texan outfit strongly influenced by the nouveau-cowboy vibe of Poco and Gram Parsons. In the late spring of 1970 they packed their bags and drove to California. Henley was an ambitious, curly-headed kid with R&B drumming chops and a sweetly frayed high-tenor voice. On arriving in L.A., his first port of call was inevitably the Troubadour. "The first night I walked in," he remembered, "I saw Graham Nash and Neil Young, and Linda Ronstadt was standing there in a little Daisy Mae kind of dress."

If Henley thought he'd arrived in the promised land, Shiloh's sole album failed badly commercially. "It was a total complete flop," he recalled. "We sat around broke and bummed out. I was hanging out at the Troub getting drunk a lot and getting ready to go back to Texas to call it quits." Salvation wasn't far away. Linda Ronstadt was walking from the Troubadour's bar to its bathroom one night when she heard Shiloh playing the song "Silver Threads and Golden Needles" in the arrangement she'd used on *Hand Sown . . . Home Grown*. With one eye on potential backing band musicians, she took note of the drummer and mentioned him to producer John Boylan.

Glenn Frey also took note of Henley. Sensing competition or camaraderie, he glared across the bar at Don but only met with hostile, suspicious eyes. Henley figured Frey was "another fucked-up little punk" and wasn't far off the mark. For Chris Darrow, the trio of Frey, Henley, and Souther—like Gram Parsons—represented a new breed of country rocker, with roots in R&B and soul rather than in folk rock. "The guys in the South that were our age, like Henley and Souther, were not playing folk music," Darrow reflects. "The melodic structures for their ballads came directly from Memphis and Muscle Shoals. All those songs that J. D. Souther wrote or cowrote, that's where they came from. And all those guys wanted to be J. D."

The scene was now set. Los Angeles had drawn these disparate musical characters to its bosom, and they in turn would reinvent the California dream. "It was the scene that attracted them," says Ron Stone, who would help to manage Souther, Frey, and Henley. "The sound may have originated in Michigan or Texas, but it was brought to Southern California and then identified as the sound from Southern California. These people found their way to California because that's where this particular music was being prized. You may be in Michigan writing Californian songs, but there comes a time when you actually have to *go* there."

5

Escape from Sin City

They all decided that the city was simply out of the question
and they wanted to be ranchers like real men.

—Eve Babitz, *Eve's Hollywood*

Home Is What Makes You Happy

For some L.A. musicians of the time, Laurel Canyon wasn't country
enough. Bucolic as it was, it was too close to Hollywood for comfort—
to the plastic dream factories that warped the nation's psyche via
screens both large and small. For the hard-core hippie, paradise lay
still farther west, close to the Pacific in the Santa Monica mountains.

Accessible from Pacific Coast Highway, which ran all the way up
the coast to Santa Barbara, Topanga Canyon was where you went if
you *really* wanted to get it together in the country—to keep chickens
and grow your own cucumbers. "When Linda Ronstadt lived in
Topanga with Tom Hammill they had horses," says Judy Henske.
"She was an amazing horsewoman, very relaxed around horses and
all animals—including men."

"Topanga really *was* the Wild West," says photographer Joel
Bernstein, who moved there in 1971. "Laurel Canyon might have

had writers and musicians and painters, but Topanga had some of those people and they were more eccentric and more reclusive." Topanga was Laurel Canyon with fewer houses and more space: you got more for your bucks there. More purist and less commercial, it had played host to an annual Banjo Contest, won five years in a row by Kaleidoscope's David Lindley. Taj Mahal, who'd swept the floors of the Ash Grove before teaming up with Ry Cooder in the Rising Sons, moved in with a Topanga girlfriend as early as 1966.

Other Ash Grove graduates—Spirit, Canned Heat, and others—followed Taj into the back of Topanga's beyond. Along with singer-songwriters Barry McGuire and Moon Martin, the Ash Grovers played regularly at the Topanga Corral at 2034 Topanga Canyon Road, described by writer Jerry Hopkins in early 1968 as "a haven for dusty cowboy boots and groups with names like the Tumbleweed Sagebrush Conestoga Wagon Boys."

"That was when Topanga was incredible," says Michael Ochs, who'd all but dropped out of the music business after quitting Columbia Records. "I'd sit there and talk to my dog and watch the mountains melt. Every morning Taj would be singing at the Canyon Kitchen. The Corral was *the* place, and they never charged us locals."

At weekends everybody would congregate at actor Will Geer's ranch. Here you mingled with artists George Herms and Wallace Berman, along with a gang of celluloid rebels who included Dennis Hopper, Peter Fonda, Jack Nicholson, Dean Stockwell, Russ Tamblyn, Harry Dean Stanton, and Brandon De Wilde. Hopper, Fonda, and Nicholson were busy scheming to make an underground, rock-oriented movie that would transcend teen exploitation. With the help of maverick *Monkees* coproducer Bert Schneider they hatched the concept of *Easy Rider*, about two hippies who set off across America on a pair of supercool choppers. "The movie industry went through a similar thing to the music industry," says Lenny Waronker. "It was no coincidence that *Easy Rider* was so much about rock and roll. People like Jack were real music guys."

But the quintessential Topanga star of the moment was Neil Young; Reprise Records went so far as to offer a free bag of Topanga dirt to anyone who purchased his debut album. In August 1968, Bernie Leadon sold Young a tall, narrow redwood house on Skyline

Trail, from which the Canadian would motor down to Pacific Coast Highway in a dusty 1956 Jeep. Among Neil's new cronies was Dean Stockwell, an actor and LSD aficionado who'd written an apocalypse-themed screenplay about Topanga called *After the Gold Rush*. "Neil hung around Topanga a fair amount," says Barry Hansen, who had a room in a house belonging to Spirit. "He'd come and listen to the band. My most vivid memory is of Neil coming up to our place after some business hassle with Greene and Stone and talking about what scum they were." In Topanga, the Canadian was able to play Lone Wolf in splendid isolation. "He was always very self-contained," says Henry Diltz. "He didn't go for the hype, and he didn't suffer fools lightly."

Young's piercing eyes and heavy brow made him look like a close cousin of Herzog's Kaspar Hauser. "People were always very afraid of him," says his manager Elliot Roberts. "He sort of glared at people and they'd freeze. He was so intense. Nothing was casual." The unearthly fragility of his voice paradoxically gave it strength and intensity. His guitar playing, too, was unique: instinctual, primitive, spat-out.

If *Neil Young* had been a commercial failure, a superior sophomore record followed quickly on its heels. *Everybody Knows This Is Nowhere*, cut in early 1969 with a grungy new backing band called Crazy Horse, featured no-frills electric classics such as "Cinnamon Girl" and the epic "Down by the River." Like *Neil Young*, it was produced by David Briggs, whose ranch on Old Topanga Road had been the scene of a 1968 bust involving Young, Stephen Stills, and a visiting Eric Clapton.

Neil had played with Crazy Horse when they were still known as the Rockets. A druggy, vaguely menacing bunch who lived together in Laurel Canyon squalor, Crazy Horse answered to Young's need for a rock and roll sound that was more intuitive and amateurish than the Springfield. Briggs, a charismatic blend of macho and poetic, was the perfect guy to capture that sound on tape. Crucial to Crazy Horse was guitarist Danny Whitten, a wounded creature to whom Neil—adept at sucking emotion from damaged souls and channeling it into his music—instantly gravitated. Dominated by the Young/Whitten guitar combo and underpinned by the thick sludge of bassist Billy Talbot and drummer Ralph Molina, *Everybody* established Neil as a giant talent and a moodily contrary man.

Out in the wilds of Topanga, an added attraction for Young was the strawberry-blond lady who ran the Canyon Kitchen. "Right in the middle of Topanga Canyon there was this small mall, and Susan Acevedo owned the coffee shop," recalls Denny Bruce. "Guys would hang there, including Neil. Topanga was Neil's Woodstock. It was, 'I don't like to go into the city' and all that stuff." Significantly older than Neil, Susan wasn't just another willowy hippie chick; she had a daughter from a previous relationship. The couple married in December 1968. "Neil was always dominated by women," Elliot Roberts told Young's biographer Jimmy McDonough. "I think he respects women more than men—he thinks they're smarter and tougher."

Another Topanga character who befriended Young was an intense, unhinged ex-con with a retinue of mainly female followers. They referred to themselves as The Family. "Charles Manson used to hang about the Topanga General Store," says Barry Hansen. "Once he wandered up our driveway to ask if he could listen to Spirit play. I said okay, but the band told me to get him out of there. He gave them the willies. So I asked him as politely as I could to leave, and he shouted at me, '*Man, you got bad karma!*'" Always one to flirt with the dark side, Neil Young was more welcoming. After Dennis Wilson took him to meet Charlie, Neil was impressed enough to recommend him to Mo Ostin, talking up such Manson compositions as "Look at Your Game, Girl" and "Home Is What Makes You Happy."*

Another acquaintance of Manson's, road manager Phil Kaufman, first brought Gram Parsons up to Topanga. Gram's pal Brandon De Wilde was now living in the canyon, so Gram decided to stay a while. Kaufman had met Parsons with his new best friends the Rolling Stones, for whom he was acting as (in Mick Jagger's phrase) an "executive nanny" while the band was in Los Angeles. "Keith

---

*One of Manson's songs, "Cease to Exist," was adapted by the Beach Boys for their 1969 track "Never Learn Not to Love." Another, reflecting the typical Topanga attitude toward Greater Los Angeles, was titled "Sick City."

Richards came in with Anita Pallenberg and this skinny southern boy in crushed velour trousers and silk scarves," Kaufman recalls. "They went out and spent a lot of money on country records, and I'd sit there and play DJ. Keith would sit there with a guitar and Mick would listen to the lyrics."

From Richards, Gram acquired the trappings of rock and roll style; from Gram, Keith imbibed the sacred laws of country soul, channeling the results into "Country Honk," "You Got the Silver," "Wild Horses," "Dead Flowers," "Torn and Frayed," and "Sweet Virginia." "The Stones were willing participants in that same mythopoetic, imagined, country America," says writer Bud Scoppa. "It was sort of a sublimated literary thing."

Some of Gram's friends thought the Stones took advantage of him. "They used him," said Burritos roadie Jim Seiter. "After Keith sang a rough version of 'Honky Tonk Women' I watched Gram sit at the piano and play 'Country Honk' just like it ended up on the record. I told Gram it was abusive that they'd taken full credit for it, but he said, 'It was an honor bestowed on me.'" Others saw Gram more as a sycophant. The fact that he could hold his own financially with the Stones didn't, in their eyes, excuse his shameless straphanging. "Gram had three strikes against him for being rich," says J. D. Souther. "We were all doing day jobs and busting our asses, and he was a trust-fund kid that could do what he wanted."

Linda Ronstadt felt a musical affinity with Parsons. "We were good friends because we both were devoted to country rock," she says. "Of necessity we became comrades." But even her patience was taxed when she found herself stranded overnight with the Stones in Laurel Canyon because Gram was too wasted to take her home. "To me that kind of living wasn't responsible," she says. "I resolved that I would never wind up in one of those scenes again without my own wheels."

Late in 1968 Gram set about assembling his own Rolling Stones— a country-soul-rock-gospel hybrid that would give vent to the music inside him. From the disparate bunch of Okies who played the North Hollywood country circuit he borrowed the name they'd used as a loose umbrella appellation: "The Flying Burrito Brothers." Abetting Gram in this new endeavor was none other than Chris Hillman, who had himself left the Byrds after taking all he could of Roger

McGuinn's control freakery. Although incensed by Gram's lack of professionalism in abandoning the Byrds on the eve of a tour of South Africa, Chris was still taken with the guy's taste in music—and his personality.

Both recently separated from their women, Hillman and Parsons moved into a house together and began writing the "cosmic country" songs that formed the basis of the Burritos' *Gilded Palace of Sin*: "Christine's Tune (Devil in Disguise)," about Miss Christine of Frank Zappa's protégées the GTOs; "Hot Burrito No. 1," about Gram's abandoned girlfriend Nancy Lee Ross; and "Sin City," an apocalyptic condemnation of L.A. with special reference to scurrilous business manager Larry Spector.

"Chris lived down the street from me in Topanga," says Tom Wilkes, at whose dining table "Sin City" was finished. "He was very quiet and unassuming, yet he chose to work with a lot of crazy people. Gram struck me as a genuinely nice guy. He was tooting a little bit, but nothing like it was at the end." Through Wilkes the Burritos signed to A&M Records, which emulated Warner-Reprise's artist-friendly approach by hiring guys such as house hippie Michael Vosse. Wilkes and Vosse went to Vice President Gil Friesen and urged him to sign the Burritos. "We said, 'This is country rock, it's something new,'" Wilkes recalls. "But we said, 'You have to let them alone.' And Gil agreed. A lot of money later, he *dis*agreed!"

Released in February 1969, *The Gilded Palace* showed the Burritos—fleshed out by Sneaky Pete Kleinow and Mississippi-born bassist Chris Ethridge—attired in their tongue-in-cheek rhinestone suits from Nudie's in North Hollywood. Like the album's songs, they subverted country and western clichés by emblazoning the band with symbols of sex and drugs. This was country rock with glam trappings and a mischievous edge. The album's cover, moreover, was shot in a place that had become as dear to Parsons's heart as Topanga: the California desert.

Ain't No One for You to Give You No Name

If Topanga was wild, the California desert was something else again—a place denuded of movie-star vanities, an alien landscape of heart-expanding emptiness. This arid expanse of rock, scrub, and cacti—with the Joshua Tree National Monument park as its focal point—had long served as a place of escape from Los Angeles: L.A. the Sin City, L.A. the *Sick* City. The alternative Palm Springs, Joshua Tree was a magnet for people with fantasies of primitive Native American mysticism, as well as for all manner of crackpots and cultists.

One such was George W. Van Tassell, who believed that aliens used the desert to land their spacecraft and who began hosting UFO conventions at an abandoned airport in nearby Giant Rock in the 1940s. Thousands of flying-saucer fanatics congregated at Giant Rock every year, hoping to attract little green men from space. Among Van Tassell's devotees were Hollywood renegades such as Ted Markland, a strapping, Peckinpahesque actor who shared a pad in Laurel Canyon with fellow thespian James Coburn. Ted came out to Joshua Tree in 1956, falling in love with Navajo Indian culture and discovering the wonders of peyote. He brought fellow Hollywood rebels Steve McQueen and Dennis Hopper to Joshua Tree, got them fried on mescaline, and dragged them up the sides of mountains. "I had everybody out there," recalls Markland, who heaved a barber's swivel chair all the way to the top of Giant Rock. "It was a great place to get away from L.A., and then you'd go back in again."

UFO-mania had peaked by the late 1960s, but Joshua Tree remained a big draw for stoned L.A. actors and musicians entranced by the space and silence of the Monument—not to mention the Joshua trees themselves, spectacular yuccas that grew only at a very specific altitude. "There's a kind of wistful, melancholy quality to the desert that's almost nonverbal," says Ned Doheny, another regular visitor. "You have this sense that you're on another planet. The thing about Southern California is that you really find it in the lay of the land—in the desert and the mountains and the ocean, the things that really transcend time."

Gram Parsons was hanging out with Keith Richards and Anita Pallenberg when the Stones' pot dealer Sid Kaiser recommended they take a trip out to the desert. "Sid said there's this place called Joshua Tree," remembers Phil Kaufman, who'd appeared with Ted Markland in the 1965 comedy Western *The Hallelujah Trail*. "He said it's very spiritual, and this friend of mine Ted knows the Indians out there. Sid said, 'You guys should go out there and take some peyote.'" At Joshua Tree, Gram and Keith and Anita ate peyote and scanned the starlit sky from Cap Rock, a two-story-high outcrop of quartz monzonite in the monument. "It seemed like an endless night," Keith Richards recalls. "It took a thousand years, but it was all over too quick."

"We had binoculars, loads of blankets, and a big stash of coke," adds Anita Pallenberg. "That was our idea of looking for UFOs. Did we believe in them? Well, it was all part of that period. We were just looking for *something*." For the remainder of his life, Parsons turned to the desert as a place of freedom and mystical release. "He used to go out there whenever he wanted to be alone or just be spiritual," says Kaufman. "It was a good place for him, a quiet place." In October 1969 Parsons was cast in a film, *Saturation '70*, based on Van Tassell's UFO conventions. Shot at Giant Rock, the movie was the brainchild of Stones insider Tony Foutz and costarred Gram, Michelle Phillips, and Julian, the young son of Brian Jones. "Everyone was convinced that we were going to see flying saucers," says editor Frank Mazzola, whose résumé included *Performance*. "Maybe that was one of the cracks in the fantasy of the time we lived in—that we were that gullible and that stoned. In the end the film was never even finished."

Not finishing things was typical of Parsons. By the time *Saturation '70* was aborted he was feeling restless in the Flying Burritos. Having squandered their entire A&M advance on a train tour that did little to promote their album, the band was demoralized and down-at-the-heels. Not to mention very stoned. The standard of live performance was the first thing to be affected by the drug intake. Sneaky Pete Kleinow claims there wasn't a Burritos show that didn't embarrass him. Parsons and Chris Ethridge were both stoned when Herb Alpert and Jerry Moss came to view their new investment at a Whisky a Go Go show. "The Burritos turned up at the Troub hoot and they were atrocious," says Bernie Leadon. "There was a big respect among people who hung out there for professionalism, so that was a big nonstarter."

The real problem was Gram's ongoing infatuation with Keith Richards. "There was a slow progression of Gram and Keith actually turning into each other," says Pamela Des Barres. "At the Troubadour, Gram came out onstage *as Keith*, with the makeup and all the scarves round his neck. Chris literally kicked Gram's guitar off the stage."

"Chris and Gram started out like brothers," says Phil Kaufman. "They were really good friends, but then Gram's drug problems put a wedge between them." By the end of 1969, when the Burritos were one of the few bright spots at the Stones' ill-fated Altamont Festival, Parsons was ensconced in Sunset Boulevard's Chateau Marmont hotel with a sixteen-year-old named Gretchen Burrell. "There was a lot of rock action at the Marmont," says producer-scenester Kim Fowley. "Gram and Gretchen, Don Johnson and Melanie Griffith, John Cale and his GTO wife, me. There was a dope dealer living there, a crippled woman who dealt from her bed." When Eve Babitz went to take pictures of Parsons at the hotel she was shocked by his physical degeneration. "The pictures I took that day are ugly," she wrote. "Gram had put on weight and a kind of sullen expression crept across his face sometimes like a bad cop and I couldn't wait to get out of there."

The fact that Gram was such a mess limited his impact on his country rock contemporaries. From their viewpoint he was a dilettantish glamour boy and not a team player. "I'd see him all the time," says Michael Ochs, by then working at A&M. "I couldn't understand why he was so fucked up. Here was this good-looking, talented kid bouncing off the walls." For years Gram's flakiness and propensity for starfucking meant that he was dismissed as a primary influence on country rock. In Britain's *ZigZag* magazine, for example, Pete Frame was obliged to revise his slightly sneering attitude toward Parsons. Only in the early 1980s did Gram's cult reputation start to grow in any meaningful way. Ultimately Parsons was peripheral to the Troubadour in-crowd. "The people that embraced the Burritos were already into the music," says Linda Ronstadt. "I wouldn't say Gram was pivotal, because he didn't get that much attention."

Yet Ronstadt's own protégés Glenn Frey and Don Henley paid

close attention to Parsons. After Longbranch Pennywhistle supported the Burritos at the Troubadour, Frey studied Gram's every
onstage move. Bernie Leadon, who joined the Burritos in September 1969 after the departure of Chris Ethridge, confirms that Frey,
Souther, and Henley all took their country rock cue from Parsons.
"Henley and Frey respected Gram, I think," Bernie says. "They
respected his take on country music, partly because it had a fair
amount of R&B in it." Parsons also remained an influence on the
Byrds, who—with Roger McGuinn as the sole surviving original
member—were remodeling themselves as a hard-edged country rock
outfit. When McGuinn persuaded the great Clarence White to join
the group it soon paid dividends. Having graced *Sweetheart of the
Rodeo* with his meticulous Telecaster picking, White was hired with
drummer Gene Parsons (no relation) in the late summer of 1968.

Post-Parsons, the Byrds of 1969–1970 became a fearsome live
unit, as one can hear from a belatedly released 1969 album recorded
at San Francisco's Fillmore. "We're talking about five years from
'Mr. Tambourine Man,'" says Bud Scoppa, whose 1971 book *The
Byrds* was the first on the group. "In those years I think McGuinn had
matured tremendously as a musician, even if he hadn't matured
much as a human being."

"We were all aware of what Roger had been through," says John
York, the Byrds' new bassist. "He had been through so many people
with really aggressive personalities. There was sometimes reference
to the fact that we were sort of like remnants after a great battle."
The mere fact that McGuinn was prepared to share the spotlight
with a guitarist as preternaturally gifted as White suggested that
he'd acquired a new humility. It helped, though, that Clarence was as
self-effacing as Gram Parsons had been attention-seeking. "Just playing with Clarence for thirty seconds was enough to know that the guy
was from another galaxy," says York, who didn't last long as a Byrd.
Gene Parsons wanted his friend Skip Battin in the group, and John
was politely elbowed out in late 1969. For him, as for McGuinn
himself, the country-rock version of the Byrds was really an extended
ethnomusicological diversion. "They wanted to show where they
came from," York says. "Like, 'This is the music my parents used to
listen to, and I wanna incorporate it into what I'm doing now.'"

Free My Gypsy Soul

Along with Poco, Linda Ronstadt, Rick Nelson, and others, the Byrds and the Burritos took country rock into the 1970s. But there was another strain of American roots rock that was less beholden to country music and more derivative of rhythm and blues and related black American forms. This was the sound that the Rolling Stones explored on their run of albums from *Beggars Banquet* (1968) to *Exile on Main St.* (1972).

L.A.'s role in this seam of funky, blue-eyed rock and soul has never been well documented. Reflect, after all, that Gram Parsons was as influenced by the southern soul of Memphis and Muscle Shoals as he was by Bakersfield or Appalachia. Reflect also that the original Flying Burrito Brothers were not a country rock band but a loosely knit group of displaced players from Oklahoma and Texas and Mississippi—guys who chilled out after sometimes soul-destroying sessions in Hollywood studios by convening in little valley clubs to play blues and rock and roll long into the California night. "On Saturday nights, after hours, musicians from all over the city would meet at a place called the Crossbow," David Gates remembers. "It was there that I met guys like Steve Douglas, Glen Campbell, James Burton, Leon Russell, Chuck Blackwell, Jerry Cole."

The core of the original Burritos hailed from the musical hotbed of Tulsa, Oklahoma: they were the tail end of the Dust Bowl migration to the Golden State. But there were connections, too, with New Orleans musicians such as Harold Battiste and Mac "Dr. John" Rebennack, who formed their own swampy clique in Los Angeles. Their influence fed through to the work of native Californians such as Ry Cooder, Bonnie Raitt, and Lowell George—aspiring "white Negroes" from the L.A. canyons.

Importantly, this was a strain of retro music that dovetailed neatly with the sound of post-blues-boom England: not for nothing did the Rolling Stones employ such L.A.-based sessionmen as Cooder, Keys, Russell, and Rebennack. Crucial to this California-London dialectic were Delaney and Bonnie Bramlett. "Delaney and Bonnie got me locked into England," says David Anderle, who signed the pair to Elektra Records. "It was American white roots blues with a real *sound*.

It was blues and it was Stax but it was very L.A., too. That whole scene was paralleled by the Burritos and was incredibly important."

L.A.'s new love affair with the South—black *and* white—was only too evident at Warner-Reprise, where Lenny Waronker and friends nurtured the talent of artists such as Van Morrison and Ry Cooder. "Van Morrison was a *huge* influence on the music out here," says David Anderle. "It was almost like, 'We gotta get Southern California to sound like Van Morrison!'" Inspired by Morrison and by the sound of Creedence Clearwater Revival, Waronker and his staff laid the groundwork for a new wave of rootsy white acts: Cooder, Raitt, Little Feat, Maria Muldaur, and more. "Lenny and Randy were *big* fans of Creedence," says Ted Templeman, who produced Morrison's *Tupelo Honey* for Warner. "When they found out Creedence were from Berkeley they were crushed."

Brought into the Warner-Reprise fold by Jack Nitzsche, Ry Cooder was even less of a joiner than his labelmate Randy Newman. Yet Cooder slowly became a linchpin of Lenny Waronker's emerging "Burbank Sound." "Ry was the youngest of all these guys, but he had the wisdom of an old man," says Waronker. "When Jack Nitzsche brought him into my office I was shocked. I had assumed he was way older than he turned out to be." Signed to Reprise as a solo artist in 1969, Cooder kept himself to himself, perfecting his magnificent technique and crafting ultratasteful arrangements of R&B/soul/gospel classics and musty Depression songs. A scholarly connoisseur of Americana, Cooder in 1970 released the first of several marvelous albums that sounded like the Band had they been curators of the Smithsonian Institution. "He was doing something so unique and special, and in an odd way he had a sort of pop sensibility with it," says Waronker.

"I made a lot of weird records that didn't make sense, that weren't fish or fowl, and that didn't advance me or them," Cooder says. "But they tolerated it. It's odd and hard to say—and you don't like to think of yourself as nothing more than a cachet for somebody to show George Harrison what's up when he comes to town—but maybe that's what it was. To Lenny's credit he never said, 'You've got to toe the line and you've got to participate and this is what we expect of you.' Nobody ever said that, thank God. I'd have run in terror. I remember once Van Dyke once said, 'A corporation shows love with money. The more money they let you spend of theirs, the more they love you.' And that's really true."

A less fastidious, more Dionysian version of Ry Cooder was Lowell George, fellow Angeleno and master of slide guitar. Lowell was a movie brat, a roly-poly beatnik who'd hung out in coffeehouses listening to Delta bluesmen. His Beefheartesque band the Factory had been a canyon fixture since 1966, living in a house in the hills above Crescent Heights Boulevard. "The Factory lived in a real hippie house," recalls writer Jan Henderson, who would run down to warn them when cops were nearby. "It had psychedelic posters on the walls, and Harrison Ford would be sitting there grooving to the music when he wasn't doing carpentry jobs." George first entered the Burbank orbit via Jack Nitzsche's *Performance* sound track. Lowell's songs—open-road country-rock classics such as "Willin'" and "Truck Stop Girl"—were also getting acclaim and being covered by the Byrds and Linda Ronstadt. "Somehow a demo of ['Willin'] got out and it was the rage of the Troubadour," George told *ZigZag*.

Warners' Russ Titelman flipped when, in 1969, he attended a rehearsal for Lowell's new group. "They were going to sign with Gabriel Mekler's Lizard label," Titelman remembers. "I said, 'You don't wanna do that. Why don't we go see Lenny? So I took Lowell and [keyboard player] Billy Payne over to Warners and they sang 'Willin',' 'Truck Stop Girl,' and 'Brides of Jesus.' Lenny just said, 'It's a deal. Make a record.'"

The first Little Feat album was a conscious emulation of the Band, with a generous dose of Stones in the mix. Although it sold next to nothing, with the band remaining in a state of desperate penury, *Little Feat* encapsulated the Reprise aesthetic as well as any album of the period. For Burbank insiders such as Van Dyke Parks, Lowell George was a talent to be treasured and fostered. "He came to me because I was . . . working for the man," Parks told Bud Scoppa. "We always looked at it as doing an inside job—we were going to bilk the corporation together."

It's sobering to reflect that, had they been making records in the first decade of the twenty-first century, Little Feat would almost certainly have been dropped after their debut. But then the same might be said of a dozen other seminal Warner-Reprise acts of the period: Neil Young, Joni Mitchell, Randy Newman, Van Morrison.

"That was the time before bean counters came in to run things," Feat guitarist Paul Barrére told Bud Scoppa. "A&R people actually had ears."

The Straight Guy

Before he knew Lenny Waronker and Russ Titelman, Lowell George's original mentor was a man who, while already an under-ground icon, was profoundly out of step with the times. The fact that Frank Zappa was one of the most prominent rock-star residents of Laurel Canyon didn't change the fact that he viewed the flower-power underground with amused contempt. "It was like Frank had X-ray vision and could see into the future," says Pamela Des Barres, then Miss Pamela of the Zappa-fostered GTOs. "He could see where all the hippie bullshit was going. And when everybody else got weirder, Frank got *less* weird. I think one of the main reasons he moved to Laurel Canyon was to make fun of it."

"I live in the middle of the great hallucinogenic wasteland— Laurel Canyon," Zappa told *Teen Set* magazine, "on one of the hot streets with the rest of the stars . . . lotsa action, having a wonderful time, wish you were here." In a *Guitar Player* column some years later, Zappa was even more cynical about Laurel Canyon and its sound, describing "folk-rock 12-string swill" as "the predecessor of the horrible fake-sensitive type artist/singer/songwriter/suffering person, posed against a wooden fence provided by the Warner Bros. Records art department, graciously rented to all the other record companies who needed it for their version of the same crap."

"Frank's music was not rich in the promises of the love genera-tion," said Mark Volman with a smile; he joined Zappa's Mothers of Invention after the demise of the Turtles. "If anything, it was as anti-hippie as it was anti-American." But Volman says Zappa got along quite amicably with the singer-songwriter clique. "Frank was never really *scathing* about anything," Volman says. "He just represented a different dichotomy to the love and peace scene." In 1968 Zappa moved from Kirkwood Drive to the big log cabin that silent-era Western star Tom Mix had built decades earlier at the intersection of

Laurel Canyon Boulevard and Lookout Mountain Avenue. Here the goateed satirist marshaled a stable of freaks who included Captain Beefheart, Alice Cooper, the all-female groupie-superstar act Girls Together Outrageously, street weirdo Wild Man Fischer, and jazz-folk megatalent Tim Buckley. Most of these artists were signed to one of two labels, Straight or Bizarre, that Frank set up with his manager, Herb Cohen. The acts on Straight were naturally no less outré than those on Bizarre.

"Frank was so far ahead of the other artists," says Volman, who metamorphosed into Flo (or "the Phlorescent Leech") in the Mothers. "He was already an entrepreneur and spending money to develop other artists." For some, Zappa's cynicism was a little too much to take. David Anderle, who'd signed the Mothers of Invention to MGM Records in 1966, balked at Frank's ethos. For Anderle, the world of the Beach Boys' Brother label (which he ran) held more musical appeal. "I always felt there was something a little totalitarian about Frank," Anderle says. "I was awed by the clarity of his vision and his ability to make it happen, but it was without warmth."

Zappa was also steeped in a different Los Angeles—the multi-ethnic metropolis of jazz, rhythm and blues, doo-wop, and Chicano pop—from the "vanilla" rock scene of Sunset Boulevard and Laurel Canyon. He was among the few white artists who even alluded, on *Freak Out!!*'s "Trouble Coming Every Day," to L.A.'s Watts riots of 1965. This is one undeniable strand of the Canyon story: how a post-surfing "Southern California" of freeway dreams and denim sex was concocted by outsiders and shunted aside the true polyethnic Los Angeles of the 1940s to the early 1960s. After all, the cheap street-corner sounds of R&B and doo-wop were what had brought such entrepreneurs as Phil Spector, Lou Adler, Herb Alpert, and Kim Fowley into the game in the first place.

One of the things that really distanced Zappa—like Fowley—from the cabal was his lack of interest in drugs. Frank preferred to stay straight, while his minitribe of bizarros ran riot on the Sunset Strip. Sometimes an artist's drug use would incur the master's wrath and he'd be turfed out of the inner circle. Lowell George, a de facto Mother on *Weasels Ripped My Flesh*, refused to conform to the regime of Zappa and was given his marching orders. "Frank just finally fired

Lowell for smoking dope all the time," says Pamela Des Barres, who worked with George on the GTOs' *Permanent Damage* album. "I don't even know what Lowell was doing in the Mothers."

Tim Buckley came to Straight from Elektra, where he'd failed to live up to Jac Holzman's expectations. A born nonconformist, this exquisite curly-haired troubadour from Orange County deliberately sabotaged Jac's plans to make him a folk-rock star. "I don't know if Tim had a chip on his shoulder, but he wasn't gonna take shit from anybody," says Jerry Yester, who produced Buckley's albums *Goodbye and Hello* (1967) and *Happy/Sad* (1969). "He resisted parts of himself that were natural. If he came up with a song that was like a beautiful ballad, he would intentionally contort it and pervert it."

By mid-1969 Buckley was heading toward the free-form madness of *Starsailor*—harsh jazz-rock without melody, a springboard for scary vocal swoops and ululations. He also was messing with heroin. "All we are saying," he sang brazenly during a Troubadour show in 1969, "is give smack a chance."

Sympathy for the Devil

One afternoon in the summer of 1969, Zappa was sitting in the living room of the Log Cabin with Wild Man Fischer and an assortment of GTOs. Suddenly a scary-looking man burst through the open front door and introduced himself as "the Raven." Zappa rose, uncertain and scared, to his feet. The Raven handed Zappa a small bottle of stage blood, announced that he had "isolated the specimen," and pulled a gun from his pants. Wild Man Fischer, himself a fairly loopy individual, turned visibly white with fear.

Zappa managed to placate the intruder by encouraging him to hide his gun. Fischer, the GTOs, and Frank's wife, Gail, joined in: "Help the Raven hide his gun!" Eventually he was persuaded to stash the weapon in a hole in the backyard. The Raven went on his way, but Zappa decided it was time to find a less accessible residence. "[Frank] was afraid of the very thing that bit the hippie movement in the ass," says Billy Payne of Little Feat. "That was the craziness of what would happen to people when they got fried on drugs."

"There were a lot of weird people around," says Joni Mitchell. "There was one guy who had a parrot called Captain Blood, and he was always scrawling real cryptic things on the inside walls of my house—Neil Young's, too." The heady sexual and narcotic experiments of the 1966–1968 period had freed some minds but damaged many others. Laurel and other Los Angeles canyons were now crawling with weird wannabes and unhinged hangers-on. The dark, unsettling music of the Doors was at moments a more accurate sound track to the scene than the warbling of Joni Mitchell. In her famous essay "The White Album," Joan Didion observed that "a mystical flirtation with the idea of 'sin' . . . was very much with us in Los Angeles in 1968 and 1969."

"Everybody was experimenting and taking it all the way," says film editor Frank Mazzola, whose exposure to the dark world of director Donald Cammell during *Performance* had seriously unnerved him. "It opened up a negative force of energy that was almost demonic." Gone was the beatific innocence of 1966–1967. Beads and bells hadn't changed the world. The situation in Vietnam was getting worse by the month. A festering unease gnawed at America's ghettos and inner cities. "What had tied so many people together was opposition to the war," says Chester Crill of Kaleidoscope. "But by 1968 it became really clear that things were not going to change in Vietnam. Things looked so black that people became flat-out paranoid."

In L.A., a kind of malevolent decadence took root in the rock scene. The drugs were getting harder. The exploitation of the scene by dealers of all kinds was rampant. "The Sunset Strip got really ugly," says Jan Henderson. "Let's face it, we were all doing shit we weren't supposed to, but the sharks moved in. I remember going to parties and seeing people screwed out on Seconals and Nembutals— the heavy sleepers."

"L.A. was a dangerous environment at that time," says Phil Kaufman, who tried in vain to keep Gram Parsons on the straight and narrow. "It was blatant drugs." Parsons's best new friends were John Phillips and Terry Melcher, both moneyed and both debauched. There was much partying at the Chateau Marmont, and perilous motorcycle rides along canyon roads. Phillips was a particularly egregious example of rock megalomania. Living in his mock-Tudor pile in Bel Air, he was at once a social aspirant and an untrammeled hedonist. With his producer, Lou Adler, he befriended all the hip new movie people: Warren Beatty, Jack Nicholson, gadfly publicist Steve Brandt, and Roman Polanski and his pretty blond wife, Sharon Tate. Commenting on *Performance*, which starred his friends Mick Jagger and Anita Pallenberg, Phillips argued that Donald Cammell's film was about estranging yourself from the world and creating your own society. "With really intelligent people," he pronounced, "it's almost a matter of inbreeding at this point."

"At the beginning everyone had been sort of on a par," says Nurit Wilde, a friend of the Mamas and the Papas. "Cass never became too big for her britches, but John changed a great deal. The moment he got some power he became a megalomaniac." The new aristocracy of rock and hip Hollywood also was a magnet for Parsons and Melcher. Like Phillips, Melcher followed Gram's lead when it came to country music, borrowing the trappings of Nashville and Bakersfield for solo material. The Stones' coupling of jet-set decadence and honky-tonk slumming entranced all of them. "I enjoyed working with Terry," says John York of the Byrds, who worked with Melcher during his stint as a Byrd. "But he had this annoying thing of being a guy who didn't have to ever worry about time or money."

When he wasn't in the studio with the Byrds, Melcher was palling around with Dennis Wilson, hippest and most hedonistic member of the Beach Boys. Handsome and priapic, Wilson hid his considerable talent behind a surfer-dude charm. The Beach Boys, their surfing days way behind them, were now part of Warner-Reprise, which distributed their David Anderle–run Brother label. If Dennis revealed the poetry and sensitivity of his inner soul on beautiful Beach Boys songs such as "Be Still" (*Friends*) and "Forever" (*Sunflower*), his chief priorities remained drugs and girls. An ample source of the latter was the stoned troupe who followed the mesmerizing Charles Manson around town. So smitten was Dennis with Charlie—"the Wizard," he called him—that he allowed Manson's Family to move from Topanga into his home in Rustic Canyon. "Terry Melcher told me about this exotic, charismatic guy who lived out near my family's ranch in the valley," says Ned Doheny. "He was writing tunes and there were all these girls hanging around, and they were living out of Dumpsters. Terry said we should go out and visit."

Manson, who'd been in jail for much of his life, excelled in the art of controlling damaged minds. The girls he collected on his travels turned their lives and wills over to his care. For more than a year they passed themselves off as just another communal tribe espousing the values of free love and organic food. "Manson lucked into a situation where the elements around him allowed him to get away with that stuff," says Pamela Des Barres. "He couldn't have done it in the 1950s and he couldn't have done it in the 1970s."

Among other things, the Wizard was just another frustrated L.A. singer-songwriter. And the more time he spent around Dennis and Terry, the more he thirsted for legitimate success as an artist. In August 1968, at the behest of Melcher's and Dennis Wilson's friend Gregg Jakobson, Manson demoed a number of songs. But when Melcher—spooked by the Family—cooled on the idea of touting him to Columbia, Manson became vengeful. "Charlie got pissed off that they didn't think he was a genius," says Denny Doherty. "His attitude was, 'Who the fuck is *Terry Melcher*? He can't even *sing*.'"

Melcher, like John Phillips, lived in a tony property in Bel Air, one he shared with actress girlfriend Candice Bergen. But he'd recently rented out the house to film director Roman Polanski, opting to spend the summer of 1969 at the Malibu beach house of his mother, Doris Day. On the evening of August 9, 1969, Manson dispatched a group of Family members to the house, at 10050 Cielo Drive. It turned out that Polanski's actress wife, Sharon Tate, was hosting a small gathering of in-crowders, heiresses, and celebrity hairdressers who moved in the John Phillips/Cass Elliott circle. Phillips, along with Denny Doherty, had intended to drop in on the party himself. "I've met so many people over the years who told me they were invited to that party," Doherty says. "But John and I really *were*."

The slaughter of the pregnant Sharon Tate and her friends that night has been recounted so many times that we need not dwell on it here. Suffice it to say that in one terrifying evening, the killings changed the L.A. music scene forever, casting a macabre pall over what architectural historian Reyner Banham termed "the fat life of the delectable canyons." Never again would anyone be able to trust a person on the basis that they looked groovy and wore their hair long. "It just destroyed us," says Lou Adler. "I mean, everyone was looking at everyone else, not quite sure who was in that house and who knew about it. And then no one trusted hippies anymore. It was a very paranoid time, and the easiest thing to do was to get out of it. Everybody went behind closed doors." Van Dyke Parks, who'd stopped by the house earlier that day, says the Manson killings were "a collective sin" that "forced everyone to think about the idealism that had gotten us to that point."

In December 1969, when Manson and his followers were arrested, rock's dabbling with devilry climaxed a few hundred miles north of Los Angeles. Honorary Angelenos the Rolling Stones, who'd only just finished mixing *Let It Bleed* in Hollywood, tried to make amends for charging high ticket prices on their U.S. tour by staging a free concert in the scraggy brown hills east of Oakland. "There was something swarming and ominous about this gathering," *Rolling Stone*'s David Dalton later wrote of the show. "Kinetic energy zinged through the air like psychic pellets. The place was a war zone." Altamont would come to symbolize the death of the 1960s. In a classic case of misplaced idealism, the Stones entrusted the job of security to feuding local chapters of the Hell's Angels. Tanked on alcohol and downers, the Angels proceeded to get rough with the crowd, beating them back with pool cues. When artists such as Marty Balin of the Jefferson Airplane intervened to protest, they, too, were attacked by the menacing, leather-jacketed bikers.

The dark flip side of Monterey Pop, Altamont was a collective bad trip—not least for the Stones, who found themselves horribly out of their depth. The spectacle of Mick Jagger ineffectually pleading with the crowd to "cool it, man" in the Maysles brothers' film *Gimme Shelter* was the logical conclusion to the Faustian pact their satanic majesties had made with the forces of darkness. In their book *Living with the Dead*, David Dalton and Grateful Dead manager Rock Scully wrote that Woodstock and Altamont were "two ends of the same mucky stick . . . the result of the same disease: the bloating of mass bohemia in the late '60s."

The Stones' flirtation with the diabolical—in their songs, in their shows, in Donald Cammell's *Performance* and Kenneth Anger's *Lucifer Rising*—was the same thing as Haight-Ashbury's sympathy with the Angels. It was decadence posing as radical chic. When the Angels stabbed Meredith Hunter to death under Mick Jagger's nose on that apocalyptic night, a decade's psychedelic frenzy came to a shocking climax. The time had come to chill out—to take it easy.

6

A Case of Me

Where do you have left to go but in?

—Joni Mitchell

Music from Big Ego

Albert Hammond was wrong—it *was* raining in sunny Southern California. Heavily. The clubs were quiet, and the Sunset Strip was soporific. People stayed sequestered in their canyon cabins and Hollywood bungalows.

At Wally Heider's Hollywood studio, three young men bonded in a loose alliance that was the next best thing to a band. Cocooned by the ultraprotective Elliot Roberts, David Crosby, Stephen Stills, and Graham Nash were at work on their debut album. The atmosphere at Heider's was euphoric. The three men—the hedonistic Californ-ian, the drill-sergeant southerner, the affable fellow from Manches-ter, England—were brothers in an open musical relationship, crafting electroacoustic rock that was the very essence of laid-back and mellowed-out. "You couldn't get these guys to work together if they didn't like each other," says Allison Caine, who worked for Elliot Roberts. "That's why some of the groups had broken up. With

Crosby, Stills, and Nash it was the love relationships, the hanging out, the smoking dope, the sailing with David."

Crosby, Stills, and Nash was postpolitical back-porch music: hippies taking stock of where the 1960s had gotten them and of what their new relationships meant. Stephen sang of sweet Judy Collins in "Suite: Judy Blue Eyes," and Crosby hymned his love Christine Hinton in the exquisite "Guinevere." Nash, meanwhile, had fallen deeply in love with Crosby's ex. "Graham ended up at David's place, where I was staying until my house was ready," Joni Mitchell remembered. "He came down sick and I took him home to my new house to play Florence Nightingale. I was looking after him and I got attached. I really felt for the first time in my life that I could pair-bond." In wide-eyed awe of these magical Americans—and Canadians—Graham moved in with Joni in her little A-frame on Lookout Mountain Avenue: "Our House," with two fluffy Persian cats in the yard. The Nash/Mitchell cohabitation was the Laurel Canyon dream incarnate. For the first time in pop, there was a direct, almost diaristic correlation between songs and relationships. Joni's "Willy"—Nash's nickname—was the first fruit of their affair, a song in which she promised to be "his lady all my life."

"This really was a moment when musicians had an enormous determination to communicate what they were feeling," says Judy James. "You could hear that at the hootenannies at the Troub, and in living rooms all over town." But it was in the studio that Stephen Stills came into his own. On fire with musical energy and inventiveness, the driven multi-instrumentalist was a one-man band and producer, overdubbing himself in endless layers into the small hours of the night. "Stephen was really a great musical anchor," said Derek Taylor. "He hasn't stamped his personality on pop history as much as Neil, but he did so much. You could understand why Crosby wanted to hang out with the Springfield guys. At the beginning, at any rate, they were a lot of fun to be around."

"[Stephen] craved success, money, and stardom so hard you could feel it in his voice," Ellen Sander wrote, "but he came on like a stone hick whenever he lightened up. His presence was a studied forbiddingness, he said little, smiled less, dropped perfectly uproarious one-liners when they were least expected." With his trademark mustache and fringed jacket, David Crosby made a striking contrast to Stills, who wore V-neck sweaters and whose hair never dropped below the shoulders. When Dennis Hopper and Peter Fonda came to shoot their counterculture classic *Easy Rider* later that year, rebel-without-a-pause Hopper modeled his entire look on the ex-Byrd. Crosby's mission was to make L.A. hip by importing San Francisco dress sense, attitude, and politics—the fabulous furry freakiness of Haight-Ashbury, where he increasingly spent time with old Bay Area friends such as Paul Kantner, Grace Slick, Jerry Garcia, and David Freiberg.

But it wasn't all right-on politics and back-slapping brotherhood at Heider's studio. For Sander, the New York journalist for whom Jac Holzman had recently left his wife, the scene was emotionally messy. "Crosby had never really gotten over Joni," she wrote in *Trips*. "Stills was sensing that his desperately involved affair with Judy Collins was coming to a real end. He spent half his time agonizing over it, the rest of it trying to convince her to marry him. . . . Graham was falling in love with Joni, and she was falling in love with him." Tensions slowly grew between David and Stephen, with Graham acting as a buffer between his more aggressive comrades. "Graham was—and still is—the only sane person in that ensemble," says Ron Stone. "He seemed so much more prepared for that first big flush of success—that wave that comes over you, where you're *it*. He had a head start on David and Stephen. Also he was comfortable in his own skin."

When Atlantic's Jerry Wexler dropped in to Heider's, he took the same dislike to Crosby as he had to Geffen. When there was talk of titles for the album, Wexler mischievously suggested *Music from Big Ego*. One cause of the egomania was the increasing use of cocaine, which had surreptitiously entered the bloodstream of the Laurel Canyon music community. "Cocaine was this *elixir*," says writer Jonh Ingham. "You never saw it and it was hideously expensive. It was considered this elusive, aristocratic drug that you'd love to try but you never knew anybody who had it." B. Mitchel Reed had dubbed Stills and Crosby "the Frozen Noses" when they taped three songs for his KMET show. An eyewitness to the effects of the drug on David and Stephen was Robert "Waddy" Wachtel, a guitarist who'd recently moved to L.A. from New York City. "Crosby brought Stills over one night to where I lived in the canyon," Wachtel recalls. "Stills was kinda weird. I never really saw anybody like that. He didn't really talk right. At one point I said to Dave, 'What's with that guy?' And Crosby goes, 'Oh, he's just coked out.' I literally went, 'What's that?' And he says, 'Not me, Waddy. I'm not gonna be the one to turn you on. You'll know soon enough.'"

Cocaine aside, there were basic inconsistencies in the CSN setup. Crosby, smitten with Stills's musical chops, also was thrown by his southern machismo. Yet Crosby himself kept a large collection of guns that seemed at odds with his ethos of free love and nude swimming. Ellen Sander remarked that even bullshit was an art in Crosby's house. "Everything is an art," Crosby whipped back at her, "and it's *all* bullshit." The totemic Crosby, torn between the elitist escapism of "Wooden Ships" and the confrontational fury of "Long Time Gone," was at the hub of a shift in political sensibility at this time. Committed but selfishly hedonistic, Crosby couldn't make up his mind whether to tune in or drop out. "The disagreements between Los Angeles people then stemmed from activism versus dropping out," says Domenic Priore. "Do we change the world by going against the grain and shoving crap in the Man's face, or do we just drop out and become an alternate society?'"

The release of *Crosby, Stills, and Nash* in May 1969 marked the true dawn of posthippie California. It announced that jangly bands with Rickenbacker guitars were over, offering in their place a loose triad of alpha males in denim jeans. It also flew in the face of power rock and heavy blues. "When we first came out it was Marshall time," Graham Nash remembered. "It was Jimi, Free, Cream, loud rock-'n'-roll, whereas our music had this fresh, sunny vibe which cut right through." Hendrix himself took due note. "I've seen Crosby, Stills, and Nash," he said. "They're groovy. Western sky music. All delicate and ding-ding-ding." Crosby, Stills, and Nash acted as a kind of salve at a point when the hippie revolution was in serious danger of overheating. "There were too many people dying and breaking up," says music producer Robert Marchese. "People were like, 'Okay, we're gonna calm this thing down.' They didn't *really* calm down. They were doing just as many drugs, but it became more sophisticated."

Crosby, Stills, and Nash was Top 10 by July 1969, remaining on the charts for more than two years. But some Byrds and Buffalo Springfield fans were turned off by the supergroup packaging of CSN, mourning the loss of the innocence that lit up the Sunset Strip in the mid-1960s. "It all started to become like a big business deal," says Tom Nolan, the first local rock writer of note. "By the time they started putting these supergroups together, it all started going downhill." Nolan wasn't alone in noting the influence of the men pulling the strings behind Crosby, Stills, and Nash. What set David Geffen and Elliot Roberts apart from the agents and managers who preceded them was that they looked exactly like their artists. They behaved like them, too: if Geffen was parsimonious in his drug use, Roberts may have smoked more pot than all his clients put together. "The first major change that happened in this era was people like David Geffen and Elliot Roberts becoming powerful," says David Anderle. "These were people from the folk dream period of the 1960s but they had their feet in both camps."

Holding down a new day job as a vice president with Creative Management Artists, Geffen simultaneously comanaged Elliot Roberts's roster of artists. Effectively, Elliot was a kind of front for Geffen. "When I worked for Elliot, David was never there but it was very clear that he had influence," says Allison Caine. "They were very careful about the propriety of his role as an agent. David never had his fingerprints anywhere."

"The association was as complex as anything in the music business," screenwriter Carl Gottlieb noted in David Crosby's autobiography. "By California law Elliot couldn't directly negotiate for the services of his clients while acting as their personal manager. As an agent David couldn't properly take a management commission on clients he was managing in fact, if not in name."

The issue of whether Geffen was only in it for the money or whether he actually cared about the music is one that divides people to this day. "I think he loved the music," says Allison Caine. "I can't believe that he did it strictly for the money. It was the emotional attachment—the love of the artists and the music." For David Crosby the mitigating factor when it came to Geffen was Roberts. Elliot, he figured, was the good cop to David Geffen's bad. "Even though we knew David was smart and would do a good job," Crosby told Dave Zimmer, "I never thought he was that nice a guy and I didn't trust him all the time. So we needed an insurance policy. A watchdog. That was Elliot Roberts. [He] was more of a *mensch*. So he balanced things out."

"Elliot was shrewd," says Allison Caine. "He fit in with the scene while being the guy that had to do the business. He always protected his artists, always. That was his focus, at whatever cost and whatever names he got called." Geffen himself was empathic enough to understand that the key to this new style of management was people. "I quickly figured out [that] the one ability I'd better have is to create relationships," Geffen said of his time in the William Morris mailroom. "It isn't about how tall you are or how good-looking you are or whether or not you can play football. It's about whether you can *create a relationship*."

Geffen wasn't tall or good-looking, and he certainly hadn't played football. Indeed, his fanatical drive to succeed was fueled by his considerable insecurities. With brazen chutzpah, David figured he could beat just about anyone at the entertainment game. The key, though, was to earn the trust of an inner circle of artists and then wage war on everybody else. "There are two schools of personal management," says Carl Gottlieb. "One in the manipulative Svengali school, the other is the nurturing, protective manager who erects a Chinese wall around the client and indulges the client's every whim and wish. Geffen-Roberts was the later."

"I never felt I was *too* protective," Geffen says today. "I felt I was functioning as a dam against the river of shit that comes pouring down on artists, and it was a job that I took very seriously." Geffen was prepared to use any means necessary to get the best deals for his artists. "He was extremely intense and preternaturally focused," Carl Gottlieb says. "He could also exploit any insecurity you had about yourself and make you feel like you weren't worthy."

An early victim of Geffen's ruthlessness was Paul Rothchild, who'd produced the first CSN demos but was unceremoniously squeezed out of the frame before recording began at Wally Heider's. "That was the beginning of the end of the love groove in American music," Rothchild told Fred Goodman. "To me, that's the moment.

When David Geffen enters the California waters as a manager. The sharks have entered the lagoon."

One of Geffen's unlikeliest allies was Stephen Stills, whose craving for success belied the self-loathing that lingered from his love-starved boyhood. Stills saw Geffen as his ticket to megastardom, and with good reason. Uptight and politically conservative, Stephen hid his uneasiness about Geffen's sexual orientation and often stayed at his apartment on Central Park South. One night in the late spring of 1969, Geffen and Stills took a taxi up to Ahmet Ertegun's swanky place on the Upper East Side. Over dinner the three men discussed ways to make Crosby, Stills, and Nash the biggest band in the land.

When Stills expressed doubts about CSN going on the road as an acoustic trio, Ahmet Ertegun scratched his goatee. "Stephen," he asked, "did you ever think about getting Neil Young in the group?"

Old Ladies of the Canyon

Though Graham Nash and Joni Mitchell were busy recording and touring during much of 1969, the couple spent many happy hours together on Lookout Mountain Avenue. "It was an intense time of, 'Who's gonna get to the piano first, who's gonna fill up the space with their music first?'" Nash recalled of their relationship. "We had two very creative writers living in the same space, and it was an interesting clash of, 'I wanna get as close to you as possible'/'Leave me alone to create.'"

Too honest to pretend he was in her league as a songwriter, Graham was mesmerized by Joni's talent. When she wrote, she seemed to be channeling. But it was hard being intimate with someone so highly strung and so consumed by herself. "Joni had the confidence of her talent," says Ron Stone, who road-managed Mitchell when she toured. "The only thing I would say about her is I think it's for *other* people to compare you to Picasso."

The success in 1969 of *Clouds*—featuring "Chelsea Morning" and "Both Sides, Now"—seemed to suffocate Mitchell. Suddenly everybody wanted a piece of her. Even Graham seemed to want too much. Significantly, she dedicated *Clouds* to the memory of her maternal grandmother, who'd sacrificed her deepest artistic yearnings to raise children. Mitchell's status as a spokeswoman for a generation of liberated women was emblematic of a new female struggle. "When [her] first album came out," says former FolkWorld artist Mary McCaslin, "a lightbulb went on in a lot of women's heads saying, 'Look at this. You're the woman singer-songwriter. If she can do it, I can do it.'" But in Laurel Canyon, while they were grudgingly accorded a new respect, women were still expected to defer to men. "It was difficult for a woman to direct men," Mitchell herself says. "They bruised very easily."

"I didn't think about being a woman at the time, but in hindsight it was plenty tough," says Linda Ronstadt. "The whole idea of sexual harassment hadn't surfaced, but there was a lot of completely outrageous and unacceptable stuff going on—from *everyone*.'" Women on the canyon scene were still viewed primarily as sexual trophies. "A lot of them were secretaries at record companies," says Denny Bruce, "and they were groupie enough to want to be involved in any kind of rock scenario."

"I used to go up to Laurel Canyon and clean these guys' houses," admits Pamela Des Barres. "We were more than willing to be taken advantage of. I mean, it was just about *being there*, with the sun coming through the windows and the guys in the other room playing guitars."

"See, it wasn't *that* long ago that women were in the '50s, and that's what a lot of us learned from," says Nurit Wilde. "The girls were there to say 'Hey, groovy' at the appropriate moments, and to hand out the joints. If you were cute you were there to make a pretty picture. But some of us were rebels right from the beginning." What cartoonist Trina Robbins calls "the great outpouring of antiwoman hostility in the undergrounds of the early '70s" was really the result of the threat men felt from such rebellious females. As feminized as guys were by their hippie apparel and flowing hair, they were unable to let go of their entrenched sexism—or perhaps simply unconscious of it. "We liked to think we were enlightened at the time," says Ron Stone. "Looking back, we were not quite as enlightened as perhaps we thought. At the time, these were not issues for us—or *seemingly* not issues."

It is also true to say that most successful female artists of the period—Joni Mitchell, Linda Ronstadt, and Judy Collins—relied to greater or lesser degrees on the patronage of powerful men. "Unfortunately," says Chris Darrow, "like many other women in the music business Linda was forced to align herself with men to get her way down the line." As late as 1974, interviewed for a book called *Rock 'n' Roll Woman*, Ronstadt was still wrestling with "the problem of people thinking I'm a piece of cheese."

Me, Myself, and I

"The world had become so mysterious from the vantage point of the '70s," Joni Mitchell said in 1985. "The disillusionment, the killing of the president, the stain of the Vietnam War. It was a natural thing for people to look into themselves."

As early as February 1968, *Time* noted that "today's troubadours are turning away from protest," adding that their gaze was "shifting from the world around them to the realms within." Two years later, youth guru Theodore Roszak saw these societal changes as implicitly conservative. "A lot of these kids are growing up now," he told *Newsweek*. "They want family, they want friendship, they want livelihood." Supreme Court chief justice Earl Warren argued that it was essential to reconcile "the daring of youth" with "the mellow practicality" of the mature.

But was maturity merely surrender? *Newsweek* saw "the appearance of a new breed of poet-troubadour" as "a move away from rock-as-cultural-offensive." The new direction was "toward contemplation, appreciation, celebration, a self-effacing harmony and poise seeking to refocus on a Utopian vision that had become fuzzy." It was as if the music had gone full circle, back to folk. Except that this wasn't folk music as Joni and friends had known it in the early to mid-1960s; it was, thanks to Dylan, Leonard Cohen, and others, far more personal and subjective than that. "Politics is bullshit," Dylan told Phil Ochs. "The only thing that's real is inside you."

"The time was right," rock critic Janet Maslin wrote, "for reactionary expressions of frustration, confusion, irony, quiet little confidences, and personal declarations of independence." The hallmark of the singer-songwriter genre, she added, was "a self-absorption complete enough to counterbalance the preceding era's utopian jive." For heretics such as Frank Zappa, the new acoustic singer-songwriters were narcissists in thrall to their own angst: "navel-gazers," in the phrase coined to condemn them. Instead of engaging with the topical turmoil of the moment, these fey creatures were mired in apolitical self-love.

"My style at that time was very intimate," one of them later reflected. "To criticize it, it was very self-centered, very autobiographical, and you could call it narcissistic. But the upside of that was that it was very accessible, and I think people liked that." The speaker was James Taylor, a gaunt, privileged singer-songwriter who'd wound up in Los Angeles by default rather than design. Though you'd never have gleaned it from his gentle, plangent songs, James also was a habitual user of heroin and a former inmate of two mental institutions in his native Massachusetts. His mentor was a short, well-educated Englishman named Peter Asher, acolyte of the Beatles and brother of Paul McCartney's ex-girlfriend Jane. Asher also had been half of Peter and Gordon, a British invasion duo that scored such U.S. hits as "World without Love" (1964). Asher signed Taylor to Apple Records in London, but the singer's first album foundered as a result of the Beatles' business problems. In 1969 Asher brought Taylor to Los Angeles in an act of pure faith, rustling up just enough cash to rent an adobe-style house on Longwood Avenue, off Olympic Boulevard. "I brought James over here because I really thought his songs were important," Asher says. "There was a genuine proselytizing aspect to it."

One October morning, Asher breakfasted with Warner Brothers' Joe Smith at the Continental Hyatt on Sunset Strip. Smith had seen Taylor stoned and lurching around at the Newport Folk Festival that summer. "Peter and I settled a deal," Smith recalls of the breakfast. "He was very bright and scheming and was going to be a wonderful manager for an act. I liked him immediately and we formed a very strong bond."

"The fact that Warners already had Joni and Neil made me think that they would know what to do with a James Taylor," Asher says. "Joni and Neil hadn't had any real success at that point, but they had the cool Stan Cornyn ads. I felt that if they were sticking by Joni and Neil, they would understand James."

Asher was as entranced by the whole Laurel Canyon vibe as he was by the laissez-faire ethos of Warner-Reprise. It was clear that something fresh was happening in Southern California. "What was really new to me from the times I'd been here earlier was the Troubadour," he says. "With musical movements like that, one always thinks that everybody knows each other. But in this case they did. Jackson Browne I remember meeting up at David Geffen's house. Joni I met at one of James's gigs."

If one album could be said to have inaugurated the new mellow sound of canyon singer-songwriting, it was Taylor's *Sweet Baby James*, produced by Asher at Hollywood's Sunset Sound studio in December 1969. James's soothing tenor voice and intimate guitar picking offered smooth respite from the horrors of the times. "James seemed like the perfect guy for the time," said Taylor's long-time friend and guitarist Danny Kortchmar. "As a young man in his early twenties, his aura was of somebody who was sensitive but not feminine, handsome but not too macho."

"We loved that James Taylor record," says Ned Doheny. "I know Jackson Browne really thought James was a force to be reckoned with. James broke the mold and made that whole scene acceptable in a way that it hadn't been before." *Sweet Baby James* was shot through with country rock touches that were pure Southern California. Peter Asher had brought in Chris Darrow to play fiddle, along with Red Rhodes on pedal steel and Randy Meisner on bass. Taylor may have hailed from the Berkshires in New England, but the title track gave us a "young cowboy" who slept in "the canyons." "Country Road" was a perfect distillation of the new rural mood.

"I never thought that *Sweet Baby James* would become what it was," says Darrow, who also brought in drummer Russ Kunkel for the first of many historic studio sessions. "James was a very nice guy—I wouldn't have known that he had heroin problems at that time." The paradox that such mellow music could be made by such a tormented man remains irresistible. But the most famous song on *Sweet Baby James*, "Fire and Rain," made it obvious that Taylor's world wasn't all country roads and sunny skies. Inspired by the suicide of a friend, the song acknowledged the darkness and depression that would haunt James for years. "At the time I didn't think my songs were personal," Taylor told Joe Smith. "[But] 'Fire and Rain' is a very personal song which drew a lot of attention, and therefore people connected me with that kind of song."

Another musician playing on *Sweet Baby James* was Carole King, the Brill Building songstress whose portfolio boasted such timeless classics as "The Loco-Motion" and "Will You Love Me Tomorrow?" King, who'd recently switched coasts and moved into actress Mary Astor's old Laurel Canyon home high on Appian Way, was recruited by Danny Kortchmar to play piano on the album. Unlike most of her Brill Building contemporaries, she was keen to keep pace with the times, emerging from the backroom shadows to form a band, with Kortchmar on lead guitar and her second husband, Charlie Larkey, on bass. The label that signed the group was Ode, a new indie launched in L.A. by Lou Adler.

Had Adler cared more about singer-songwriters, Ode might have been the definitive independent label of the late 1960s and early 1970s. "Lou had made so much money from the Mamas and the Papas," says the group's biographer Matthew Greenwald. "He didn't really give a shit." A hip warlord, Lou was already looking at the bigger entertainment picture. "Lou really had a production deal called a label, whereas we had a real label," says David Geffen, comparing Ode to his own Asylum label. "We had a great many artists, whereas he had very few. Lou also produced most of the stuff that came out on Ode. We were not producers."

Carole King's move from New York to California simultaneously saw her move from a writer-for-hire to a singer-songwriter mentality. "Her brain changed as much as her hairstyle did," says Peter Asher. "And I think James had quite a bit to do with that. To go from 'The Loco-Motion' to 'You've Got a Friend' . . . I mean, we'd always treasured Carole's demos of those famous 1960s songs, because you realized how special she was in her own right."

"Carole moved to the canyon around 1969," recalls Adler, whose other artists included Spirit and Merry Clayton. "I'd been too busy to cut her *Writer* album, but by 1971 I was free to do an album with her. I simply tried to re-create her demos. The timing was perfect. There had been a transition from cool to mellow, I guess, with James Taylor as the leader of them all."

"L.A. is a more relaxed environment than New York and it has affected me that way," said King. "I'm speedy for the L.A. pace." The very title *Writer* was significant. In the new canyon milieu, the accent was on the craft and introspection of composition itself— the idea of the songwriter in her living room, channeling her feelings and beliefs. Here was Carole King the earth mother, the Brill Building beehive queen repositioned as a rocking-chair honey. "I want songs of hope, songs of love, songs of raw feeling," she said. "I'm really hung up on that. I love seeing why relationships work and just watching them work more than even figuring out *why* they work."

Although *Writer* sold modestly, Lou Adler kept faith with King. In January 1971 she went into A&M Studios to record a new album with Adler, Kortchmar, Larkey, Kunkel, and others. The sound was tight, simple, economical, and soulful—and it would come to dominate the musical flavor of L.A. in the early 1970s. "The rhythm sections that we used had a lot to do with the sound of those records," says Adler. "The 1970s brought in a whole new set, and it was James who really introduced the guys who would become The Section."

The classic *Tapestry*, released late in 1970, was a feel-good experience extraordinaire. Petrified, King debuted its songs at the Troubadour in May 1971. "Carole was squeezing my hand so hard," Lou Adler remembered. "I knew she was churning on her way up to the stage." By the late summer, thanks to its double A-side smash "It's Too Late"/"I Feel the Earth Move," *Tapestry* had spent fifteen weeks at No. 1. "Funnily enough, Kootch and those guys weren't that thrilled with *Tapestry*," Adler says. "Kootch asked me what I thought of it and I said that it was the *Love Story* of the record industry. It hit a nerve."

Tapestry has for so long been a byword for singer-songwriter serenity that it's easy to forget how good it is. Not only was King one of the supreme melodists of the era, but her singing on the album was intimate and wonderfully vulnerable. "My production values were right because of what I learned listening to James Taylor albums and Neil Young albums," she told *Rolling Stone*. "I was able to get naked in my sound. I became more honest by listening to those records and by working with those people."

Keeping a close eye on the runaway success of *Tapestry* was a host of singer-songwriters who'd long viewed Carole as their front-runner. For Randy Newman, a longtime admirer, the new status of the singer-songwriter was problematic. Too acerbic and self-effacing to be a rock romantic in the Neil Young/Joni Mitchell mode, Newman distanced himself from the confessional canyon clique. "Laurel Canyon has got an awful lot of musicians living in it," he said in 1970, "but I really don't know anybody." In any case he questioned the supposed transparency of "confessional" songwriting. "I never believed it was naked baring of the soul," he says today. "I think you could take a guess and know a lot more about me than you could guess about Joni or Neil. When you met them you weren't so sure that that's what they were writing about."

Using third-person characters—or singing *in character*—Randy's songs were suffused by irony, often stunningly funny. Musically they were anchored in Tin Pan Alley and in the piano-based rhythm and blues he'd soaked up during childhood vacations in Louisiana. Despite the late Ian MacDonald's verdict that his debut is actually his best album, commercially it failed. For its follow-up, Lenny Waronker suggested they dispense with coproducer Van Dyke Parks and make a proper rock album. The sinewy, sensual *12 Songs* in 1970 almost featured a cameo by his labelmate Jimi Hendrix. "I wrote 'Suzanne' with Hendrix in mind, and I talked to him on the phone about it," Randy recalls. "He said, 'You're a Sagittarius, too, huh?' He was so lacking in confidence, it was unbelievable." It's odd enough to hear Clarence White applying his languid country licks to this stalkers' anthem, one of the creepiest items in the Newman catalog.

If he had little affinity with the CSNY-Joni-Jackson canyon-cowboy community, Newman benefited greatly from the new wave of interest in artists who did it all themselves. "Dylan and others like him made it all right for your voice not to be bel canto," he reflects. "Maybe [there] was some kind of interest in the creator like there was at the end of the eighteenth century, where people were interested in Beethoven anyway."*

---

*Typically, Dylan himself mocked the school of introspection by releasing an album called *Self-Portrait* (1970). It consisted almost entirely of covers of other people's songs, many mawkishly sentimental.

But Newman's luckiest break was simply being on Reprise Records, where talent such as his was nurtured and developed over several albums. The mood in Burbank was more upbeat than ever. Early in 1970, Mo Ostin took over from Mike Maitland as president of Warner-Reprise, with Joe Smith named executive vice president. Instrumental in the switch was Ahmet Ertegun, who urged Kinney Corporation chief Steve Ross to empower Ostin and Smith. And Ertegun wasn't alone in regarding Warner-Reprise as both super-shrewd and ultratasteful. "At *Rolling Stone* we just began to realize that this was an extraordinary company," says Ben Fong-Torres. "They were the first hip brand among the major labels."

In 1971, in an unprecedented step, *Rolling Stone* publisher and editor Jann Wenner conducted a feature-length interview with Joe Smith. That Mo Ostin remained behind the scenes, allowing Smith to be the company's public face, did not go unnoticed by Warner insiders. As he himself had been empowered, so Mo chose to extend more slack to Lenny Waronker, whose shaping of what came to be known as "the Burbank Sound" he recognized as critical. "Being made a vice president was almost like a joke," Lenny claims. "But from Mo's and Joe's point of view, I think that to have somebody who came from the studio and who supported artists become head of A&R was a great signal."

The continuing presence of Van Dyke Parks was another signal. In September 1970, Mo Ostin appointed him Warners' director of audiovisual services. "Warners hired people like Van Dyke just because they liked having him around," says Barry Hansen, who worked for the company before hosting a popular novelties radio show as Dr. Demento. "None of us had long hair," says Lenny Waronker. "We had long *sideburns*, but that was it. I mean, it was never about hair for Randy or Van Dyke or me. We were so snotty at the time that anything anybody else was doing was not cool."

Following the failure of *Song Cycle*, Parks took a hiatus from recording his own material. Instead he dedicated himself to the work of such fellow artists as Newman and Cooder. "We didn't know who we were selling Randy or Ry to," he says. "It was strictly on a wing and a prayer." The hothouse atmosphere at Burbank didn't always make for harmony, in *or* out of the studio. "There were times when we would get on each other's nerves," Parks reflects. "Randy had a real serious sense of what he was doing, as did Ry. But we all outlived it and we're all still speaking." As straight as he was, even Newman dabbled with drugs. "I had a family real early, so I was different in that sense," he says. "But I wasn't free of ending up in places I shouldn't have been at three in the morning."

For anyone looking in from the outside, the Warner-Reprise singer-songwriter stable suggested that the old Tin Pan Alley era of invisible tunesmiths in cubicles was finished. As Carole King had done, writers such as Jimmy Webb and Harry Nilsson emerged from the shadows to become stars in their own right. And in time, Brill Building veterans such as Barry Mann (with 1972's *Lay It All Out*) and Ellie Greenwich (with 1973's *Let It Be Written, Let It Be Sung*) would attempt to emulate the breakaway success of their old rival's *Tapestry*.

"By 1970 you had an entirely different radio," says Mark Volman, whose AM-friendly Turtles found themselves beached by FM rock. "Everything changed between 1965 and 1970, and radio allowed that transition to happen. You had James Taylor, Carole King, Jackson Browne—the 1970s writers—and also Stevie Wonder. Music began to make this really strong metamorphosis after the Beatles laid the groundwork and then broke up." The Turtles tried to stay hip with tracks such as "Earth Anthem" and "Chicken Little Was Right." They even formed their own Blimp Productions publishing arm to scoop up such undiscovered singer-songwriters as Judee Sill. But things were moving—and changing—too fast. After a last unreleased album, produced by Jerry Yester, the Turtles breathed their last. "I think you could say that the Turtles got left behind," Volman says. "The musical scene was discovering this new, young, hip counterculture that was much more influential because of the drugs that were happening."

For some veterans of the folk scene, the new introspection of Laurel Canyon's singer-songwriters seemed trite. "A lot of the confessional stuff seemed to me a jackoff," says Judy Henske. "I didn't think it was good poetry, and I didn't think it was good show business. But everyone else seemed to think it was great." The culmination of the confessional period was *Sweet Baby James* being certified a million-seller and its creator making the cover of *Time* magazine on March 1, 1971. "After *Sweet Baby James* I knew what it felt like to work for a living," James Taylor said, "and be this sort of hypothetical entrepreneur with a record company, agent, manager, whatever."

Phil Spector, left behind by the L.A. scene despite his association with the Beatles, was scathing about the all-singing, all-writing stars who'd made producers like him redundant. "I'm getting a little tired of hearing about, you know, everybody's *emotional problems*," he told *Rolling Stone* editor Jann Wenner. "They're not writing songs anymore, they're only writing ideas." Spector sounded like Norma Desmond in Billy Wilder's *Sunset Boulevard*: "I *am* big . . . it was the pictures that got smaller!" As with Norma, however, nobody was listening.

Legend has it that when the Laurel Canyon rock community got the news about the butchering at Terry Melcher's house on Cielo Drive, Stephen Stills ran around shrieking, "They're killing everybody with estates!"

Estates were a concept that Stills, Crosby, and Nash were now all too familiar with, given that their debut album was selling so well. But there also was the small problem of how CSN were going to translate their layered studio sound to the stage. Uneasy as the prospect made him, Stills was giving serious thought to Ahmet Ertegun's suggestion that his old sparring partner Neil Young be bolted onto the trio to augment their live power.

Elliot Roberts for one was surprised that Stills had even considered it: "It still always shocks me that it was Stephen's call to invite Neil back into the fold when he knew he wouldn't be able to intimidate him." For his part Graham Nash felt threatened by the idea of Young joining the group. He'd found the perfect harmony trio and now suddenly Stephen's old Springfield buddy was entering the picture. "With CSNY it was like the Yankees adding another starter," says Ben Fong-Torres. "Whereas most teams are content to have a couple of guys who can throw the ball, this group had four."

Young's ego made itself felt from the outset. The Canadian instructed Elliot Roberts to inform the trio that equal billing was "non-negotiable." Whether that made CSNY a genuine rock and roll group was another matter. "Everybody was tryin' to do their own thing," Young told Jimmy McDonough. "I don't think it was ever supposed to be a band. It *wasn't* a band." When Young was cut in for a considerable percentage, drummer Dallas Taylor was incensed. It didn't help that Taylor was one of the first heroin addicts on the L.A. rock scene. Onstage, he deliberately tried to throw Neil off balance by changing time signatures during the guitarist's solos. Soon, Taylor was ousted from the band.

The decision to join CSNY was attributed at the time to the thrill Young got from dueling live with Stills. More plausible as an explanation was that the group afforded him greater exposure than he could possibly attract by himself, for Young was as interested as David Geffen in making money. He intuitively understood that Geffen's modus operandi was to make money off the backs of stars who ostensibly cared nothing for filthy lucre. This was pop capitalism's Trojan-horse strategy: to sell anticapitalism to the kids, the longhairs, the dropouts. "I'm not going to say that I don't like the money, you know," Young told Ritchie Yorke. "I do like the money and it's going to make me a lot of money and it definitely plays a part in my being here, you know."

With Joni Mitchell playing support, the quartet opened in Chicago on August 16, traveling on to upstate New York for a rock festival whose scale would dwarf the Monterey Pop Festival two years earlier. "We're scared shitless," Stills announced from the stage of the Woodstock festival. It was only their second gig.

Famously, Joni never made it to the festival but composed its anthem, "Woodstock," anyway. David Geffen, more concerned about her TV appearance on *The Dick Cavett Show* the next day than about the festival, urged her to remain in New York. "I picked up the *New York Times* at the airport," Geffen remembered. "It said '400,000 People Sitting in Mud,' and I said to Joni, 'Let's not go!'" In the event, CSNY flew out of the festival in a helicopter and appeared on the Cavett show themselves. Geffen also leveraged CSNY's appearance in the Woodstock film to stipulate that "Woodstock" be the movie's theme song. "The producers were either going to give me what I wanted or that was it," he told Carl Gottlieb. "Let's not kid ourselves. I was a formidable figure always."

With Neil Young in CSNY came a whole extra dimension of danger and unpredictability. His intensity was soon felt in the solo songs he inserted into the CSN repertoire. Long versions of songs such as "Down by the River" were vehicles for Young and Stills to revert to their staglike guitar sparring. During these testosterone sessions Graham Nash was obliged to stand at the side of the stage, impotently rattling a tambourine. Yet Stills was the most affected by Neil's growing confidence. Stills's insecurities were obvious when he hogged the limelight at New York's Fillmore East. Backstage afterward, an ugly squabble broke out. The dressing room wasn't big enough to contain these egos.

It didn't help that Geffen, Roberts, and their lackeys sealed CSNY in a bubble of smugness that might have been good for their art and their bank balances but wasn't great for their humanity. "That's what got them out of touch with reality," says Nurit Wilde. "It exacerbated their already growing megalomania and their belief that they were gods." The wall that Elliot Roberts erected around the sessions for CSNY's *Déjà Vu* at Wally Heider's in San Francisco only made the competitiveness among the four men the more claustrophobic. "When we did the first CSN record, we were very much in love with each other and each other's music," Nash told rock critic Robert Sandall. "By the time of *Déjà Vu* that had all turned to shit."

The tension between control freak Stills and the lazy but mouthy Crosby was especially toxic. It was Stills's arrogance and assumption that he was the leader of Crosby, Stills, Nash, and Young that created the most tension in the group. "The conflicts then were between me and Stills and Nash and Stills and a little between Neil and Stills," Crosby recalled. "Stephen felt as if Neil had taken the group away from him in some fashion or other, even though it was Stephen who invited Neil to join us in the first place."

Young was especially frustrated by CSN's overly intricate arrangements. "What we've got to do is listen with an eye to simplicity," he muttered as he watched Stills at work with engineer Bill Halverson. "Think how we can make it bigger by simplifying it." At one point the vibes at Heider's got so bad that Nash called a band meeting. As he attempted to express his misery at the niggling resentments within the group, he burst into tears. "Nash had to work so hard to be the diplomat and keep things together in that group," says Denny Bruce. "He said that Stephen Stills some days could be judged to be insane, or words to that effect. And Geffen said he had never seen anyone lose his temper like Stills. He said the veins in Stephen's neck came out through the shoulders."

Nash, who'd cherished the original trio's camaraderie, also was galled by Young's unwillingness to really commit to CSNY, as well as by what he later described as "Neil's insatiable need for control." As someone who'd always subsumed his own ego to the collective musical good, Nash's patience with Neil started to wear thin. There also was a political schism between Crosby and Nash on one hand and Stills and Young on the other. When Hugh "Wavy Gravy" Romney invited CSNY to play a benefit for the "Chicago Seven" arrested at the 1968 Democratic National Convention, Stills and Young declined to participate. Nash's song "Chicago" was a direct plea to his bandmates to follow their consciences.

It didn't help that *Déjà Vu* was recorded against a backdrop of loss and tragedy. Stills had split up with Judy Collins, which only made him the more driven and monomaniacal in the studio. Nash was having problems with Joni, who felt hemmed in by cohabitation. Much worse, on September 30, 1969, Crosby's girlfriend, Christine Hinton, was killed in a head-on car collision while running errands near their Marin County home. Her death sent Crosby into a catatonic depression that colored the rest of his life. Such decimating loss was uncommon for musicians in their midtwenties. David's use of heroin increased dramatically, burying grief that would catch up with him later. "After Christine died David became guarded, afraid to give of himself," Elliot Roberts said. "He didn't want to make decisions anymore."

Heroin and cocaine both played their part in the problems surrounding *Déjà Vu*. Dallas Taylor, who claimed that he, Crosby, and Keith Richards had turned "half of Hollywood" on to smack, was mainlining it in the studio. "Heroin was more prevalent than you'd think," says Essra Mohawk, who'd been turned on to the drug by her junked-out husband, Frazier. "I mean, *James Taylor* was doing it! This guy used to come to our house in a nice car, dressed real collegiate, and he would deliver the little package. It seemed so neat and clean."

Cass Elliott, always keen on prescribed opiates (Dilaudid, Demerol, Percodan, et al.), also was still doing the big no-no. "The whole idea that Cass Elliott was doing heroin at this point would have been so shocking to the likes of me," Joel Bernstein says in hindsight. "I mean, when Laura Nyro went into a bathroom to do cocaine with her limo driver I was *horrified*. Because cocaine was *serious shit*."

Stills, meanwhile, was drinking and manically snorting coke to fuel all-night recording marathons. Like more than a few users of the drug, he clung to the fact that he didn't do heroin, as though that redeemed his intake of other substances. "A lot of times CSNY was pretty crazy, and I couldn't understand why," Young later mused. "I mean, everybody was, like, toasted. *I* wasn't doing drugs, but drugs were starting to surface in other places—and were having a negative impact, I might add. Was I naive? I think so." Young's compatriot Joni Mitchell was similarly innocent. Shielded from debauchery by Graham Nash, she had little idea of what was really going on at Heider's. "People tended to be protective of me," she said. "Even in the scene when cocaine was around, people would shelter me from it."

Making regular appearances at Heider's were Elliot Roberts and David Geffen, busy arranging tour dates and overseeing other business. Whereas Elliot loved to hang out and minister to his artists' needs, David grew increasingly impatient with their petulant feuding. By nature he also was less interested in the San Francisco scene where CSNY were making a second musical home.

Déjà Vu, completed by mid-November 1969 and released early the following year, was pompous and ponderous after *Crosby, Stills, and Nash*. Nash's "Teach Your Children" was a charming country rock song, but Crosby's "Almost Cut My Hair" was the kind of blowhard hippie rhetoric that Dennis Hopper's Crosby-based character spouted in *Easy Rider*. "The first album, you put it on in the middle of the afternoon and you're boogieing and laughing by the time it's over," Crosby rightly said. "It doesn't happen with the second one." Downer it may have been, but the weight of expectation on *Déjà Vu* helped Atlantic shift millions of advance copies. America had belatedly discovered its own instant Beatles—the Four Horsemen of the counterculture. The acclaim and general fawning went quickly to their heads. "What the trick is with us is that we're mass artists," Crosby told Ben Fong-Torres. "There's never been that kind of stuff before until Gutenberg."

If sex and drugs now took up most of Crosby's time, he was careful to stay abreast of politics, viewing himself as a radical messiah of youth. Fong-Torres was present at a Laurel Canyon dinner chez Stephen Stills, where Crosby asked Stills, Nash, Young, Joni, Elliot, and their friends to contribute to campaigns being waged by Jesse Unruh, Jane Fonda, and Dr. Benjamin Spock. The spring of 1970 presented CSNY with the perfect political flash point. When four student protesters were shot dead by military police at Ohio's Kent State campus on May 4, Neil Young wrote the charged, harrowing "Ohio"—reflex agitprop born of sincere outrage and the greatest song the band cut with Young in the lineup. Atlantic rushed out the single in late June, and CSNY consolidated their heroic status.

"Ohio" notwithstanding, CSNY in 1970 really represented the death of rock's innocence. In the words of San Francisco light-show pioneer Joshua White, "We were now applauding the *presence* of the artist rather than the performance." Crosby in particular became insufferable. "In my experience, there was never anything quite like the egos in CSNY," said David Geffen. "It was not easy. David was obnoxious, demanding, thoughtless, full of himself—of the four of them, the least talented. And I think that he *felt* the least talented." Even so, Geffen was keen to keep his cash cow working. But the CSNY tour in the summer of 1970 was what finally destroyed the band's remaining camaraderie. The main cause this time was Stills's overbearing need to be in control. "It was my instinct for giving orders," he admitted, ". . . that led to a lot of hassles." On July 9 the quartet played its last show for four years.

When Neil Young sought respite from Crosby, Stills, and Nash via Crazy Horse, the situation wasn't much better: Danny Whitten was himself in the viselike grip of heroin. "I photographed Crazy Horse in January of 1970," says Joel Bernstein. "By this point Neil had already had guitars ripped off and sold by Danny without Neil even *knowing* it. That was how naive Neil was." In the early summer, Young retreated to Topanga to record the lo-fi songbook that was

After the Gold Rush. A sound track for homegrown canyon consciousness, the album was cut in part at Young's home on Skyline Trail
before being finished at Sunset Sound in Hollywood. Featuring Jack
Nitzsche on piano, Greg Reeves on bass, and a young East Coast
guitarist named Nils Lofgren, *Gold Rush* was pronouncedly sans
Crazy Horse: Whitten and Molina played, but there was no Billy
Talbot in evidence.

Cameron Crowe later reported that "Whitten's strong aura of
junk" scared Young out of his wits. "My job was to sit next to Danny
and make sure he didn't go to the bathroom," says Jan Henderson,
who set up the equipment for the *Gold Rush* sessions at Sunset
Sound. "The other guys kept saying, 'Don't let him get up and run
away. Keep him entertained.'" In addition to the Whitten problem,
Young had to contend with an almost schizoid Jack Nitzsche. "One
second [Jack] would be sitting there drivelling away about how
much he loved Neil's music," said Nils Lofgren. "Then next thing
he'd be yelling and screaming at him, calling him names and refusing to play."

A reaction of sorts to the overproduced *Déjà Vu*, *Gold Rush* also
leaned more heavily toward the raggedly acoustic than *Everybody
Knows This Is Nowhere* had done. "I Believe in You," "Only Love
Can Break Your Heart," and the version of Nashville stalwart Don
Gibson's "Oh Lonesome Me" exuded a dragging beauty, a wavering
melancholia. "I Believe in You" suggested that all was not entirely
idyllic in Young's marital nest. Despite the crunching "When You
Dance I Can Really Love" and the righteous "Southern Man," *After
the Gold Rush* remains a definitive statement of patched-denim
sensitivity. "When Neil came out with the Levi's and the patches on
the cover of *Gold Rush*, it was a uniform," says Denny Bruce. "Suddenly everybody had to dress that way."

A package the image may have been, but what set Young's music
apart from the overly cozy music of the period was the strain of dis-
comfort beneath the surface of even his most laid-back acoustic
songs. In the crude delicacy of his melodies and the wistful femi-
ninity of his voice, something troubling always lurked in Neil's
shadows.

You Probably Think This Song Is about You

When Joni Mitchell opened for CSNY in Chicago in August 1969, Neil Young took his fellow Canadian aside and whispered that they should be opening for *her*. It was a generous sentiment and one that Joni appreciated. What she thought of Neil's songs wasn't clear, but there was a mutual respect between these expatriates that was only enhanced by the absence of romantic frisson between them. "I feel very kindred to Neil," she later told *Musician*. "We're caught between two cultures—we're neither-nor."

Young, though, was secretly shocked by the confessional transparency of Mitchell's songs. "[Joni] writes about her relationships so much more vividly than I do," he told Cameron Crowe. "I guess I put more of a veil over what I'm talking about." It was ironic, therefore, that Neil's "Only Love Can Break Your Heart" was a song about the end of Joni's affair with Graham Nash. Maybe it was easier for him to observe the relationship problems of others than for him to confront his own. That said, the Nash/Mitchell breakup affected everybody in the immediate Geffen-Roberts circle. The two singers had loved each other deeply and respectfully, but now Joni felt torn between her love and her art. Notes Nurit Wilde, "A monster talent like Joni's wasn't going to be kept down by being someone's old lady."

Mitchell's torment dramatized the struggles many female artists faced as the 1960s folded into the 1970s. Haunted by the conformities of the 1950s, when women stayed home and stifled their ambitions, the folk generation became part of the feminist uprising. But for Joni this came at a painful cost. Just as she had suffered dreadful loss after giving up her baby in 1965, so she now forsook her best shot at conjugal happiness. "Graham is a sweetheart, and we didn't part with any animosity," Joni told Dave DiMartino. "[He] needed a more traditional female." Actually there *was* animosity. Rather unwisely, Joni chose in the early summer of 1970 to embark on a brief affair with Stephen Stills. Perhaps it seemed the easiest way of disentangling herself from the intimacy she'd shared with Graham.

"I remember the week that Joni and Graham broke up," says Carl Gottlieb. "Elliot Roberts was at our house, and the news came that Graham and Stephen weren't talking. There was an explosion, and

Joni and Graham and Stephen all called the Lookout Management office that afternoon and said, 'Cancel the tour, cancel the studio, I'm going to Hawaii. . . .' And Elliot was just wringing his hands. My wife, Allison, told him, 'Cheer up, you're gonna get at least three great songs out of this!'"

"Joni and Graham wanted to end it while it was pure, I think, rather than get into the nitty-gritty," says Henry Diltz, who'd photographed the couple in touchingly intimate moments. "Then again, there was a lot of that back then. And it was poignant because there was still love there, but people would go on the road and while you were on the road things would happen." Nash and Mitchell officially ended their relationship in June 1970, by which time Joni's third album, *Ladies of the Canyon*, was in the Top 30. Among its songs was "Willy," an early statement of love for Nash that reversed the dynamic and made *him* the doubting, distancing partner. The album found her branching out and jettisoning her folk past, using a broader palette of instrumentation to paint a twelve-part picture of turn-of-the-decade life in Laurel Canyon. "I want my music to get more involved and more sophisticated," Mitchell said. "Right now I'm learning how to play a lot of new instruments."

On the title song Joni sang of Trina with her "wampum beads," of Estrella with "the gypsy shawls," and "songs like tiny hammers." When Stan Cornyn put together the Reprise ad for the album, he created an imaginary canyon girl named Amy Foster, who sat in "her orange inflatable chair listening to Neil Young's second album" and "waited for the Country Store delivery boy to arrive with her groceries." If "Ladies . . ." and "Conversation" and "Morning Morgantown" suggested a new kind of lifestyle music, the album also featured the ambiguous Utopianism of "Woodstock" and the euphoric eco-anthem "Big Yellow Taxi." Meanwhile, "The Arrangement"—a piano-based song that anticipates the great Mitchell midperiod of *Court and Spark*—spoke for all women who felt as trapped as she did.

Joni felt stifled not just by the pressure of intimate relationships but by the pressures of success. "There's a tremendous pocket of adjustment where you either take drugs or kill yourself or something," she said in 1998. "You say you're not gonna change, but everything around you changes, and you eventually have to change."

In the spring of 1970 she told Elliot Roberts she no longer wished to perform live. "Joan was never one who liked touring," he says. "Touring was not very kind to her. Audiences were fine, but she couldn't sleep after shows, so she'd be exhausted all the time. And she wouldn't take pills."

"I liked small clubs," Mitchell says. "But with the big stage, timing is of the essence, and I work in fifty different tunings. Standard tuning would have been easier, but then I wouldn't have had all of that original chordal movement." In the summer, Mitchell fled L.A. for Europe. On the Greek island of Crete she fell in with a group of wild hippies who lived on a beach and barely knew who she was. It was the escape from herself that she had long craved. On a dulcimer she'd brought with her she wrote a clutch of songs that would appear on her next album. "Carey" and "California" told of the fun she was having in Europe but acknowledged a longing for home and the displacement she felt.

When Mitchell finally returned, she met and fell in love with James Taylor, who was writing songs for his next album, *Mud Slide Slim and the Blue Horizon*, but also was back in the throes of his heroin addiction. The two were already an item when Taylor began filming Monte Hellman's *Two-Lane Blacktop* in New Mexico in the early fall of 1970. Joni visited the set, bringing her guitar and dulcimer with her. The affair was markedly different from the relationship she'd had with Graham Nash. Whereas Nash had been solicitous and emotionally available, Taylor was as introverted and self-absorbed as any other junkie. "I was pretty unconscious around then," Taylor remembered, "but she was writing 'A Case of You' and *Blue* in a single-story, rough-cut wooden house up on rock piers in Laurel Canyon."

"James and Joni had their tempestuous moments," says Peter Asher, "but for a while they were mutual fans and friends. I was on James's team, so it was hard for me to tell. Some days it was very obvious that something had gone wrong, but I never knew exactly what had happened." Taylor's addiction plunged Mitchell into despair. When she came to record *Blue* at Sunset Sound, she was fragile and anxious to the point of agoraphobia. Most of the sessions were closed to everybody except Mitchell and producer/

engineer Henry Lewy. Taylor himself was only allowed in to add guitar to songs such as "California," "A Case of You," and the opening "All I Want." "I was at my most defenseless during the making of *Blue*," she later reflected. "I guess you could say I broke down but I continued to work. In the process of breaking down there are powers that come in, clairvoyancy and . . . everything becomes transparent."

"You had to take your hat off to singer-songwriters of that era, because they really exposed themselves," says Allison Caine. "Talking from a woman's standpoint, what Joni did was really brave. The singer-songwriters gave you everything in their art, and maybe that's why they held back privately." When *Blue* came out in 1971, Taylor felt as exposed as Mitchell. "Joni's music is much more specifically autobiographical than [that of] a lot of other people," he remarked. "Everyone who writes songs writes autobiographical songs. But hers are sometimes alarmingly specific." Yet it was the specificity, the personal detail, of Joni's despair that made *Blue* a touchstone for the period. People clung to the album as though it were a friend guiding them through their own darkness. "It turned forever on its head the notion of what a singer-songwriter was expected to be," writer Bill Flanagan noted. "Joni became enormously popular through that, and people didn't just love her the way they loved the Rolling Stones or Motown, they really felt, 'This woman, by the light of this record player, is looking into my soul.'" Other commentators had less sympathy with Mitchell's self-pity. "The ultimate irony," wrote Penny Stallings, "is that it is shy, circumspect Joni herself who's to blame for making her life an open record: she's the Woody Allen of rock."

On "River," Mitchell simultaneously voiced the desire to disappear and rebuked herself for being so difficult to live with. When she talked of losing "the best baby I ever had," it was unclear whether she was talking of Taylor or still in mourning for Graham Nash. "I was really mad at show business at that time," she says. "I became kind of contemptuous of the audience. Critics seemed to praise me when I felt I was poor and slam me when I felt I was at my peak." With *Blue* behind her, Joni decided to get herself back to the garden—in her case the garden of Canada, specifically the rugged Sunshine Coast of British Columbia north of Vancouver. After three years on Lookout

Mountain Avenue, she built an austere house that overlooked the crashing Pacific. "She built this spectacularly beautiful, almost monkish house," says Ron Stone, who for many years rented Joni's Lookout Mountain home. "It was out on this little point on the water. It did not have the creature comforts. It was pretty stark but it was a piece of art."

The self-imposed exile wouldn't last long. Although she continued to spend time in British Columbia, Mitchell found herself ineluctably pulled back to Los Angeles and the music scene she had fled. And when she got back, David Geffen was waiting for her.

7

With a Little Help from Our Friends

If you want to talk about what happened in the L.A.
music scene in the first half of the seventies, you can
sum it up with one name—David Geffen.

—David Anderle

Degrees of Separation

David Geffen was now a millionaire. Three Top 10 smashes in a row for his protégée Laura Nyro had added huge value to her Tuna Fish Music publishing catalog. In November 1969 Columbia's Clive Davis took control of the fledgling company in a deal worth more than $3 million. Now everybody wanted Geffen to represent them and fight for them. He acquired Johnny Rivers's house—at a knockdown price—high above Sunset on Alto Cedro Drive. On hoot night at the Troubadour, people sidled up to him to pay homage. "Geffen was *always* at the Troub," says former music-business lawyer Bill Straw. "He was this very straight guy, dressed in chinos and very preppie-looking."

From their adjoining offices at 9130 Sunset Boulevard—once the base for Phil Spector—Geffen and Elliot Roberts built their musical empire with remorseless drive. Yet the vibe was low-key and folksy. Guitars were casually strewn around. Neil Young's piano sat in a corner. "You could walk into that office anytime and there would be Crosby or David Blue," says Henry Diltz, by now court photographer to the scene. "You could stop by and use the phones, say hello to the secretaries, get a Coke."

Too impatient to deal with the on-the-road machinations of band life, Geffen left Roberts to massage the egos of Crosby, Stills, Nash, Young, Mitchell, and company and instead concentrated on the next phase of empire-building: launching his own label. Yet it was those temperamental, self-preoccupied artists who gave Geffen the leverage to go for the big kill. "We were very fortunate in that Joni and Neil drew great people to them like magnets," Elliot Roberts reflects.

"David was quite brilliant on the business side of it," says Ron Stone, "but it was Elliot's intuitiveness about the music that was the key. He had an uncanny ability to see through to the heart of the issue, which was the creative nucleus of that particular group." Peter Asher claims that first impressions of Roberts—as some kind of glorified pothead—were misleading. "Elliot actually had a mind like a steel trap," Asher says. Together, Geffen and Roberts plotted their route to world domination. Crucial to their strategy was the creation of an insulated elite, a pampered aristocracy of Geffen's significant artists. "Geffen-Roberts definitely changed the tone of things," says John York. "It created this whole stratum of stardom that was complete nonsense but was a great way to market the music."

"You have to remember we came out of the early 1960s and the whole Brill Building mentality," says Ron Stone. "Dylan and the singer-songwriters came along and changed the dynamic. We were all reinventing the business." Stone was constantly astonished by Geffen's all-consuming ambition. When he arrived in the morning David had already been in the office for three hours. When he left at night, Geffen would remain there for three more. It was though he had no life outside of 9130 Sunset.

Geffen discovered that he possessed an important weapon: he

could shout louder than anyone else in the business. The sound of David on the telephone—screaming the terms of a deal or haranguing some hapless lackey—was relentless. "I met David at a *Top of the Pops* taping in London," says artist manager Tony Dimitriades. "He was standing outside the studio in a callbox and shouting at the top of his voice, '*I need to speak to Ahmet Ertegun!*' I was in awe. Here was this young guy . . . in dirty jeans and a T-shirt, and he was talking to the suave head of this legendary record company."

Geffen was a ruthless schemer. Invariably the first victim of his insatiable need to win was the truth. After manipulating Richard Perry into producing Barbra Streisand's album *Stoney End*, Geffen urged Nyro to tell Streisand that "Wedding Bell Blues" had been personally written for her. Nyro was appalled and refused. "It's not a *big* lie," Geffen said, sulking. Not yet thirty, he hungered to be an industry heavy-hitter, a colossus like Mo Ostin or Ahmet Ertegun. His dream would come true in an interestingly circuitous way.

In June 1969, Warner–Seven Arts—of which Atlantic Records was now a part—was sold to the Kinney Corporation in New York. Miraculously, Kinney was headed not by a soulless mogul but by a CEO named Steve Ross, who saw that the way to grow was to empower talented executives. As a result, Ertegun's power base would mushroom. It was he who urged Ross to replace the mediocre Mike Maitland with Mo Ostin at the helm of Warner-Reprise. "We got the break of our lives," says Joe Smith. "Steve believed that the management of creative companies was the key. The artists will come and the artists will go, but Mo and Joe and Ahmet and Jerry will always be there." David Geffen observed the power shifts with rapt attention. Though Ertegun was mildly irritated by David's pushiness, he saw him for the formidable force he was. The two men had conspired to make CSNY happen. Now Geffen wanted more of Atlantic's money to develop a young artist he'd taken a shine to.

David Crosby had suggested that Jackson Browne mail a tape to Geffen in late 1970. After several years in the business, always somehow about to make it, Browne was still dealless. "Geffen had helped a friend of mine, Essra Mohawk," Browne recalled, "and I hoped he could do something to save me the misery of traipsing round to record companies staffed by people who shook hands like a trout and then kept you hanging for weeks because they wouldn't take any responsibility."

"The letter said, 'I'm writing to you out of respect for the artists you represent,'" remembered Geffen, his desk already cluttered with tapes by hopeful troubadours. "And it went on and on and on and on and on. I figured, 'My God, this guy can't be any good,' so I threw it in the garbage pail." When Geffen's secretary Dodie Smith retrieved an 8" by 10" glossy of the doe-eyed twenty-two-year-old from the bin, David was persuaded to give Jackson's tape a spin. "It was the only tape we ever took that was unsolicited," Elliot Roberts remembers. "We put it on because we had nothing else to do one morning. It was 'Song for Adam.'"

Geffen was quickly smitten by the singer's good looks. "Jackson was very pretty," he told writer Michelle Kort. "[He] is classically good-looking, matinee-idol good-looking." Similarly taken with Browne's looks was Laura Nyro, who was introduced to him by Geffen and whom Browne supported on a short tour through the winter of 1970–1971. The singers embarked on a brief and tempestuous affair that surprised their mentor—Nyro's taste usually leaned to rugged Italians. Geffen was as taken by the soothing grooves of Browne's songs as he was by his beauty. There was a fresh, ardent quality to them, a graceful kind of wisdom. For the coalescing Laurel Canyon community, Jackson was the scene's emotional Boy Scout. "He was a real soulmate," says Bonnie Raitt. "There was something so truthful and at the same time so heartbreaking about his songs."

Geffen went to Ertegun and urged him to sign Browne. Ertegun, unconvinced, declined. When Geffen pushed harder, Ertegun protested. He suggested that Geffen start his own label and sign Jackson himself. David decided he would do just that, if only to prove how shortsighted his mentor had been in turning Browne down. But Ertegun did more than encourage his disciple; he also offered to be Geffen's 50 percent partner in the label, then to be called either Benchmark or Phoenix, with Atlantic handling distribution and covering all expenses. "It was an astonishing deal that would not cost Geffen a cent," Geffen's biographer Tom King wrote.

"Geffen was eager, attentive, psyched up, intense—always turned

on like a light switch," says Stan Cornyn. "He was also a great listener, like Mo. They were probably the two best listeners to people
that I've ever come across." In late July 1971, Geffen gave his first
interview about the new label, now to be called Asylum. With typical
chutzpah he told *Record World* that Joni Mitchell and Laura Nyro
would be joining the label. He spoke too soon: Nyro herself was
courted directly by Clive Davis and chose to stay with Columbia.
Geffen was deeply hurt and added Nyro's name to a growing list of
resentments. "I was devoted to her," he told Nyro's biographer
Michelle Kort. "And let's not kid ourselves, to be Laura Nyro and
have a guy like me devoting himself to you is quite a thing."

"I know it broke his heart," Ellen Sander said of Nyro's decision.
"I remember Elliot had to go to New York and get David to go somewhere because he was so depressed." With or without Nyro, the
name Asylum spoke succinctly of David's desire to create a talent
sanctuary that would give artists the freedom to create without
music-industry pressure. "We were looking at A&M, which was a
small boutique record company at the time," Geffen says. "Fortu-
nately there were a tremendous amount of talented people floating
around at that time, and the big record companies didn't seem to
have any interest in them. Elliot and I had our pick, practically, of
everybody that was around then."

"They somehow created their own stable of artists *and* plucked
some of the best artists from larger labels by offering them more creative control," says Ben Fong-Torres. "It was just a more personalized
management style that created kind of a hip vision."

"I was young and naive," Geffen says. "When we started Asylum
we never expected it would turn into the company it became. We
were as excited and thrilled as it unfolded as the artists were when
their records came out and succeeded." Geffen's impact was felt
throughout the West Coast music industry. Whereas Lou Adler had
been the tall, dark godfather of Hollywood pop in the previous
decade, now this short, slim New Yorker was running rings around
everybody in the business. It was a wake-up call for anyone growing
lazy and complacent. "A bunch of hippies had become major players
and were now calling the shots," says David Anderle, by then an A&R
man at A&M. "All of us stopped smoking pot and got serious."

Play It as It Lays

For some people the shunting aside of "the old breed of hustlers" was precisely what killed the maverick spirit of American pop. Geffen had upped the stakes, turning back-porch folkies into Learjet superstars. He saw there were millions to be made here—maybe as many as in the film industry—and fantasized about becoming rock's very own Louis B. Mayer, a biography of whom he'd devoured as a teenager. And he was vain enough to seek celebrity for himself. "This is one of the few places in show business," he told *Time*, "where an executive like me can be a star too."

Privately, Geffen was fed up with Crosby, Stills, Nash, and Young. In 1970, realizing the money would be "pissed away," he'd recommended that United Artists pull the plug on a movie project they'd set up for David Crosby. "I took my relationships seriously, not just with the band but with the people we dealt with," he told Carl Gottlieb, who'd been hired to write Crosby's script. "I had to go back to those people. I had to ask them for favors." Publicly, though, Geffen never messed with CSNY's status as the American Beatles. They remained the platform for his dreams. "I remember David once leaping to Crosby's defense like a dog onto a bone, even though he and Crosby were fighting at the time," says Jackson Browne. "He stood up there and took on this room full of people."

Geffen had slight misgivings about Browne's singing, but trusted enough in his talent to bankroll what turned out to be expensive recording sessions. "I met Jackson with Geffen in a hotel room in Boston," says Bud Scoppa, who gave *Jackson Browne* a rave review in *Rolling Stone*. "Geffen was as magnetic as Jackson was. Just being in the same room as those two guys, it seemed like they had their own illumination."

"We were all young and we were all inventing our careers," Geffen says. "I was very close to Jackson, just as I'd been very close to Laura Nyro. With each person I had a unique relationship." When Browne's "Doctor My Eyes"—with David Crosby and Graham Nash harmonizing behind him—reached the Top 10 in March 1972, the fresh-faced angel-boy from Orange County had finally arrived. Browne's soulful sensitivity gave the introspection of Neil Young and

James Taylor a new twist. And he made some of the established L.A. songwriters feel old.

"The truth is that I felt deeply envious of people like Jackson, because I couldn't find an identity like that for myself," says songwriter Jimmy Webb, for whom Geffen had secured a new deal at Reprise. "I felt somehow lost in a much older and more conservative group, so I immediately began to plot some way out of this cul-de-sac." Despite the fact that his biggest hits came via pop/MOR artists—Glen Campbell ("Wichita Lineman"), Richard Harris ("MacArthur Park"), the Fifth Dimension ("Up, Up, and Away")—Webb himself was desperate to align himself with the counterculture. Purchasing the former Philippines consulate near the corner of LaBrea and Hollywood Boulevard, Jimmy turned the twenty-three-room mansion into a den of benign iniquity. "There was this amazing scene going on there," recalled guitarist Fred Tackett. "There was a constant parade of people: you'd walk in and Jimi Hendrix or Mitch Mitchell would be sleeping on the couch."

Webb had never quite recovered from his first major L.A. show as a singer-songwriter, when he bombed at the Dorothy Chandler Pavilion in February 1970—with a fifty-five-piece orchestra behind him. "You could have picked someone randomly from the audience and handed them lyric sheets and they would have done a better job than Jimmy did that night," says Bill Straw. Webb's three Reprise albums (1970's *Words and Music*, 1971's *And So: On*, 1972's *Letters*) were full of melodic marvels but sold disappointingly. One evening he visited Browne at Geffen's house and experienced a disconcerting déjà vu, for he had often dropped by the property when it belonged to his sometime mentor Johnny Rivers. "Jackson was Geffen's protégé in exactly the way that I'd been Johnny's protégé," Webb recalls. "Jackson played all his songs in front of the fireplace just as I'd played *my* songs for Johnny. That was such a weird kind of repetition and it made me feel like an old man."

As much as he was Geffen's golden boy, Browne was also, crucially, a conduit for talent—Asylum's de facto head of A&R. Through him would come the majority of the label's hit acts. "David relied entirely on artists recommending each other," adds Peter Asher. "It wasn't based on *his* artistic vision. It was Jackson talking about Linda Ronstadt, or Glenn Frey talking about John David Souther. David basically just followed *their* noses."

"That idea of artists sitting around together and bouncing off of each other, David took that to another level," says Lenny Waronker. "He was an artistic business guy, and as a powerful manager he was always right on the money. Elliot did the day-to-day, but I think David was the deal." Browne himself has always stressed his debt to Geffen. "Some people would never get on record at all," he told Cameron Crowe, "if it weren't for the more ambitious people with an eye on careers and managing people's lives." Among the hopefuls Browne brought into the Asylum fold were his old Echo Park buddies Glenn Frey and J. D. Souther. One night Frey joined Souther and Linda Ronstadt for dinner at the Nucleus Nuance on Melrose Avenue. Halfway through the meal, Souther turned to Frey and suggested he go on the road with Linda, who needed a band.

Frey had by now bonded with Don Henley, the curly-haired Texan he'd sized up at the Troubadour. With his own band, Shiloh, going nowhere, Henley was at a similar impasse. Frey asked if he'd be interested in a short-term gig with Ronstadt. "Glenn was our suggestion," Ronstadt says. "But he was the one who discovered that Henley could sing. He used to call Don his secret weapon."

After the tour's first night—a date at Disneyland on July 12, 1971—Frey and Henley made a pact to start their own band. David Geffen had told Frey that he should be in a group, whereas Souther thought he should be a solo artist. It was a shrewd insight, because Souther was a born loner and Frey a natural gang member. Frey and Henley looked no farther for bandmates than the other hired guns in Ronstadt's band: Bernie Leadon, recently of the Burritos, and Randy Meisner, youngish veteran of Poco and Rick Nelson's Stone Canyon Band. The band was to be called the Eagles, as much because it sounded like a Detroit gang as because the bird in question was a symbol of Native American mysticism.

"John [Boylan] and Linda gave us our blessing," Henley told Cameron Crowe. "I really respect Linda Ronstadt. She's got a good heart. She's never been selfish enough to hold anybody back." Frey, Henley, Leadon, and Meisner all played on *Linda Ronstadt*, released in early 1972. Ronstadt and Boylan had high hopes for the album, which included a version of Jackson Browne's "Rock Me on the Water" recorded at the Troubadour. "A lot of people in L.A. were trying to figure out the perfect country-rock sound," Boylan said in 1996. "We knew that if we could get the combination right and the songs right we could have something big. And we thought we had." They hadn't—the album never rose higher than No. 163 on the charts—but out of it came the Eagles, along with Ronstadt's own stellar 1970s career.

As pleased as they were to have Leadon and Meisner on board, Don and Glenn were determined not to repeat the mistakes Poco and the Burritos had made. Great things had been expected of both those bands, but neither had delivered on their promise. And Gram Parsons was unraveling before everybody's eyes. "Jackson said, 'These guys are gonna make more money than us put together,'" says J. D. Souther. "They'd watched Gram fall apart onstage and Gene Clark disintegrate at the Troubadour bar, and they were going to go ahead and play tight and clean and they were going to get it done."

For a moment, Frey and Henley contemplated a version of the Eagles that included Souther. "It was about three or four months into the band's life, when we were all officially part of the Geffen-Roberts hang," says Bernie Leadon. "It was probably based on the fact that J. D. could write and was another good-looking guy. But then it was like, 'Well, what's J. D. gonna *play*? We don't *need* another guitar player.'" Souther remained an unofficial sixth Eagle, however. As ambitious as David Geffen himself, he and Don and Glenn were determined to write hit singles for the group. They were going to sign with Asylum and become stars. "The Eagles weren't going to fail," says Geffen. "It was a group that was put together with clear intentions."

"This was going to be our best shot," Frey said. "Everybody had to look good, sing good, play good, and write good. We wanted it all. Peer respect. AM and FM success. No. 1 singles and albums, great music, and a lot of money." If Bernie Leadon was hired for his musicianship, he, too, was clear about the Eagles being a meal ticket. "We had lofty goals," he says. "We made some very good decisions about who to work with. Geffen was the top of the heap. Our attitude was, Why not *try* for the top?" Interestingly, it was Leadon who did all

the talking when the Eagles trooped into 9130 Sunset to offer themselves to Geffen. "We marched into David's office and said, 'Here we
are. You want us or not?'" he says. "He came down to a rehearsal and
said that yes, he did." Geffen, Roberts, and underling manager John
Hartmann stopped by at a little rehearsal hall in the San Fernando
Valley. A stack of boxes sat in the middle of the room, forcing them
to watch the band over a small cardboard mountain. "We knew and
committed to them right then," Hartmann recalled. "It was *nothing*
to believe in the Eagles."

Geffen not only bought out Henley's and Frey's Amos contracts,
he also paid for them to get their teeth fixed. "What David did in
terms of piecing together various people and putting together the
Eagles was absolutely brilliant," Jac Holzman said in early 1973.
"[He] happens to have a great deal of patience, an incredible
amount of taste, and is an excellent father confessor to his artists."
By August 1971, Geffen had the core of Asylum's roster in place:
Browne, Souther, the Eagles. Also along for the ride was Browne's
old Paxton Lodge buddy Ned Doheny. "I think David wanted me to
be involved largely because Jackson spoke highly of me," Doheny
says. "I don't think he really heard what I was doing." Geffen may
not have heard what Doheny was doing but he thought he was cute—
among the Laurel Canyon cognoscenti it was believed that Geffen
had a crush on him.

One hot afternoon in August 1971, Geffen sat in his sauna on
Alto Cedro Drive, sweating alongside Frey, Henley, and Doheny.
Geffen told his charges that Asylum would never be larger than the
number of artists he could fit in the sauna. "David took the crème de
la crème of that scene," says their gal pal Eve Babitz. "And he signed
them on the basis of their cuteness." Not that Geffen ever contemplated making a pass at them. "I think he was far too smart ever to
make a move on any of these guys," says Nurit Wilde. He was also far
too ashamed. His mother, Batya, still labored under the delusion
that King David might someday present her with grandchildren. "I
don't think David ever got a ripple of disapproval about it," says
Souther. "It was probably more of an issue among people he was
doing business with, because there weren't many gay men out of the
closet at the time."

Geffen knew he couldn't have these boys—the hippie tolerance of the times embraced almost everything but homosexuality—but he could live through their relationships with women. "David hadn't come to terms with his sexuality, so I think he lived vicariously through a lot of people in his immediate purview," says Doheny. "He assigned himself the role of protector and benefactor. I mean, everybody *knew* he was gay, but nobody talked about it. I cornered him on it once, but he sort of made light of it and said, 'Yeah, I was checkin' out your butt!'"

Two of the original Asylum artists—David Blue and Judee Sill—did not fall into the pretty-boy category. Blue, whose *Stories* album was the third release on the label, was a Greenwich Village veteran and Dylan acolyte who (as David Cohen) had been one of the four folkies on a seminal 1965 album called *Singer-Songwriter Project.* "David was like a conduit for all the Village folkies who'd stay in my house when they came to L.A.," says Elliot Roberts. "That was a big part of the Joni-folk–Laurel Canyon axis—Tom Rush, Dave Van Ronk, and company."

Blue had been one of the early hip signings on Reprise, brought into the Warner Brothers fold by Andy Wickham. Dropped by that label, he fell into depression and heroin addiction, states from which Roberts temporarily rescued him. "I found myself in dire straits, in terms of being a human being," Blue said in 1974. "Elliot said I could go on Asylum, which was a lesser deal in terms of money. To me, it had nothing to do with money, but it had to do with my relationships with Elliot and David as people, and their concept of what sort of record company they were going to make of Asylum."

Sill, whose eponymous debut was Asylum's first official release in early 1972, also had been a junkie. Running away from home as a troubled middle-class teenager in the San Fernando Valley, she spent three years as a street addict, prostituting herself and holding up liquor stores to support her habit. Unlike Blue, a workaday folk talent, she was possessed of something like genius. Happily she managed to kick heroin long enough to write some of the most intricately beautiful songs of the period. "Judee had been in Hollywood sort of poking around," recalls Mark Volman, who signed her to the Turtles' Blimp Productions publishing company. "Our hope at the time was that giving her a place to make music and write songs might help her through her problems."

When David Geffen discovered Sill he thought he'd found his new Laura Nyro. Meanwhile, Sill thought she'd found her savior. "I remember her coming home one night swooning over Geffen and telling me he was the man for her," says Jim Pons, the producer who'd brought her to Blimp. "She also thought he was going to help her get to the top."

Like many women on the Troubadour scene, Sill fell under the enigmatic spell of J. D. Souther. Their subsequent affair was born at least partly of his sincere admiration for her talent. "There's no one more important in my musical life than Judee," he says. "Jackson was the furthest along as far as having learned songwriting, and then I met Judee and I thought, 'Fuck, man, she's school for all of us.'" Judee, fragile at the best of times, was shattered when Souther left her. "I remember going to a birthday party for Judee," says Bill Straw, who did legal work for her. "There was a large group of people there, including Linda Ronstadt. Judee was interested in J. D. Souther, and basically he then got interested in Linda."

When *Judee Sill* came out in early 1972, it featured such wondrous examples of what Sill called her "country-cult-baroque" style as "Ridge Rider" and "The Phantom Cowboy." Also on the album was the single "Jesus Was a Crossmaker," produced by Graham Nash. It was about Souther, describing him as "a bandit and a heartbreaker." "I knew very little about Judee," says Nash. "But I do know that she was a very bright, talented, funny lady. She kept to herself a great deal—a *great* deal. Personally I had no idea she was taking drugs on that scale."

On the sleeve of her album Judee gushed, "David Geffen I Love You." But *Judee Sill* had the misfortune to be followed swiftly on the Asylum schedule by the debut albums by Jackson Browne and the Eagles. It wasn't long before she was lost in Geffen's shuffle. "When I first met him I thought he was some kind of knight in shining armor, you know," she said. "But I didn't understand the other things, the things that made him such a ruthless businessman."

The subject of "Jesus Was a Crossmaker" was busy working on his own Asylum debut in early 1972. Anchored in his Amarillo roots and drawing on the influence of heroes such as Hank Williams and Tim Hardin, *John David Souther* embodied the country spirit of early 1970s Los Angeles. On tracks such as "It's the Same" and the near-classic "Jesus in ¾ Time," southern soul and gospel influences offset the reedy ache of J. D.'s voice. Souther's decision to tread a solo path was the making of him as a songwriter. Jackson Browne had shown how much integrity was to be gained in going it alone. Yet J. D. remained solidly at the heart of the extended family that was the Canyon/Troubadour community. "I always thought he was the pivot of that whole Laurel Canyon scene," said the late Derek Taylor. "He was a good packager of musicians and everyone liked him."

With his reddish hair and piercing blue eyes, Souther was a magnet for the young honeys of Hollywood. "He had girlfriends who were *Playboy* centerfolds," says Judy Henske. For a good year he and Ronstadt were the scene's hottest couple, the new Joni and Graham. "They were the best couple I ever saw at that time," says Chris Darrow. "I thought that was a great male-female matchup." Souther and Ronstadt set up home in Beechwood Canyon, east of Laurel Canyon and Cahuenga Pass. The canyon spawned a loose crew who dubbed themselves "the Beechwood Rangers" and at different times included Jackson Browne, Warren Zevon, Kris Kristofferson, and actor Harry Dean Stanton. In their cozy Beechwood nest, Ronstadt would sit and listen to the Louvin Brothers and the Stanley Brothers while Souther tried to turn her on to *Frank Sinatra Sings for Only the Lonely*. "Linda had great taste in songs, and she was also brilliant," says Souther. "She was always depicted as saying ditsy things at the wrong time, but she was the most well-read person I knew."

A regular hangout for Ronstadt and Souther—and for everybody else within the Geffen-Roberts orbit—was Lucy's El Adobe restaurant on Melrose Avenue. Run by Frank and Lucy Cassado, the El Adobe was a sanctuary for musicians both successful and struggling. The Cassados themselves were surrogate parents to the scene. "All of us spent countless hours in the company of Frank and Lucy," says Souther. "Frank was feeding me way before I could afford to pay him."

Souther was delighted to be on Asylum Records. In a few short months he and his friends were at the threshold of success. With Geffen and Roberts guiding their careers, they were like made guys.

"Asylum was definitely shelter from the storm," Souther says. "There wasn't a huge panic to get us packaged. I think there was a sense of the Blue Note days, where a school of jazz guys got to play what they actually wanted and were treated as artists." Roberts was more explicit still about sheltering Asylum's artists from the storms and stresses of modern life. "They're not out there on the street," he said. "I mean, they're really, truly . . . artists. They are all very—not closed, necessarily, because they're all actually very open, but . . . they only see a certain spectrum and they expect us to fill them in on the rest of the spectrum. And we do."

Looking on with interest were the executives at Warners in Burbank, for what Geffen and Roberts had created was a kind of micro-Reprise. "Asylum had one style where Warner-Reprise had many styles," says Stan Cornyn. "But it had that one style at the right time to have the style." The boutique aspect of Asylum's roster was reflected not just in the clique of artists but also in the session musicians who played on albums by Browne, Souther, and others. "The Asylum vibe was very different from anything I'd seen before," says Craig Doerge of the Section. "A relatively small group of studio musicians was allowed to form as a little family. We got this reputation as the focus of the Southern California sound. Maybe half the hit records made in that period featured the same twenty guys."

The only downside to this was an increasing homogeneity, with the sound a close cousin to the one Lenny Waronker, Russ Titelman, and Ted Templeman had incubated in Burbank. Along with the homogeneity came a distinct whiff of cronyism, something that incurred the resentment of those not invited to the party. "Asylum was a very pompous thing," says Robert Marchese, who saw the label's artists up close most nights at the Troubadour. "And they were nonstop. They were ruling the roost."

"They've all become very successful with us, extremely wealthy," Geffen said. "No one has beaten them or tried to take unfair advantage of them. It's very much of a family scene, we're all very close." The more money he made, the more Geffen liked the power it gave him. He loved outsmarting people, beating them into submission by the sheer force of his intelligence. He was the new potentate of Sunset Boulevard. But his canniest trick was the way he blended into the scene. The artists on Asylum believed that he was one of them, a hip guy who cared about their art. And on one level he was. But behind the scenes he was flouting rules to maximize his gains.

Behind the veil of what Carl Gottlieb called Asylum's "benevolent protectionism," Geffen worked things to his own advantage. Paying out nominal advances and dispensing with paperwork, he and Elliot effectively controlled every aspect of their artists' careers: record deals, publishing, gate money from touring. "David and Elliot were cunning, Geffen especially but Elliot, too," says Ned Doheny. "It was enlightened self-interest. But they were also very kind. People don't wind up in those positions by being assholes."

Doheny, whose well-connected Beverly Hills family knew Ahmet Ertegun socially, watched Geffen emulate the crafty charm of his mentor. "Ahmet was extremely erudite and worldly and David was none of those," Doheny says. "With people like David there's always a lot of bullshit around the fact that they basically just want to make money. It's not that they don't believe themselves—honestly I think David really did believe in his ideal of what Asylum was going to be. But what he had going for him was the fact that artists are self-involved to the point of being autistic." Geffen and Roberts were the perfect double act, with Elliot playing stoned good cop to David's sober bad cop. If any of the Geffen–Roberts/Asylum artists expressed unease about Geffen, Roberts quickly soothed their fears. "Elliot Roberts had a ritual," says Denny Bruce. "When he'd leave the office he'd drive through the canyon and visit his clients. He was considered cool for that."

"Elliot was our personal Woody Allen," says J. D. Souther. "He was absolutely the funniest man ever to be in the music business. He also had a deal-making technique that at the time was probably foolproof. He would smoke a copious amount of fantastically great dope and then make these deals. You'd see guys stagger out of his office as though they just did not know what had happened. He was like some kind of peace-pipe salesman."

For all their benevolence, there was undeniable favoritism in the Geffen-Roberts stable. With Jackson Browne and the Eagles, no expense was spared. But with other artists under their patronage—such as Judee Sill, David Blue, Ned Doheny, and Essra Mohawk—less effort went into building their careers. Mohawk, placed with Reprise in 1970, had been groomed by Geffen as a new Laura Nyro. But after the release of her *Primordial Lovers*—a lost singer-songwriter classic—Geffen and Roberts became distant. "I asked them why I ran into so many walls," Mohawk says. "People would kind of imply that there was somebody out there holding me down. And I said to Elliot, 'Did David do that?' Elliot said to me, 'Don't even *think* like that!' It was the first time he ever talked as though he was threatening me."

"Who Is David Geffen and Why Is He Saying These Terrible Things about Me?"

The return of Joni Mitchell from the wilds of British Columbia—and her subsequent signing to Asylum—may explain why Essra Mohawk, Judee Sill, and others were "held back." There were whisperings that Mitchell didn't want other women on the label. Ironically, she was present at 9130 Sunset the day Sill stopped by to sign her Asylum contract. "Joni knew who Judee was," says guitarist Art Johnson, who accompanied Sill. "Let's just say their cautious conversation was memorable."

"We were sorry to lose Joni at Reprise, of course," says Lenny Waronker. "I think David Geffen's sense with Asylum was that if you go with talent, the probability was that you would be successful." Reunited with her original champion, Elliot Roberts, Joni surprisingly became friendlier with his partner. With Ron Stone renting her Lookout Mountain Avenue house, Joni moved into Geffen's new Bel Air home on Copley Drive as a houseguest. "We were roommates," Geffen said. "It was a very heady time, very tumultuous and a lot of fun. I kept on telling Joni I wanted her to write a hit, and she was always kind of making fun of me about the idea that she should have a hit. But I wanted her to sell a lot of records."*

---

*In a *New Yorker* profile of Ahmet Ertegun, the catty George S. Trow Jr. observed the Atlantic boss overhearing Geffen on the phone to Mitchell. "He must be talking to an artist," Ahmet whispered in a snide aside to Trow. "He's got his soulful look on. He is trying to purge at this moment all traces of his eager greed."

Mitchell found that the scene had changed in the months she had been away. Geffen's wealth now placed him at the center of a glamorous network that included the hippest Hollywood actors of the day: Warren Beatty, Jack Nicholson, and others. After Lou Adler introduced him to Beatty, Geffen became an avid supporter of the actor's political activities. Mitchell was his date at a big fundraising concert for South Dakota senator George McGovern, staged by Adler in April 1972 and featuring Carole King and James Taylor among the performers.

When Mitchell played L.A.'s Dorothy Chandler Pavilion on March 13, 1972, she brought Geffen and Roberts onstage for the encore. Supporting her on the date, as he'd done for her whole tour, was Jackson Browne; the two had recently become lovers. Geffen took a voyeuristic pleasure in the ups and downs of the affair. Joni would come home and at night and unburden herself to the supportive Geffen. She also poured her feelings into the songs for her Asylum debut *For the Roses*, though most were about the pain of her relationship with James Taylor. "Cold Blue Steel and Sweet Fire" explicitly detailed the realities of Taylor's addiction. "Blonde in the Bleachers" acknowledged the impossibility of sharing her life with this "rock and roll man." "For the Roses" itself was on one level an expression of envious bitterness, on another a lament for the innocence of the early folk scene. "I was watching [James's] career and I was thinking that as his woman at that time I should be able to support him," Mitchell said. "But everything I saw him going through I thought was ludicrous, because I'd thought it was ludicrous when I'd done it."

The inclusion on *For the Roses* of "You Turn Me On, I'm a Radio"—a Top 30 hit in late 1972—was telling because it was self-consciously written to be a hit. "I remember when she sang it to me," David Geffen said with a smile years later. "It was almost kind of making fun of my attempt for her to write a hit record." The calculated nature of the song rankled with Mitchell, striking a false note that she was determined to avoid in the future. An overlooked album, *For the Roses* is where Mitchell found her mature musical voice. Bringing in players with a blacker, more jazz-based feel, she inches here toward the mid-1970s masterpieces *Court and Spark* and *The Hissing of Summer Lawns*.

Mitchell's affair with Browne didn't last long. When he ended it she spiraled into another dark depression. Despite her success she felt increasingly alone in Los Angeles. "I don't have a large circle of friends," she said. "I have a few very *close* friends, and then there's a whole lot of people I'm sort of indifferent to." It didn't help that *Rolling Stone* bestowed the title "Old Lady of the Year" on Mitchell when 1972 closed. "Oh, it was a low blow," she says. "I was not abnormally promiscuous, especially within the context of the free-love experiment." Furious on Mitchell's behalf, friends such as Graham Nash offered to write to editor Jann Wenner and complain. B. Mitchel Reed, with whom she had never had a sexual relationship, was perplexed to find himself on the list of her lovers. "Assumptions were made in interpreting the lyrics, as they always are," Mitchell says. "All of that nonsense destroyed the ability of the listener to identify with songs."

Years later Mitchell would exact revenge on Browne with a song ("Not to Blame") that was ostensibly about O. J. Simpson but implicitly alluded to Browne's alleged physical abuse of actress Daryl Hannah in 1992. "I'm not trying to exonerate Jackson," says Ned Doheny of the Hannah incident. "I'm just saying that these situations are sometimes best left to some degree unjudged. I think Joni clearly had some bitterness toward Jackson." Other veterans of the scene are less generous. "She was one of the worst," says one. "She went through all those guys and used all of them, from Graham Nash to Jackson. And then she could write about it and say, 'Fuck you.'"

Geffen claimed Mitchell was the only star he'd ever known who wanted to be "ordinary"—a relative term in Los Angeles. "I guess what he meant was that in some areas I needed exceptional treatment," she says. "But in other areas it was stupid to offer me that treatment—and lonely-making."

"Artists tend to be difficult," Geffen muses today. "And Joni was certainly an artist. It's likely that the more talented artists are, the more difficult they'll be. And by that I don't mean more difficult for *me*—I think their lives were more difficult for *them*. Joni is one of the great artists of the twentieth century, but the bigger a star she became, the more difficult it was for her to live in her own life."

Graham Nash, perhaps the great love of Joni's life, was busy surviving the fallout from *Déjà Vu* and the often rancorous CSNY tour of 1970. The group had splintered in different directions, nursing wounds and writing songs for solo albums. The CSNY orbit shifted to northern California and the Bay Area. Crosby, Nash, and Young all bought property in or around San Francisco. In the fall of 1970 Young invested in a ranch near Redwood City, complete with 140 acres of land. Even Elliot Roberts temporarily moved his base of operations to the city of ocean fogs and gingerbread mansions. For his part, David Geffen was glad to put some distance between himself and Crosby and Stills, especially when the mixing sessions for the subpar 1971 live album *Four-Way Street* proved as fractious as the *Déjà Vu* recordings. Geffen got along fine with Nash—"an extremely quiet and modest gentleman," in his view—and with Young, whom he saw as "very shy and not interested in all the big pop-star bullshit." But he'd had enough of the other two, whose rampant egotism was compounded by their drug intake. After Crosby threatened not to go onstage if Geffen didn't arrange for some grass to be flown from LAX to a concert, Geffen told Elliot Roberts, "I'm finished. This is the end."

"It was the straw that broke the camel's back," Geffen says. "It's not that I didn't think it was a worthwhile job, I just didn't think it made the best use of my abilities and I didn't want to be that close to the artists any longer." In an interview with *New Musical Express* in the fall of 1972, Geffen thought it "very doubtful" that CSNY would record together again. The friction among the four of them stemmed, he claimed, from the fact that "Stephen kinda thought it was his band, while all the others thought they were pretty equal." He added that "when I see Stephen doing things that I consider to be wrong I tell him so and he doesn't listen, that's the time when we have to come to a parting of the ways." Stills, smarting from what he perceived as the favoritism accorded Neil Young, got wind of Geffen's remarks and had a bumper sticker made up for his car that read "WHO IS DAVID GEFFEN AND WHY IS HE SAYING THESE TERRIBLE THINGS ABOUT ME?" He later claimed that the band's "attendant managers and various functionaries" had "actually got off on all that destructive competition between me and Neil and would, in fact, goad us on."

Things were acrimonious in the CSNY camp, and not simply because of Stills's overweening competitiveness. Nash, who'd felt deeply betrayed by Stills's affair with Joni, exacted revenge by luring Rita Coolidge away from Stills. David Crosby said, "Nash took Rita away from Stephen so fast it was absurd." When Graham attempted to set things straight with his friend, Stills spat in his face. Stills now spent much of his time in Colorado and in England, where he rented a rambling mansion in the leafy county of Surrey, south of London. With his love of Thoroughbred horses, he reveled in his new role as rock lord of the manor. Hurting from the loss of Coolidge, he sought solace in the arms of French chanteuse Veronique Sanson. But despite the Top 20 hit he'd had in late 1970 with the anthemic "Love the One You're With," he remained restless and angry.

David Crosby, against the odds, made one of the better solo albums of the era. A product of the musical accord between Laurel Canyon and Haight-Ashbury, *If I Could Only Remember My Name . . .* featured an all-star cast of California cronies, with members of the Grateful Dead and the Jefferson Airplane playing alongside Neil Young, Joni Mitchell, and Graham Nash. Stephen Stills was conspicuous by his absence but made a cameo appearance as a character in "Cowboy Movie," a labored allegory of the Stills-Nash-Coolidge love triangle. In 1971 he wrote his own song about the messy swaps in "Change Partners." No wonder Nash, in an interview with Ben Fong-Torres in August 1971, bemoaned the fact that "people can't listen to a song for the song's sake, they've got to know who it's about."

Dedicated to the memory of Christine Hinton, *If I Could Only Remember My Name . . .* was haunted by her ghost. "The trouble is the words all come around to, 'Why is it like this?'" David forlornly told Fong-Torres. "They are all mostly about Christine . . . [they're] pretty sad and they don't draw any useful conclusion." One person who did not appreciate the diffuse melancholy of *If I Could Only Remember My Name . . .* was David Geffen. He was particularly niggled by "Song with No Words (Tree with No Leaves)," which was just that: six minutes of "da-da-da"s and "doo-doo-doo"s that Geffen saw as conclusive proof of Crosby's stoned idleness. Geffen needn't have worried. After he sheepishly played the track to Ahmet Ertegun in New York, the canny Turk smiled and placed a reassuring hand on the shoulder of his golden boy. "Don't worry," Ertegun said with a grin. "We've already shipped a million."

Neil Young, meanwhile, was happy to be out of Los Angeles. Even Topanga hadn't been remote enough for him. "You never knew what was gonna be happening when you went home," he told Jimmy McDonough. Broken Arrow, his secluded ranch, made Young happier. "I like the country better," he said. "Somebody's comin' at ya, you can see 'em." Also behind him was his marriage to Susan Acevedo, who filed for divorce early in October 1970. A very different kind of woman now commanded his affections. Neil had seen actress Carrie Snodgress in 1970's award-winning *Diary of a Mad Housewife*, falling in love with her neglected, vulnerable character. Young was in a heavy-duty brace after damaging his back on the ranch, and Snodgress became his emotional nurse. But he also was taken with Carrie's nonconformist, noncareerist attitude to the entertainment business. She walked on the wild side in ways that Neil never had.

Harvest, in 1972, came out of a brief period of contentedness, the back brace and painkillers notwithstanding. Young thought he'd found his heart of gold. Yet it was a strangely autumnal record for a twenty-four-year-old rock god to make. "I was saying, 'OK, let's get really, really mellow and peaceful,'" Young reflected. "'Let's make music that's just as intense as the electric stuff but which comes from a completely different, more loving place.'" More overtly countrified than *After the Gold Rush*, *Harvest* featured a new backing band, the Stray Gators, with Ben Keith on pedal steel and Kenny Buttrey on drums. Jack Nitzsche and former James Brown bassist Tim Drummond fleshed out the lineup. The album started life in Nashville, where Young was a guest on Johnny Cash's TV show. Cash, always alert to new music, had both James Taylor and Linda Ronstadt on the show as well. After the taping, Neil asked James and Linda if they'd sing with him at the nearby Quadrafonic Sound studio. "Old Man" and "Heart of Gold" resulted from the session, with Taylor playing banjo on the former.

Early in 1972, "Heart of Gold" hit No. 1. It was as close as Neil Young ever came to the commercial mainstream. The song fixed him forever in some people's minds as the soft-voiced minstrel with the battered guitar and patched jeans. *Harvest* was the year's essential singer-songwriter LP, aural comedown music for befuddled survivors of the long, strange 1960s trip. In his *Rolling Stone* review of the record, Laurel Canyon dweller John Mendelssohn wrote disparagingly that Young had "all but abdicated his position as an authoritative rock and roller for the stereotypical laid-back country-comforted troubadour role." But even here, amid the ramshackle ambience, disquiet lurked like a serpent. "The Needle and the Damage Done," one of his greatest songs, turned its light on Danny Whitten's heroin addiction.

By the fall of 1972, it was as though Young had taken Mendelssohn's assessment to heart. He decided to upend everything with a loud, brash, disheveled tour of America. Crucial to Neil's plans was Whitten, whom he decided to add to his new Stray Gators backing band in hopes that they would reactivate the chemistry of 1969–1970. The guitarist had managed to get through the sessions for *Crazy Horse*, a rough but infectiously grungy album that Jack Nitzsche coproduced for Reprise in late 1970. Among Whitten's songs on the record was "I Don't Want to Talk about It," a timeless anthem for emotionally wounded men. Nitzsche himself was living near the ranch when Whitten made it up to Broken Arrow for rehearsals in mid-November 1972. Hardly in the best shape himself—a combination of booze and black magic was making him ever more abusive to Neil—Nitzsche quickly perceived that Whitten was lost to smack. A few days in, it was clear to Young and everybody else that Danny could barely play, let alone tour. On November 18 he was given $50 and put on a flight back to L.A. That night his latent death wish came true: he overdosed on a combination of alcohol and the tranquilizer Diazepam. The shadow of Whitten's end— a suicide in all but declared intention—hung over the subsequent tour like a grim cloud. Neil felt unavoidably guilty. The day after Danny's death he wrote the impassioned "Don't Be Denied," a mini-autobiography that remains one of his greatest songs.

The *Time Fades Away* tour kicked off at the dawn of 1973. With the sturdy Drummond/Buttrey rhythm section anchoring the barroom groove and the cantankerous Jack Nitzsche supplying barrelhouse piano, Young sang a new selection of angry, bilious songs: the *Time*

Fades Away album, for the most part. It was the last thing fans of *Harvest* were expecting. "Everybody said that *Harvest* was a trip," Young later told Bud Scoppa. "To me I'd happened to be in the right place at the right time to do a really mellow record that was really open, 'cause that's where my life was at the time. But . . . I don't know where I'd be right now if I'd just stayed real mellow."

The atmosphere on the *Time Fades Away* tour was dark and uncomfortable. There was no team spirit here. At one point the band threatened mutiny unless they were paid more money. "[That] turned him against everything," Elliot Roberts told Cameron Crowe. "He didn't know how to handle his friends constantly hitting on him for more money." Jack Nitzsche's malign influence spread through the touring party. Resentful of Young's power over him, Jack began to hate his employer. "The tour was torture," Nitzsche later told *Crawdaddy.* "Everyone in the band was bored to death with those terrible guitar solos. He would turn and face the band with this stupid grimace while he was playing, and I would nearly roll on the stage laughing."

Young's relationship with Nitzsche verged on the masochistic. "The ridicule Neil suffered at the hands of Jack's opinions was ruthless," recalled Carrie Snodgress. "And that's what turned him on." At some level Nitzsche felt that Neil owed him—that he hadn't fully acknowledged the role Jack had played in the early stages of his career, helping to shape masterpieces such as "Broken Arrow" and "Expecting to Fly." "Jack always felt he deserved at least a percentage of some of the songs he worked on," says Denny Bruce. "Neil hinted that there would be a 'taste' for Jack but it never came." Bruce concedes that Nitzsche was his own worst enemy, pushing away anybody who could have helped him. His alcoholism had already estranged his old friends in Burbank. Ry Cooder told Mo Ostin that Jack wasn't together enough to be his producer. "At Warners there was this country club of Lenny and Ry and Russ [Titelman]," Bruce says. "Jack wasn't allowed in that club anymore. But he thrived on drama. He almost *looked* for it."

Badly stung by the *Time Fades Away* tour, Neil Young slunk back to Broken Arrow to continue work on a film he was making. *Journey through the Past* was as self-indulgent as any artistic product of the

California singer-songwriter era. "I thought what was happening in my life was very interesting," Young told Jimmy McDonough. "Should be documented . . . and then I found out that, y'know, I had no perspective and was an egomaniac because I did that." Warners clearly agreed, because they reneged on their commitment to distribute Neil's $400,000 home movie. It was, he said, the only instance of lack of cooperation he ever had with the label. "For the first time in my life," he told Cameron Crowe, "I couldn't get anything to turn out the way I wanted."

Don't Even Try to Understand

Whereas Neil Young and Joni Mitchell were intuitive and unpredictable, Glenn Frey and Don Henley set about success with the pragmatism of a Tin Pan Alley partnership. "The Eagles were *made* to sell a million records," Elliot Roberts says. "They wrote to be huge."

Yet it was the pressure that Frey and Henley felt in the exalted sphere of Young and Mitchell that spurred them on to prove themselves. "Being around Geffen, and in close proximity to Jackson Browne, Joni Mitchell, Crosby, Stills, and Nash," Frey said, "this unspoken thing was created between Henley and me which said, 'If we want to be up here with the big boys, we'd better get our game together.'" Frey and Henley, who shared a pad in the hills near the Hollywood Bowl, decided they didn't want to risk being exposed to the Troubadour crowd too early. Better to get out of town and hone their craft. Geffen agreed and dispatched the Eagles to Aspen, Colorado. As "Teen King & the Emergencies," the Eagles held down a short residency at a club called the Gallery in the late fall of 1971. When they returned to L.A. they were ready to take on the world.

Among the songs they earmarked for their Asylum debut was one Jackson Browne had started back in the Echo Park days. It was called "Take It Easy" and to Frey's ears it sounded like a hit single. The sentiment seemed to encapsulate the freewheeling dream of Southern California. Jackson told Glenn to run with the song. Classic Frey lines such as "It's a girl, my Lord, in a flatbed Ford" were inserted into the existing lyric. The result was an anthem for every stringy, footloose youth at large in the Golden State: *"Lighten up while you still can/Don't even try to understand."* "'Take It Easy' was 'Mr. Tambourine Man' for the next decade," says Domenic Priore. "The guy is saying 'Fuck this, I've dropped out . . . you find a place to make *your* stand.' That line epitomizes the second generation of country rockers."

Along with "Take It Easy," the Eagles rounded up a bunch of other songs for their album. Don Henley and Bernie Leadon had collaborated on a sultry slice of rock and soul called "Witchy Woman." Jackson Browne pitched in with "Nightingale," an easy-rolling rocker inspired by his affair with Laura Nyro. Troubadour buddy Jack Tempchin offered the band the Pocoesque "Peaceful Easy Feeling," the prototype midtempo country-rock track of the time. It was the peaceful easy side of the Eagles that appealed to English producer Glyn Johns when they flew to London to work with him in February 1972. This created an interesting tension at Olympic Studios, where Johns had worked with the Rolling Stones and Led Zeppelin. To his dismay, the band wanted a tougher, grittier sound. The friction between producer and band was not the best news for David Geffen, who was presented with a whopping $125,000 bill for the sessions. But Asylum wound up with three sure-fire hits: "Take It Easy," "Witchy Woman," and "Peaceful Easy Feeling." Hiring a new promotion man, Paul Ahern, Geffen was confident that his label could make the band a success. "The way we actually broke the Eagles was much more conventional," says Elliot Roberts. "They were a bridge between avant-garde and commercial."

There was already a buzz about the band when they returned to Los Angeles. On April 2, 1972, they performed at the opening of an exhibition of works by Texas artist Boyd Elder, whose decorated cow skulls would become part of the Eagles' iconography. Elder's private showing, at a gallery in Venice, turned out to be a gathering of the entire Geffen-Roberts clan. Geffen himself was there, as were Joni Mitchell, Jackson Browne, Ned Doheny, and Cass Elliott. What better occasion to unleash the Eagles, who were set up in a corner of the gallery to run through a short set of the few songs they'd worked up? "They stood in the corner, and there was beer on the floor from a keg that was leaking," Henry Diltz remembers. "They sang 'Witchy Woman' over and over, plus a couple of other songs they'd written."

For those outside the inner sanctum, the vibe around Asylum's new darlings was less appealing. "I saw the Eagles' first proper L.A. gig," says Jonh Ingham, then a correspondent for the English music press on the West Coast. "The place was just *awash* in sycophancy."

When "Take It Easy" was released in June, it became an inextricable part of the summer's sound track. It was the new sound of sunny Southern California—Poco with a turbo engine. "The Eagles fine-tuned the whole machine," admitted Poco's Paul Cotton. "The difference between *Pickin' Up the Pieces* and *Eagles* is huge. They could be played on AM and country radio and we couldn't."

"The weird thing about the Eagles was that nobody was from California," says Chris Darrow. "And most of the California guys resented that, because the *world* looked at the Eagles as the essence of California."

"The singer-songwriter thing *did* get very identified with L.A., and I thought that was rather unfair," says Peter Asher. "We once did a show in Japan with James, Linda, and J. D. Souther, and they said they were going to call it 'California Live'. We said, 'Not one of these people is actually from California.' They went, 'Oh, it doesn't matter.' But it mattered to *us*." The fact that "Southern California" was a kind of construct, a mythical mirage created by outsiders, was central to the Eagles' music. Not for nothing did they head off to Joshua Tree in the California desert to create the cover for the album. "None of us were native Californians," said Glenn Frey, who called Joshua Tree "a power spot," "but we were all really into the mysticism of the high desert."

When "Witchy Woman" cracked the Top 10 in September 1972, both the Eagles and Asylum Records had arrived. "It's my assumption that David Geffen called in a lot of favors for 'Doctor My Eyes' and 'Take It Easy,'" Frey told Fred Goodman. "At the moment," Geffen said in the wake of the success, "we're getting the same thrill from seeing the Eagles, Jackson Browne, Jo Jo Gunne, and Judee Sill happen. . . . It's as hard to do it with Jackson Browne as it was to do it with Joni five years ago."

Elsewhere in L.A., Geffen's peers looked on with envy and mild unease. Says Lenny Waronker, "I looked at Asylum and thought, 'Wow, country rock finally worked.'"

Exile on Sunset Boulevard

For Gram Parsons, the success of the Eagles was galling. He derided Frey and Henley as purveyors of "bubblegum." It was no coincidence that in the summer of "Take It Easy" his own career was in trouble.

"After I joined the Eagles I ran into Chris Hillman and he asked me what it was like," says Bernie Leadon. "I said, 'Well, it's a *little* bit like the Burritos.' But after he saw us he said, 'I don't see it. I don't see what you're saying.' He didn't think Frey was a very good singer." Parsons didn't think so either, but he was too wasted to mount a challenge. He'd spent the previous two years in the limbo of addiction. His involvement with the second Burritos album, *Burrito Deluxe*, was negligible. In June 1970 Chris Hillman kicked him out of his own group.

Parsons spent much of that year in the company of John Phillips. It was "Papa John" whom Gram was following on a Harley-Davidson one morning in May when the bike broke apart at 50 miles per hour and hurled him across the road. He spent several weeks recovering in the hospital. Phillips, who'd separated from Michelle to live with actress Genevieve Waite, released a solo album—the Parsons-influenced *Wolfking of L.A.*—in that same summer of 1970. Its jaunty country-rock flavor partially obscured the fact that several of its songs were about the wreckage caused by hard drugs. "Wolfking" was an apt nickname for a man who, when he wasn't consorting with the likes of Mick Jagger and Jack Nicholson, was running around L.A. with the "junkie bums" he sang about in the song "Drum."

The other Mamas and Papas weren't in much better shape. Michelle Phillips was briefly married to an out-of-control Dennis Hopper. Cass Elliott was playing Vegas but otherwise surrounded herself with a small court of spongers. "Cass had given up," Denny Doherty says of the original canyon hostess. "She had her own demons to deal with. But I didn't see that she was dabbling in the dark side with her little rat-faced friends." Doherty, who cut his own countrified solo album—1971's *Whatcha Gonna Do*—was himself in a desperate mess. That year he rented out his Appian Way house to film director Hal Ashby. "I stayed up in the canyon until we started burning the furniture," he says.

Parsons's friend Terry Melcher had been living in a state of near-terror ever since the Manson killings. In Gram he found a kindred spirit and fellow rich kid with whom he could while away the long summer nights and take the edge off his paranoia. "Terry liked witty, funny people, and Gram was extremely funny," says Eve Babitz. "They were two dilettantes together." Melcher was still enough of a force in the business to persuade Jerry Moss at A&M that Gram Parsons was "the white country Hendrix." Moss agreed to finance some sessions, and the two men set to work recording a jukebox selection of classic country songs. Unfortunately they were so blasted on pills and coke for the entire duration of the sessions that not even the involvement of musicians such as Clarence White and Byron Berline could rescue them.

Parsons cooled his heels for the remainder of 1970. Secretly he felt he'd blown it; he wondered if he would ever have a record deal again. In March 1971, despairing of the L.A. scene, he and Gretchen flew to England to accompany Keith Richards and Anita Pallenberg on a short tour by the Rolling Stones. At this time he first became addicted to heroin. When the tour was over, he and Gretchen were summoned to Nellcôte, the château Keith and Anita had rented at Villefranche in the south of France. They didn't last long there. "It must have been a week or two at the very beginning," says Pallenberg. "At the time I was very aloof from all these California girls. Gretchen was a bit moany and reproachful. And that's why they left, I think." Pallenberg's account smooths over the truth, which was that Parsons was booted out of Nellcôte. "They told me, 'Okay, you will take Gram to the airport and you will put him on a plane *out of here,*'" said Stones factotum Jo Bergman.

"There's a history of people getting pulled into the Stones' vortex," says Perry Richardson, then an assistant to photographer and Stones insider Michael Cooper. "Then for whatever reason they feel they've been rejected from the inner circle. It was a crushing blow to Gram." So crushing, in fact, that Parsons actually attempted suicide by overdosing on his return to London. He would never see Keith Richards again.

Back at the Marmont, Parsons nursed his wounds and attempted to stay off heroin by sticking to alcohol. His weight ballooned. "He blew up, he became huge, yet he was wearing the same clothes he'd worn when he was 30 pounds lighter," says Chris Hillman. "It was a sad sight." Ever forgiving, Hillman still believed in Gram's talent enough to want to help him. When he and fellow Burrito Rick Roberts happened on a pretty girl singing folk and country songs in a tiny club in Washington, D.C., he telephoned Gram and said he had to hear her. In October 1971, Parsons went to see Emmylou Harris sing at the club, the Cellar Door.

It wasn't until the following year that former Byrds/Burritos manager Eddie Tickner succeeded in procuring Parsons a new recording contract. This time it was with Mo Ostin, who'd tried to sign the Burritos in 1968. "I went with my hat in my hand and said, 'Mr. Ostin, sir, I sure am sorry about that deal I pulled a few years ago,'" Gram said in 1973. "'What do you think about me doing an album now?' He said, 'Great.'" In June 1972 Parsons returned to London at the behest of former Blind Faith bassist Rik Grech, who wanted to make an album with him. Perry Richardson remembers Gram expressing "an element of frustration" over his lack of success, particularly in the light of the Eagles' meteoric rise. "I think he felt he was doing the real thing, as opposed to some rock-country thing," Richardson says. "I mean, so Bob Dylan had liked *The Gilded Palace of Sin*, but what difference did that make?" In a letter to an old friend written when he'd returned to L.A., Parsons said that his music was "still country" but that he perceived no boundaries between "types" of music. "I keep my love for variations," he wrote in gonzospeak, "even tho I've some sort of 'rep' for starting what (I think) has turned out t'be pretty much of a 'country rock' (ugh!) plastic dry-fuck." He said the Eagles' music had "too much sugar in it."

At the Marmont, Parsons would sit around getting smashed on tequila and listening to tapes of Holy Roller revival-meeting tapes. Asked if he ever made a serious attempt to sober up, Gretchen Burrell (now Carpenter) replies: "Never. And you can only beg someone so many times, 'Please don't bring these people over.' I couldn't fight it." It was Gretchen who insisted they move out of the Marmont and into a new home on Laurel Canyon Boulevard.

For his Reprise debut, Parsons told Mo Ostin he wanted to hire Elvis Presley's backing band, whom he'd heard on Mike Nesmith's

Nevada Fighter album. Ostin, aware of Gram's trust fund, told him he'd have to use his own money. In August 1972 Parsons went with Rik Grech and Eddie Tickner to see Elvis play the Hilton International in Las Vegas. The band—including legendary guitarist James Burton—agreed to do the sessions. The album did not start promisingly. Rik Grech got sick and went to the hospital; a nervous Gram got drunk. But the next day things picked up, and Gram toned down his drinking for the remainder of the recordings.

The presence of Emmylou Harris made all the difference. Frustrated by Parsons's self-destructiveness, she nonetheless knew there was something magical about the blend of their voices. "He'd flirted with decadence and sort of rediscovered himself on the back of that," says Bud Scoppa. "Emmy was the incarnation of something very strong and positive, and if anybody understood him it was her." The desperate frailty of Parsons's voice on the *GP* album has drawn comparisons with the Billie Holiday of *Lady in Satin,* and it is not unlikely that its trembling, torn-and-frayed quality was the result of the shakes. There is beauty in its wounded vulnerability, as though the ghost of Hank Williams had taken up residence in the body of Fat Elvis. Outside the studio, Parsons couldn't keep it together. In December he was ejected from Chris Hillman's birthday party at the Marmont—by Hillman himself. "He was the kind of person who, when he did drink, was just horribly abusive to people around him," Chris remembers. "And I had to literally throw him out of my party."

Things weren't going too well for another of Laurel Canyon's troubled country-rock legends, Gene Clark. But at least Clark had a song on the Eagles' first album. "Train Leaves Here This Morning," which Gene had cowritten with Bernie Leadon in Dillard and Clark, was the sixth track on the debut album by Leadon's new group.

Clark had earlier come close to joining the Flying Burrito Brothers after Parsons's departure from the band. Both Clark and the Burritos were mainstays of A&M Records' country rock roster. "The A&M lot itself was one of two meccas for the record business in L.A.," says Bud Scoppa, who joined the company in October 1973. "There was a studio with a big sound stage and you'd have all these great bands rehearsing there." In the spring of 1971 A&M green-lighted a new Gene Clark solo album—his first in four years. But just as *Gene Clark and the Gosdin Brothers* had been a quasi-collaboration, so *White Light* (aka *Gene Clark*) was the result of a partnership with Jesse "Ed" Davis, a Native American guitarist who'd played with Taj Mahal.

"Gene and Jesse were close pals but not—I mean *not*—good for each other," said Gene's younger brother Rick. "Poor Jesse had a bad heroin problem; for Gene in the early '70s it was still more pot, though he was starting to get worse." Though it sold as poorly as any of A&M's country rock albums, *White Light* turned out to be one of the great singer-songwriter LPs of the early 1970s. If Clark and Davis were rowdies it didn't show on this sparse, austere, poetic record—part Dylan, part Orbison, part *American Beauty*. Clark had never forsaken his folk roots: however countrified his sound, they were always there in his elegant phrasing and courtly, metaphysical lyrics. Dylan himself thought "For a Spanish Guitar" one of the greatest songs ever written. Inspired by the Pacific Ocean at Mendocino, where Clark wrote most of the album's songs, the track was about the very birth of music in "visions" that "pulsate through my brain."

The following year, Clark—dropped by A&M—was trying to stay out of trouble when he was invited to be part of a Byrds reunion album on Asylum, a scheme hatched by David Geffen in cahoots with Terry Melcher, who invited him to join Clark, McGuinn, Hillman, and Clarke on a sailing trip from Marina Del Rey. The move was typical Geffen: having signed up the elite of the L.A. canyon scene who had evolved out of the Byrds, he couldn't resist charming the original quintet into a reunion. But *Byrds*, released in March 1973, was universally condemned as tired and uninspired. A dearth of original material forced the group to record covers of Joni Mitchell's "For Free" and *two* Neil Young songs—"Cowgirl in the Sand" and "(See the Sky) About to Rain," the latter as yet unreleased by Young himself—and had Crosby lazily reworking his own "Laughing." Only Gene Clark came good with his songs "Changing Heart" and "Full Circle."

Byrds was a strange experience for all five men, Roger McGuinn more so than anybody. He had, after all, been leading new versions of "the Byrds" for the previous six years, throughout the formations and dissolutions of the Burrito Brothers, Crosby, Stills, and Nash, Dillard and Clark, and other offshoots of that seminal band. The reunion was also a mortifying reminder that Crosby had sold millions more records than he had. "My real feelings are that Crosby was trying to get back at me for firing him," McGuinn later said. "Because he had David Geffen, Elliot Roberts and the financial power of Asylum, he had more say in the matter than he used to, and that's why Gene Clark did more vocals than he normally would have."

If that was true, it had negligible long-term impact. All five original Byrds soon went their separate ways. By June 1973, Gene Clark had been put back in his place: he was the opening act for a two-week Roger McGuinn residency at the Troubadour.

Left to right: Columbia's Billy James with Taj Mahal, Jesse Lee Kinkaid, Gary Marker, and Ry Cooder of the Rising Sons in Hollywood in 1966.

The Byrd that wouldn't fly: Gene Clark in Hollywood in 1966.

Jackson Browne at Billy James's Laurel Canyon Home in 1966.

Kaleidoscope, featuring Chris Darrow (*left*) and David Lindley (*top right*), in the stairway behind the Laurel Canyon Country Store in 1966.

160

Barry Friedman, record producer and canyon crazy man, in 1967.

Neil Young in Laurel Canyon in 1968.

The Troubadour, epicenter of L.A.'s folk and country-rock scenes.

Andy Wickham in 1967.

Linda Ronstadt in
Hollywood in 1968.

Mama Cass Elliot, "Elsa Maxwell meets Sophie Tucker," in
Laurel Canyon in 1968.

David Crosby (*center*) presents Joni Mitchell to a spellbound Eric Clapton (*right*) chez Mama Cass in 1968. Cass's daughter, Owen, sits in the foreground.

The Fantastic (but ill-fated) Expedition at the Troubadour in December 1968. *Left to right*: Bernie Leadon, Michael Clarke, Gene Clark, and Doug Dillard.

Joni Mitchell pens the lyrics for "Willy" as she and lover Graham
Nash drive to a Crosby, Stills, and Nash photo session in 1969.

Elliot Roberts at the Geffen-Roberts management office at 9130 Sunset Boulevard in late 1969.

Joni Mitchell at the window of "Our House," her A-frame cottage in Laurel Canyon.

INTER-OFFICE MEMO

WARNER BROS.-SEVEN ARTS RECORDS, INC.

TO: MO OSTIN   FROM: ANDY WICKHAM

SUBJECT:

DATE: 8TH SEPTEMBER 1969   COPIES TO: RICHARD PERRY, LENNY WARONKER, JOE WISSERT.

Mo:

In view of the recent activity in the
industry generated by the spate of pop
festivals, there seems to be emerging
the sort of tedious situation that
haunted us all after the Monterey Pop
Festival (new groups demanding high
advances etc. etc).

Bearing this in mind I attach here
Nik Cohn's lucid article on the Isle
of Wight festival which, I think, puts
the above nicely in perspective.
Please give this a careful reading.

ANDY WICKHAM

Encl.

Memo to Mo Ostin from Andy Wickham, the British "house hippie" who brought
Joni Mitchell to Warner-Reprise.

Acoustic supergroup Crosby, Stills, and Nash in West Hollywood in 1969.

James Taylor in late 1969.

The Flying Burrito Brothers in Laurel Canyon in late 1969. *Left to right*: Michael Clarke, Sneaky Pete Kleinow, Chris Ethridge, Chris Hillman, and Gram Parsons.

The Section. *Left to right*: Russ Kunkel, Lee Sklar, Danny Kortchmar, and Craig Doerge.

Carole King in Laurel Canyon in 1970.

Cap Rock at the Joshua Tree National Monument.

Neil Young's favorite band, the troubled Crazy Horse, in New York in January 1970. *Left to right*: Danny Whitten, Jack Nitzsche, Billy Talbot, and Ralph Molina.

Stills, Nash, Crosby, and Young rehearse for the 1970 CSNY tour with Johnny Barbata on drums and Calvin "Fuzzy" Samuels on bass.

Stan Cornyn, Joe Smith, Mo Ostin, and Lenny Waronker of Warner-Reprise Records, circa 1971.

Judee Sill, the first artist on Asylum, in 1972.

Randy Newman in 1972.

Lowell George (*far right*) with the original Little Feat in 1972. *Left to right*: Richie Hayward, Billy Payne, Roy Estrada.

Linda Ronstadt and J. D. Souther in 1972.

Don Henley with David Geffen at artist Boyd Elder's private showing in Venice in April 1972.

Joni Mitchell with boyfriend Jackson Browne at the Boyd Elder show.

An Asylum song circle at the Boyd Elder show. *Left to right*: Jackson Browne, Joni Mitchell, Cass Elliott, David Geffen, and Ned Doheny.

Doug Weston outside his Troubadour club in November 1972.

J. D. Souther and Jackson Browne at the *Desperado* album shoot in Agoura Hills in 1972.

"Los Desperados." *Left to right*: Jackson Browne, Bernie Leadon, Glenn Frey, Randy Meisner, Don Henley, and J. D. Souther.

The original Byrds reunite for Asylum in 1973. *Left to right*: Roger McGuinn, Chris Hillman, David Crosby, Michael Clarke, and Gene Clark.

Neil Young headlines for the opening week of the Roxy, co-owned by David Geffen, Elliot Roberts, and Lou Adler, in September 1973.

The augmented Eagles in 1973. *Left to right*: Glenn Frey, Don Felder, Randy Meisner (in car), Bernie Leadon, and Don Henley.

J. D. Souther and Jackson Browne on the road in 1973.

Tom Waits in 1973.

Joni Mitchell with Jack Nicholson and an unidentified man in 1974.

Left to right: David Geffen, producer Peter Asher, and Glenn Frey in 1974.

Ladies of the canyon. *Left to right*: Bonnie Raitt, Linda Ronstadt, and Maria Muldaur at the Santa Monica Civic Auditorium in 1974.

Asylum artist David Blue, who wrote the Eagles' "Outlaw Man," lighting Glenn Frey's cigarette in 1974.

Center, David Geffen's nemesis Irving Azoff in 1974 with clients Glenn Frey (*left*) and Dan Fogelberg.

Geffen's ill-fated supergroup Souther Hillman Furay in 1974.
Left to right: J. D. Souther, Chris Hillman, and Richie Furay.

Neil Young (*far right*) with the new Crazy Horse in Zuma Beach in 1975.
Left to right: Ralph Molina, Billy Talbot, and Frank "Poncho" Sampedro.

Noir merchant Warren Zevon (at right) with producer Jackson Browne (at left)
and guitarist Waddy Wachtel, 1976.

The Machinery vs. the Popular Song

I set out to become a singer. The star part is just
something they made up in Hollywood in 1930.

—Linda Ronstadt

Fool's Gold

For Neal Preston, a New York photographer who'd moved to L.A. in the fall of 1971, the city had become a veritable musical paradise. "Every record company had great offices and everyone was mellow and everyone would offer you a joint or more," he reminisces. "It wasn't about the Brill Building or any of that New York stuff anymore. To me, the whole record business was now based here."

Yet for some the euphoria was tinged with sadness. "The open boomtown quality of the Monterey days had passed," Eve Babitz wrote in 1973. "The older rich stars, people I knew, I watched as they all followed such an easily predictable path that you could have closed your eyes and known what they were doing. The rock stars who had no money either went to Hawaii and took drugs or went to

Topanga Canyon and took drugs, and meanwhile they waited for the next thing."

At Warner-Reprise things just got better. The years 1970 and 1971 had already delivered a harvest of hits by James Taylor, Neil Young, Joni Mitchell, Gordon Lightfoot, Norman Greenbaum, the Grateful Dead, and Van Morrison, as well as successful heavy or progressive rock albums by Black Sabbath, Deep Purple, Alice Cooper, and Jethro Tull. Meanwhile, the cachet that came with such modest-selling "prestige artists" as Ry Cooder, Randy Newman, and Maria Muldaur was still being felt in Burbank. Warners' music sales were rising at an average of 28 percent a year, with the company's music division accounting for close to 40 percent of overall sales. "The mood was pretty buoyant," says Barry Hansen, who compiled cheap sampler albums for Warners. "On Friday afternoon they'd usually break out the champagne and toast their latest hit record."

Ironically, one of the sole dissenting voices at Warners was that of Andy Wickham, the Englishman who'd played such a key role in making Warners hip. In a memo to Mo Ostin in early 1973, the now politically reactionary Wickham wrote huffily that "we have developed a looseness, a smugness, an appalling lack of civilized behaviour (secretaries using filthy language, 'executives' shambling around in ragged jeans and dirty sweat-shirts, endless silly parties in the conference room, cocaine-snorting in the lavatories etc.) which I believe is seriously impairing our efficiency as part of a streamlined industrial complex hitherto widely respected for its ability to plumb successfully the avant-garde." It's hard to know how seriously Ostin took his protégé's rant. It was fitting that Wickham was now based in Nashville, overseeing the company's country division.

The Mo Ostin/Joe Smith double act remained central to the Warner-Reprise ethos, with Mo remaining almost invisible while Joe presented the company's avuncular public face. "I was much more gregarious than Mo," says Smith, by now a noted after-dinner speaker. "With me it was kind of, 'Hey, Uncle Joe's here!' Mo was more of an inside guy, but he formed friendships with Paul Simon and Neil Young that remain deep friendships. I maybe didn't go as deep in some of those relationships."

Smith certainly went deep for James Taylor, who'd followed up the seminal *Sweet Baby James* with the equally successful *Mud Slide Slim and the Blue Horizon*, featuring a chart-topping version of Carole King's shoulder-to-lean-on classic "You've Got a Friend." Smith was there for Taylor after the singer met and fell for Carly Simon, a New York beauty four years his senior, at the Troubadour. Simon had paid her own dues on the East Coast folk circuit, singing with her sisters before being groomed by Albert Grossman as a "female Dylan." She'd had relationships with Cat Stevens and Kris Kristofferson, and had also suffered from depression and anxiety. Together, with Taylor on methadone, the couple quickly became the new king and queen of laid-back. "I've felt often in our relationship that I've been addicted to James," Simon admitted to *Rolling Stone*. "I have a dependency upon him that's almost like a drug I couldn't do without."

When they married in Manhattan on November 3, 1972, Joe Smith organized their wedding reception at the Tower Suite of the Radio City Music Hall. "The scene of the two families was something to behold," he says. "The Simons were a very uptight German-Jewish society family, where the Taylors were livestock-owning New England WASPs. When I had to give a toast I said, 'Could everybody get a little bit closer, please?!'" Back in California, Smith threw a party for the newlyweds at his Beverly Hills home on North Roxbury Drive. Guests were instructed to be on their best behavior: Joe's wife, Donnie, would not countenance drug use around her children. "All rock and roll heaven was there," Smith says. "I told everybody, 'We got twelve bathrooms in this house and two of them are outside. If you're gonna do anything, go outside because otherwise my wife will empty the house.'"

Another Warner-Reprise mainstay with kids was Randy Newman, who slowly continued on his singular singer-songwriter journey. Living up in Mandeville Canyon with his wife, Roswitha, Newman's life—by his own admission—was "boring." He wrote songs, watched TV, bought groceries, and made people laugh despite bouts of depression. "Randy was one of the funniest people you've ever met in your life," says Russ Titelman, who coproduced *Randy Newman Live* (1971) and *Sail Away* (1972) with Lenny Waronker. "We had so much fun making his records. We were free to do what we wanted, to let our imaginations go." Titelman's recollections mask the fact that it was sometimes difficult to get Newman in the studio at all. When *Rolling Stone*'s David Felton asked Waronker about Newman in the summer of 1972, the producer admitted that "half of the time was spent in cancellations and crap-outs . . . you know, a lot of midnight calls: 'Jesus, this is shit. Can we cancel?'" It didn't help that Newman viewed rock and roll with mild disdain. He admitted to Felton that he felt "kinda outside" the music scene *Rolling Stone* was covering.

Sail Away was Newman's finest album yet. With its mix of satire ("Sail Away," "God's Song," "Political Science"), evocative melancholia ("Old Man"), tongue-in-cheek nostalgia ("Dayton, Ohio—1903"), undefined menace ("Last Night I Had a Dream"), and leering sensuality ("You Can Leave Your Hat On"), the record stood apart from the narcissism of Randy's navel-gazing peers. Yet the latter group all worshiped him and envied the black humor of his songs.

Lowell George shared Randy Newman's humor and his love of the South, both in evidence on Little Feat's second album, *Sailin' Shoes*. But as much as they were Burbank's favorite sons, something jinxed Little Feat. People felt that George wasn't a charismatic enough front man to carry the band; more to the point, he eschewed the accessible California rock that helped the Eagles go platinum. There was always something gritty about Little Feat that worked against their success. George began to doubt Warners' commitment to his band. "If you have a Black Sabbath that has a platinum record the week before it's released," he said, "it's an easy situation and they jump on it. Somewhere along the line the Randy Newmans and the Ry Cooders and the Little Feats are somehow accommodated, but these people mean hard work and they shy away from them."

Lowell's friend and collaborator Martin Kibbee called him "the best-kept secret of the '70s Mellow Mafia . . . the finger in the slide on the syncopated pulse of that decade." But if "Easy to Slip" wasn't a hundred miles from CSNY, the caustic raunch of "Tripe Face Boogie" or "Teenage Nervous Breakdown" was harder and blacker than any other rock and roll coming out of California at the time. Then there was the deranged album packaging. *Sailin' Shoes*, for instance, featured an unsettling parody of a Fragonard's *Girl on a Swing* by L.A. artist Neon Park. George remained one of the great canyon characters. Van Dyke Parks treasured the tragicomedy of his work. Jackson Browne learned slide guitar from him. Linda Ronstadt routinely sought his feedback. "Lowell was so incredibly generous with his time, his praise, and his encouragement," future Feat guitarist Fred Tackett told Bud Scoppa. "I remember him convincing Linda that she could sing. Because it was coming from him, you believed him."

A regular social stop-off for George was a Laurel Canyon house on Wonderland Avenue belonging to Three Dog Night singer Danny Hutton. A drop-in den of debauchery, the Hutton house featured a bedroom with black walls and a giant fireplace. Lowell would often swing by and entertain the likes of Brian Wilson or Harry Nilsson. "I had the party house of all party houses," says Hutton. "Lowell was often there, ingesting huge amounts of cocaine yet somehow getting fatter and fatter."

Little Feat's commercial failure was only underscored by another up-and-coming Warner Brothers band, the Doobie Brothers. The fact that *Sailin' Shoes* producer Ted Templeman masterminded their sound only made it worse. "The Doobies were just a hard-core rock band that played for Hell's Angels up in San Jose," he says. "Joe Smith let me take a shot with them." A free-flowing, easy-on-the-ear amalgam of country, rock, and funky R&B—a kind of West Coast Allman Brothers—the Doobies scored big in 1972 with the driving "Listen to the Music." An even bigger hit, "Long Train Runnin'," followed in 1973. As the Eagles were to Gram Parsons, so the palatably funky Doobies were to the ornery Little Feat.

Yet there was justice of sorts, for the Burbank ethos dictated that just as Gordon Lightfoot's AM success paid for cult FM artists such as Randy Newman, so the Doobie Brothers bankrolled the likes of Little Feat. "Lenny was the catalyst and cornerstone for all of this," says Templeman. "He and Mo constantly let us do what we wanted, kind of like the way Steve Ross let Mo do what *he* wanted. We were the only A&R staff in the world, I think, who were all producers at the same time."

As Warner-Reprise gave Randy Newman and Little Feat free rein to develop, so David Geffen and Elliot Roberts played up the notion that Asylum was a talent hothouse. Behind the scenes the reality was slightly different. Geffen was increasingly aware of the value of Asylum as a brand. He was also feeling less and less inclined to babysit his acts. "Many times I felt I was too close to my artists," he says. "It had become too personal."

"What happens is that as the next wave of artists comes into the system, they're not your compadres," says Ron Stone. "And it becomes more businesslike. Even with the Eagles, a half generation behind CSNY and Joni, I think David cared less." When in late 1972 Steve Ross asked if he'd be interested in selling his label to Warners, Geffen jumped at the opportunity to cash in—especially since Ross assured him he'd stay on board as label president. For $2 million in cash and $5 million in Warner stock, Asylum was conjoined with Atlantic Records.

The news was received by Asylum's artists with stunned disbelief. The seductive words Geffen had uttered in the sauna evaporated. A deep feeling of betrayal permeated 9130 Sunset. "Asylum was an artist-oriented label for about a minute, until the big money showed up," Don Henley told author Marc Eliot. "Then my, how things changed." Geffen didn't flinch. He offered no words of apology. Secretly he regarded half his artists with mild contempt, even when they questioned the blatant conflicts of interest he'd overseen in simultaneously running Asylum, Geffen-Roberts, and the quaintly named publishing arm Companion Music. "I think Geffen stiffed everybody," says Ned Doheny. "I happen to be the guy that pointed out to the other artists the fact that the record company and the publishing company were essentially the same thing."

"When he first started out, David dealt almost completely from the heart," says Jimmy Webb. "Anyone who could take poor, pitiful Laura Nyro under his arm at Monterey and say, 'Don't worry, darling, we'll make them eat this crow they've heaped on you' proved that. But to be honest, I believe he became so wealthy that it became more about money than about the artists. And it may have even become *all* about the money, for all I know. Once money has accumulated to a certain amount, people have a tendency to go into alternate realities."

By their own admission, Jackson Browne and the Eagles had been oblivious to what was going on. Amazing as it seems today, none of them even had lawyers. "Manager-client relations are really an extension of parenting," says Carl Gottlieb, who got a front-row view of the commotion. "A lot of artists never hit emotional puberty and outgrow that need for authority figures. I think the Eagles and Jackson did. They got past the artist-as-child and got in touch with their inner business adult."

Geffen himself denies the sale caused a rift between him and his artists. "At the time I don't recall that there was a lot of talk about it," he says. "Nothing really had changed. We continued to operate in exactly the same way as we did before I sold it." Yet one consequence of the Asylum sale was that he was obliged to turn over his 75 percent stake in Geffen-Roberts Management to Elliot Roberts. "After I decided to sell to Steve Ross, I didn't want to be in the management business anymore. I felt it had potential conflicts of interest, and so I gave Elliot the company. And I've never regretted that. I've always thought it was the right decision to make at that time." He nonetheless continued to make his presence felt behind the scenes.

Another consequence of the sale was the increased responsibility of the company's undermanagers. The duo of John Hartmann and Harlan Goodman, for example, looked after non-Asylum acts Poco and America. (The addition of America to the Geffen-Roberts stable entailed the shunting aside of British manager Jeff Dexter. "Geffen sent them a ticket and flew them over when I thought they were rehearsing here in England," Dexter told *Rolling Stone*. The group's Dan Peek described Dexter as "a little pea with absolutely no pull and no money up against a big conglomerate corporation.") More fearsome than either Hartmann and Goodman was Irving Azoff, a tiny terror of a manager who'd moved to L.A. from his native Illinois to secure deals for his clients Joe Walsh and Dan Fogelberg. Azoff landed the latter a deal at Columbia after label chief Clive Davis came west to court singer-songwriters. "Clive had everything laid out—caviar, canapés, the whole deal," Fogelberg recalled. "He played me Paul Simon's first solo record, which had yet to come out, and kept talking about a kid named Springsteen and a guy named Billy Joel that he'd signed. Clive said, 'I'm signing singer-songwriters, and I think you belong here too.'"

Azoff's arrival at Geffen-Roberts coincided with the firing of

Hartmann, who'd suggested to the Eagles that he take them under his own wing. According to Hartmann, Geffen threatened to "bury the band" if they left. Azoff seized his opportunity. "I immediately made the Eagles my business," he said. "We were all just a bunch of punk kids who were the same age." To the Eagles, Azoff was exactly the kind of ruthlessly single-minded manager they wanted—their very own five-foot-four knight in shining armor. "Irving said he had all the drive that Geffen had and he would take us to the next stage," Leadon remembers. "There was no doubt that he was very bright, and that he consciously wanted to emulate Geffen. Which he in fact did. He emulated his business style, the way David yelled at people on the phone." When Azoff realized that the Eagles' business manager, Jerry Rubinstein, was also business manager for Geffen-Roberts, he wasted no time in alerting the band to the conflict of interest.

"I never liked Azoff," says Ned Doheny. "I thought Ahmet had a somewhat princely demeanor, and I thought Geffen was the cheap-seats version of that. Irving was kind of the cheap-seats version of Geffen." Geffen and Roberts, understandably, were unhappy about Azoff making off with the Eagles and insisted he stay. "I went back to all the acts and said I was going to stay," Azoff said. "Henley and Frey talked me out of [it]." In their new manager's hands the Eagles would fly higher than any L.A. band in history—perilously close to the California sun.

Song Power

As Irving Azoff entered the frame, the Eagles were grappling with the relative failure of 1973's *Desperado*, the follow-up to their successful debut album. A concept album based around the rather specious conceit that rock stars were modern-day outlaws, *Desperado* was born of the camaraderie between Glenn Frey and Don Henley. Rescued from penury by the hits on *Eagles*, the two men had moved into Laurel Canyon to live the L.A. high life they'd always dreamed about.

Frey's pad, at the corner of Kirkwood and Ridpath, was the scene

of much revelry. In abundant supply were wine, women, and song—
not to mention poker and cocaine. Regularly gathering at the house
was a gang of blue-jeaned honchos who included J. D. Souther, Ned
Doheny, Paul Ahern, and Boyd Elder. Farther up Ridpath, in a house
on stilts formerly occupied by Roger McGuinn, dwelled the more
introspective Henley. But it wasn't all fun and games. Frey and
Henley also got down to the hard grind of writing together. "Our life
then was simpler," Henley later reflected. "All we had to do was get
up in the morning and think about songwriting . . . and girls." When
Glenn chipped in on "Desperado," a song Don had begun back in
Texas, their partnership was established. The song's Wild West
theme inspired the idea of an entire LP devoted to pistol-toting
renegades.

"We'd all been to the Troubadour to see Tim Hardin," Frey
recalled. "Later the four of us, Jackson, J. D., Don, and myself went
to somebody's house. . . . That's when the idea came together about
us doing an album of all the angst-meisters. James Dean was going
to be one song, and the Doolin-Dalton gang was going to be
another." Frey had been into cowboys since the Echo Park days,
when Jackson Browne showed him an illustrated book on gun-
fighters he'd received as a birthday present from Ned Doheny. Frey
also liked the notion of the album being a grand artistic statement.
At least that was how he sold the outlaw theme to Bernie Leadon and
Randy Meisner, neither of whom was part of the Frey-Henley gang.
"Glenn was enamored of this analogy between outlaw groups and
rock and roll," says Leadon. "Some of the first reviewers of the album
said that that was a bit of a stretch."

"The metaphor was probably a little bullshit," conceded Henley.
"We were in L.A. staying up all night, smoking dope, living the
California life, and I suppose we thought it was as radical as cowboys
in the old West. We were really rebelling against the music business,
not society." At least some of that rebellion was aimed at their own
label—specifically against David Geffen, the man they felt had
betrayed their trust. Pained that Asylum was no longer the cozy
refuge Geffen had sold them in his sauna, the Eagles intended
Desperado to be a covert attack on what Henley saw as "the evils of

fame and success." The band also was pissed off at the attention America had been getting from Geffen-Roberts. Viewing the trio as ersatz Neil Young lightweights, Frey and Henley were annoyed that they had followed up the No. 1 "Horse with No Name" with two further Top 10 hits, "I Need You" and "Ventura Highway."

With Browne and Souther contributing to *Desperado*'s principal theme song, "Doolin Dalton," Henley was suddenly coming into his own as a writer. The piano-based title track was finished, and Don and Glenn banged off "Tequila Sunrise"—a hymn to the quintessential 1970s rock tipple—inside a week. Although Leadon and Meisner came in on other tracks, the Frey-Henley team would prove to be the band's creative core for the next three years.

Desperado's cover photography, shot in a run-down movie lot in the Malibu Hills, completed the band's cowboy conceit. Rounding up the gang—J. D., Jackson, Ned, Boyd Elder, and more—to help out, the band spent a day in costume, tearing around as they fired off rounds of blanks for Henry Diltz. "I think we all have an affection for those pictures when we see them," J. D. Souther said. "It represents a time before we all kind of fragmented and went our separate ways. It was really the last stand of Los Desperados." In New York, Asylum's new parent label, Atlantic, was not amused. "They made a fucking cowboy record," griped label president Jerry Greenberg. Sales of the album seemed to bear out Greenberg's gripe: neither the LP nor any of its singles cracked the Top 40.

Atlantic wasn't too ecstatic about the new album by Jackson Browne either. Like *Desperado*, Browne's *For Everyman* failed to produce the hit single that its predecessor had done—ironic, given that its first track was Jackson's own version of "Take It Easy." Another collection of plangent, midtempo musings on life and lost love, *For Everyman* swung between wide-eyed wonder and sorrowful gravitas. Like Joni Mitchell, whose heart he'd broken, Browne saw songs primarily as vehicles for self-exploration. "The process of writing a song," he noted years later, "is really the process of confronting something internal." Among the album's tracks was "These Days," the weary-before-his-years ballad Browne had written back in 1967, and the tellingly titled "I Thought I Was a Child." Janet Maslin wrote in her *Rolling Stone* review, "Jackson seems equally divided between teacher and searcher, mock-adult and mock-child." Meanwhile, the title track rebutted the elitist Utopianism of David Crosby's "Wooden Ships." An early declaration of Browne's sense of community, "For Everyman" also was an explicit rethink of the dropout complacency of "Take It Easy."

The sound of *For Everyman* was Laurel Canyon incarnate: a winning blend of *Sweet Baby James* and *Music from Big Pink*. Supplying much of its woodiness was ex-Kaleidoscope guitarist/fiddler David Lindley, whose work on the dobro and other string instruments would become a core part of Browne's sound. "Lindley is perfect for me," Browne said. "I'm very structural-minded, and it's Lindley who draws emotion out for me." The yang to Jackson's clean-cut yin, Lindley supplied the organic resonance that saved Browne from proto-AOR blandness. "We got together at the Troubadour," Lindley recalled in 1990. "He was opening for Linda Ronstadt, and I went down to see Chris Darrow, who was playing in her band. I borrowed Chris's fiddle and sat in with Jackson and Ned Doheny."

Doheny was struggling to complete his own Asylum album. Toward the end of the sessions Geffen pulled the plug, informing the trust-fund kid that he'd have to pay for the remainder of the recording himself. *Ned Doheny*, featuring the great "Postcards from Hollywood," came out later that year. "I think the reality of just how much Jackson's first album had cost was hitting home," Doheny says. "And Jackson was really David's favorite, after all."

A song on *For Everyman*, "Ready or Not," recounted how Browne had courted and then impregnated model-actress Phyllis Major. The beginning of the romance did not augur well. Jackson met her "in a crowded barroom/One of those typical Hollywood scenes." When her drunken boyfriend Bobby Neuwirth insulted her, Browne valiantly took a swing at him and was knocked off his feet. "That girl came home with me," he sang smugly in the song. "Ready or Not" was candid about Browne's unwillingness to settle down with Major, and no less candid about his unpreparedness for fatherhood when she announced she was pregnant. But ready or not, Jackson was presented with a son, Ethan, at Cedars-Sinai in L.A. on November 2, 1973. As if to build a nest, moreover, he and Phyllis had moved into the imposing Browne family home in the tony, old-money neighborhood of Highland Park. Built in a California mission style by his grandfather Clyde, its inner courtyard provided the setting for *Everyman*'s sepia-tinted cover. The album was a virtual roll call of the Asylum/Geffen-Roberts inner circle—featuring cameos from David Crosby, Don Henley, Glenn Frey, Bonnie Raitt, and Joni Mitchell, as well as from a visiting Elton John (aka "Rockaday Johnnie")—and confirmed Browne's status as the nexus of the scene.

About the only luminary absent from the proceedings was Linda Ronstadt, whose signing to the Asylum label Browne had much to do with. "Like Jackson, Linda was a very powerful figure in the artists' community," says Lenny Waronker. "I remember going with Randy Newman to see her perform, and when we went backstage Jackson was sitting there talking to her about how she should be with David Geffen." Even though she wasn't a singer-songwriter, Ronstadt was a must-have for Geffen—the reigning queen of the Troubadour scene. Still under contract to Capitol, who couldn't get her post–Stone Poneys career off the ground, she was deeply frustrated. Geffen told her to finish her deal and let him work out the details of defecting to Asylum. "I thought Linda would be a star from the time I first heard the Stone Poneys," Geffen says. "But she was very insecure in those days. She didn't realize how good she was, and she was concerned about being in the company of other people on the label that she thought were more talented than she was."

Ronstadt was complex and highly-strung. She was far too smart to play the California sex kitten, but she played men like instruments, conducting relationships with numerous producers and songwriters. "Linda would hear a song and fall in love with the writer through the song," says David Jackson. "She was definitely a songwriter's woman. Not that she cared, because she was *about the song* consistently. What a joy she was. So beautiful and so effervescent."

"Linda went out with a lot of guys, from Kris Kristofferson to Lowell George to Jerry Brown," says Denny Bruce. "She enjoyed being around men who were bright, intelligent, had their own viewpoints, and didn't talk about the music business all day." J. D. Souther was certainly bright, and he certainly had his own viewpoint. Linda was deeply in love with the Texan mysterioso when David

Geffen suggested he produce her Asylum debut—an album that would include her versions of "Desperado" and Randy Newman's "Sail Away." More than anything, Linda adored Souther's soulful ballads—songs such as "Don't Cry Now," which became the album's title track. In the end, though, the relationship told on the creative process. Ronstadt's inability to separate the personal from the professional made *Don't Cry Now* hard work. "Tough situation, eight or ten hours in the studio, then home for another ten hours," Souther reflected. "It was real tense."

"We were like kids in the studio, just inept, and we took a lot of time," Ronstadt admitted. Rumors circulated that Linda and J. D. had chalked up $100,000 worth of studio time—a profligacy that did not endear them to David Geffen. At home the couple competed for what Ronstadt called "airtime." "Someone's got to cook breakfast," she told Tom Nolan, "while somebody else gets to sit down with the guitar and write a song. In a situation like that, the stronger of the two ends up . . . the stronger of the two." For Linda, that was plainly Souther. "She had a number of producers who had been lovers," says Ben Fong-Torres. "And I think having to work alongside someone who was that much a part of your life emotionally and romantically made it tougher for her to do what it was that she heard in her mind." When the sessions for *Don't Cry Now* ran aground, Geffen suggested that Souther seek external input. John Boylan helped out on three tracks. Then came the idea of asking Peter Asher to step in. It would mark the beginning of the most successful L.A. artist/ producer relationship of the 1970s.

"J. D. and I used to go to dinner at Peter and his wife, Betsy's, house," Ronstadt recalls. "Peter liked J. D.'s songs. We went to their house because they had a nice house and they could cook. Betsy would say, 'We don't get invited back very often.' And I'd say, 'Well, I don't know how to cook!'" Asher was an increasingly popular figure on the Canyon/Troubadour scene. His low-key, respectful English temperament singled him out in a business where brashness was the norm. "He's reserved and different from a lot of people in this business," said James Taylor. "He's not a terribly flamboyant person." More than anything it was Peter's intuitive understanding of musicians that got people's attention. "He knew what to do in the studio," says Waddy Wachtel. "He knew that if you could make people feel like playing, they would play well. If you wanted a joint, there was one there; if you wanted a bump, there was one there."

For Ronstadt herself, Asher was the first male producer who treated her as an equal. "Most guys had a tendency to behave like guys do when they're fixing cars," she says. "The girl was never under the hood, or at least if she got under the hood she was considered a tomboy. Peter was different because he was prepared to validate my musical whims." For his part, Asher felt an instant respect for Ronstadt. If she struck him as "the ultimate Californian, tanned and barefoot and gorgeous," her song choices were unerring and her seriousness about her work unusual. Through her he acquired a new understanding of what country rock meant. "Linda was my educator in that world," Asher says. "All I knew about country music really was that it was old guys in hats singing songs that had nothing to do with *me*."

As her professional and platonic relationship with Asher developed, Ronstadt's intense personal one with Souther hit the skids. His inveterate infidelity broke her heart, as it had shattered Judee Sill's before her. This time the other woman was none other than Joni Mitchell. "There's not a girl singer who ever set foot in Los Angeles in that era that John David didn't have a relationship with," says Asher, who regularly hung out chez Souther. "There was a famous moment when Joni and Linda met on his doorstep—one leaving, the other arriving."

"A lot of times, things that people do that are hurtful are simply unconscious," says Ned Doheny. "J. D. unfortunately had a tendency to shit where he ate. His reputation as a ladies' man was more important to him than his friendships. He and I had a major falling out over a girl, and I think that probably that was the case with most of his friends."

Ronstadt was devastated by the betrayal. Partly as a result of it she began overeating and for six months saw a shrink. In a 1980 *Playboy* interview she described the pain it had caused. "I went over that line only once," she said. "It was really frightening and it took me about two years to come back."

On the Rox

Linda Ronstadt claims she never enjoyed cocaine. "It made me nervous," she says, "and it made it hard for me to hear." But that didn't stop her, or almost anyone else at the time, from doing it. Lots of it. "You kinda did," she says. Supporting Neil Young on his 1973 *Time Fades Away* tour, Ronstadt did enough coke to necessitate twice having her nose cauterized. She even confessed to Ben Fong-Torres that she'd tried heroin.

Cocaine was ubiquitous in the L.A. music scene by mid-1973. The perfect drug for the unbridled rock ego, it gave musicians and scenesters alike a temporary sense of omnipotence. It also deadened much of the emotional rapport that music requires. "I wrote some songs on cocaine because initially it can be a creative catalyst," Joni Mitchell reflected. "In the end it'll fry you, kill the heart. It kills the soul and gives you delusions of grandeur as it shuts down your emotional center. Perfect drug for a hit man but not so good for a musician."

Cocaine, its effects tempered by alcohol and marijuana, became the essential accompaniment to the new glamour of 1970s rock, and nowhere was it more rampant than at the Roxy, a new Sunset Strip club—complete with private VIP enclave On the Rox—opened by Lou Adler in partnership with David Geffen and Elliot Roberts. Designed to break the stranglehold the Troubadour had on the L.A. club scene, the Roxy launched in early September 1973 with an after-show party for Elton John. A host of music and movie stars was invited. Among them was Cher, who would shortly begin dating David Geffen as he belatedly attempted to convince himself—and everybody else—that he was heterosexual. Hanging on Lou Adler's arm, meanwhile, was actress Britt Ekland. "The Roxy was a big threat for everybody," recalls Robert Marchese, then running the Troub for Weston. "They could afford to pay more money. And Doug was fading. He was fucked up on coke."

The Troubadour was rife with the drug. As Marchese walked through the club to the kitchen, he'd pass along a row of record company executives, each of whom would press a vial of powder into the hand he'd extended in greeting. In Los Angeles coke was inseparable from sex. Both the Roxy and the Troubadour teemed with women who—if they weren't born like that—made themselves over as blonde, tanned California girls. Foxy women liked cocaine, and they liked fast men with the money to buy it. "You had to have coke or you didn't get laid," says Denny Bruce. "If you didn't have coke, a pad in the canyon, and a Porsche, there was a good chance you weren't going to get laid." The paradox was that the pharmaceutical use of cocaine was to blunt sensation, an effect that explained the increasingly sterile sound of Los Angeles as it entered the era of adult-oriented rock. "There were a lot of feelings stuffed down, a lot of anguish and desperate embarrassment," says Linda Ronstadt. "Everything was spoken with a very tight throat and a very flat mask."

"There was a period when people would proudly wear their little gold spoons on a chain around their neck," says David Geffen. "For me it was something I didn't care for and wanted to distance myself from. And it's not a pleasant position to be in when you're telling people what they shouldn't be doing. I had a very hard time watching a lot of what I considered to be self-destruction." For the late Danny Sugerman, sometime Doors gofer and comanager, L.A. circa 1973 "conjured up images of decaying mansions . . . an uncleaned pool, palm fronds afloat . . . sunlight was out, nightlife was in."

The contrast with the scene on the Sunset Strip in 1965–1966 couldn't have been more pointed. Now musicians emulated the sense of distance and mystique that movie stars had long embodied. There was little kinship with the audience that had made them stars in the first place. In the words of Linda Ronstadt, "The very people that had stood up and said 'We're the ones self-righteously proclaiming that this is the right political way to act in the world' were the very ones who now stepped on other people in the most hideous way—sleeping with each other's girlfriends or criticizing each other in front of their friends."

Elitism dominated the mid-1970s nightlife of the Sunset Strip. "Whatever gig you went to," says Jonh Ingham, "there was now some kind of VIP situation—an inner sanctum that everybody was trying to get into. The Roxy codified that with On the Rox."

"The Roxy and the Troub could almost be judged by the restaurants next door to them," says J. D. Souther. "Whereas it was almost embarrassing to pull up at Dan Tana's or the Troub in a limousine, at the Roxy or the Rainbow it was not only normal but predictable."

When Nick Kent of London's *New Musical Express* came to L.A. in 1973 he was struck by the cosseted incestuousness of the music scene. "The Byrds had just finished their reunion album, so Crosby was floating around like some unofficial mayor of the Strip," he remembers. "Jackson Browne was hanging out at Asylum with David Blue and everybody. They were always wearing denim. Most of them were indoors, doing drugs at Irving Azoff's house or wherever. They'd done their hanging out and they were incredibly snobbish."

Kent was attracted instead to a new street-level scene coalescing around Rodney Bingenheimer's English Disco club northeast of the Strip on Hollywood Boulevard. A revolt of sorts against the canyon mentality, the English Disco spawned a minor glam-rock revolution in the land of denim. "Everybody got really bored with the canyons," writer and Bomp Records founder Greg Shaw said. "People were falling asleep in their shoes. I never liked Jackson Browne or Joni Mitchell. To me it was all lifestyle wallpaper music."

The glam androgyny of David Bowie and T. Rex—was anathema to the Asylum crowd. L.A. country rockers referred to Alice Cooper and his contemporaries as "spectacle bands" or "costume people." When the Eagles played Madison Square Garden they sneered at the New York Dolls and wore T-shirts that snootily proclaimed the words "SONG POWER." "Glenn Frey is one of the best friends I have now," says Joe Smith, "but during those years with the coke it was always *'Those assholes!'* Everyone was an *asshole.*"

"I remember seeing Frey outside the English Disco, obviously high on coke," Nick Kent says. "His eyes were like slits looking at these people he detested." Kent often spent time in L.A. with Led Zeppelin, who held court in the company of groupies and dealers at the Hyatt on Sunset. For Zeppelin singer Robert Plant, the L.A. scene evinced mixed feelings. "The people who lived in Laurel Canyon avoided us," Plant recalls. "They kept clear because we were in the tackiest part of the Strip with the tackiest people. I wanted to know about the history of the Hollywood Argyles, and

I would never have found that out at a candlelit dinner halfway up the canyon."

Yet Plant had been a devotee of Joni Mitchell and the Buffalo Springfield, his love of whom was reflected in the acoustic side of Led Zeppelin—not least in the 1971 song "Going to California." Back in 1969, indeed, Plant had attempted to meet Neil Young. "Robert desperately wanted to meet Neil," recalls Nancy Retchin, a friend of the Monkees. "Peter Tork said that CSNY were rehearsing at the Greek Theater and we could take Robert round there. Unfortunately on the day itself I took mescaline. We were so stoned that we ended up driving Robert in my mother's car all the way down to Watts. I'll never forget Robert yelling out of the car, *'Where is the Greek Theater?!'* in this neighborhood where nobody had ever heard of it."

"The canyon scene," Plant says, "was a continuation of the artistic will to continue some sort of aesthetic and respectable role for pop music, so that there was an intention beyond "Rock-a-Hula Baby.'" Yet Led Zeppelin's antics at the Hyatt (or "Riot House") were the apogee of rock debauchery in Hollywood Babylon. "The downfall of the '60s dream was very disappointing, because we'd really thought we could change things," says Pamela Des Barres, Jimmy Page's L.A. consort of choice. "As much as I loved Zeppelin, they kind of fucked things up in L.A. The magic really went out of rock and roll."

The only star in the Geffen-Roberts firmament not to sneer at glam rock was Neil Young. In a radio interview with B. Mitchel Reed in September 1973—the month he played the opening residency at the Roxy—Young tacitly embraced the new decadence. "The '60s are definitely not with us anymore," he told Reed. "The change into the music of the '70s is starting to come with people like David Bowie and Lou Reed . . . this is much more of a dope generation that we're in now." But drugs were closer to home than Bowie or Reed. When Crosby, Stills, Nash, and Young—together with their partners and kids—convened on the Hawaiian island of Maui in late May 1973, Stephen Stills was in full-blown cocaine addiction. For the last year he had been leading his new band, Manassas, an all-star R&B/country ensemble featuring Chris Hillman. Now, despite his marriage to Veronique Sanson, Stephen was a mess. Drugs and alcohol compounded delusions that he had served a tour of duty in Vietnam.

"I short-circuited there for a while," Stills admitted to Dave Zimmer. "Things were moving too fast. I got a little crazed. Too much drinkin', too many drugs. What can I say?" Things hardly improved when CSNY assembled at Young's Broken Arrow ranch. "We'd been at each other's faces for too long," Crosby said. "Graham is the *only* nice guy and if you put all of us together for very long we drain on each other quite a bit." A planned album, *Human Highway*, was aborted as a result. "Neil didn't want to be with Stephen doin' the dope," said Carrie Snodgress, who the previous September had given birth to Young's son Zeke. Cocaine hyperbole was getting Neil down. "I don't want to talk about how incredibly famous we are," he told Cameron Crowe, "or how we could set the world on fire if we got back together. I want to play. I want to sing. I want to make good records." Crosby and Nash were equally antsy about working with Stills, preferring to perform as a duo while Stephen toured with Manassas. "I know I've blown my music and offended my friends because I was crazy behind coke," Stills said after a show in Saratoga Springs in August 1973.

Haunted by the death of Danny Whitten, Neil Young got another shock when CSNY roadie Bruce Berry—brother of Jan of Jan and Dean—overdosed on heroin and died in his Santa Monica apartment in early June. Berry had flown out to Maui to deliver coke to Stills, only to be sent home by an irate Crosby and Nash. When the roadie's body was found he had been dead for three days. David and Graham felt the same uneasy guilt that Neil had felt over the loss of Whitten. Yet another CSNY tragedy occurred when Graham Nash's girlfriend, Amy Gossage—daughter of a San Francisco PR guru—was murdered by her own brother in a drug-related killing. "Tragedy was written across Amy's every action," said Nash, whose grief dominated his bleak 1973 album *Wild Tales*. "Her loss affected me deeply, because she had been a big part of my life. I felt helpless and really empty."

With the ragged *Time Fades Away* tour behind him—the album itself would appear in October—Neil Young headed still farther into the darkness. "I just didn't feel like a lonely figure with a guitar or whatever it is that people see me as sometimes," he later reflected. "I didn't feel that laid-back." Neil was taking his own walk on the wild side. "He's had a lot of bad breaks, bad relationships, and they've all affected what he does," says Elliot Roberts. "It's not like the art is separate from the life, it's one and the same with Neil." The first thing he did was saddle up once more with Crazy Horse and David Briggs, the only people who could do justice to the dragging, tequila-soaked rock of "Tonight's the Night," "Tired Eyes," "Lookout Joe," and other new songs of Neil's. "He likes to surround himself with real people, which is why he plays with Crazy Horse," said Nils Lofgren, who augmented the band's lineup on guitar and piano. "They may not be the best musicians in the world, but they have soul and there's a communication there that you can't buy."

In August, Young and Crazy Horse played two nights at the Topanga Corral—a fitting venue for "Tired Eyes," a song inspired by a coke-related double murder in Topanga Canyon in April 1972. If *After the Gold Rush* had embodied "the spirit of Topanga" for Young in 1970, "Tired Eyes" revealed what Jo Jo Gunne's Mark Andes called the canyon's "dark side." Later that month, and continuing into early September, Neil and the Horse hunkered down at Studio Instrument Rentals on Santa Monica Boulevard. Wired on coke and Cuervo Gold, the band—with Lofgren and pedal steel veteran Ben Keith—played as if they were at a wake. "Neil's always been very conscious of his health," Lofgren told *ZigZag*. "Then he started getting into tequila, not heavily, but he got into it and started to get real loose." The result was *Tonight's the Night*. Harsh and almost defiantly sloppy in places, the album also showcased the stumbling country beauty of "Speakin' Out," "Mellow My Mind," and "Albuquerque." Years ahead of its time, *Tonight's the Night* was rejected by Reprise and shelved till 1975.

By the time Young and Crazy Horse began a short British tour in early November 1973, Neil was clear in his mind about the *Tonight's the Night* concept. Deconstructing not only the myth of "Neil Young: Sensitive Singer-Songwriter" but also the bogus fiction of rock as artless confession, Neil designed the set as a sleazy parody of lounge entertainment, set in some run-down version of Miami where "everything is cheaper than it looks." It was punk theater before its time, and the band was having a ball. Yet British fans were shocked. Echoing the reception given to the electrified Bob Dylan in 1966, audiences at venues such as London's Rainbow Theatre were left angry and confused. With an exquisite irony, Young's support act was the band that defined the new mellow sound of Southern California. "I took the Eagles on the *Tonight's* tour for the exact reason that here was the roughest thing Neil was ever gonna do," says Elliot Roberts. "I mean, Neil was sort of dribbling out of the side of his mouth, following on from 'Take It *Eeeee*asy.' He was getting booed off the stage on that tour, the mood was so down. He wasn't playing *one hit*, one song from *Gold Rush* or *Harvest* that you came to lay down your good poundage for."

"Neil had a unique place in our scene," adds Bernie Leadon, who saw the tour up close. "He had a lot of latitude. Geffen used Neil's popularity to get us booked. I remember him screaming, 'You want Neil Young, you're gonna take the Eagles as an opening act!'" The Eagles were as shocked as any of Young's fans by the *Tonight's the Night* material. Counting him as a major influence on their country-rock style, they now watched him sabotage his own role as Pendleton-shirted dreamer.

Another of the Eagles' primary influences was acting out the very self-destruction Young was singing about. Gram Parsons had picked himself up one more time in early 1973 and gone out on a cross-country tour with Emmylou Harris and the Fallen Angels. At Houston's Liberty Hall in late February, they were joined onstage by Young himself, then halfway through the *Time Fades Away* tour, along with his support act Linda Ronstadt. "Gram was real easy to hang out with," says John Lomax III, a Nashville writer who caught the Houston show. "'Course he was blasted out of his gourd, and it was pretty sad."

Back in L.A., Parsons hung out with Clarence White, who had recently played the final shows by the Byrds and was now rehearsing a new version of his Kentucky Colonels. "A lot of it had to do with the fact that Clarence had a family with kids and Gram didn't," says John Delgatto, who later released a live album from the Fallen Angels tour. "Gram was finally seeing that you could have a normal life in rock and roll." On July 14 White was killed by a passing truck while loading equipment into a van. Parsons was distraught: only the year before, he'd lost Brandon De Wilde in a Colorado car crash. He told

Crawdaddy, "Death [is] something that comes up on the roulette wheel every once in a while."

At White's funeral, Parsons lifted the heavy Catholic gloom by breaking spontaneously into the traditional gospel song "Farther Along." Harmonizing alongside him was Bernie Leadon, who'd sung it with Gram in the Burritos. It was the cathartic trigger everybody needed. Tears rolled down the faces of musicians who found it hard to show emotion other than through music. Parsons himself wept on the shoulder of Chris Hillman. As the mourners dispersed, he spoke with Phil Kaufman. "If I die," he told him, "I want you to take my body to the desert and burn it. I don't wanna go like this." Kaufman gave Gram his word.

A week after the funeral a fire tore through Parsons's Laurel Canyon Boulevard home, most likely caused by his falling asleep with a lit cigarette. The blaze incinerated many of his possessions— including his beloved Nudie suits. The event precipitated a separation from Gretchen, who moved into her father's plush Mulholland Drive mansion. Finding refuge in Phil Kaufman's house in the Valley, Parsons began work on the follow-up to *GP*. The new songs ("$1,000 Wedding," "Ooh Las Vegas," and others) were shot through with glitz and guilt, dime-store romance and slot-machine tack. Once again Emmylou Harris sang heavenly harmonies; once again the band was the core of Elvis Presley's backing musicians, fleshed out by such country-rock guests as Bernie Leadon and Linda Ronstadt. Released in 1974, *Grievous Angel* would become a country-rock classic. "The things I like of Gram's were when he was singing with Emmy," says Ronstadt. "She was very strong and was able to see the uniqueness in what he did. With Gram, most of it was sloppy, but Emmy was able to make it clearer." Harris aside, nobody knows whether she and Gram physically consummated the feelings they had for each other. She herself has always denied it.

Exactly two months after Clarence White's funeral, Parsons drove out to his beloved California desert and checked into the Joshua Tree nn. "Joshua Tree represented a quest," said his photographer friend Andee Cohen. "It wasn't about running out to the desert, trying to get loaded. It was searching for a meaning to all of it." On the night of September 18, Gram injected a heroin-and-cocaine speedball in Room 8 of the inn. As he began turning a fateful shade of blue, two girlfriends—Margaret Fisher and Dale McElroy—tried to keep him from slipping away. Frightened, they resorted to an old OD standby: inserting ice cubes into the rectum. For a brief moment it seemed to work. Gram's eyes blinked back to life.

It didn't last long. When Fisher left the inn to find food, Gram again lost consciousness. McElroy desperately attempted mouth-to-mouth resuscitation. At about ten o'clock Al Barbary, son of the inn's manager, did the same. "I've been to Vietnam and he was dead as a doornail," Barbary said. "His body was so full of poison that I about died myself. He'd been dead for maybe a half hour." At 12:30 A.M. of the nineteenth, Gram was pronounced dead at Hi-Desert Memorial Hospital in nearby Yucca Valley. "He'd cleaned up, and that was the reason he died," Keith Richards says. "He was recuperating out there, but he got seduced one time. He was clean and took a strong shot. It's the one mistake you don't wanna make."

On September 21, two days after Gram's death, Phil Kaufman and roadie Michael Martin drove a hearse to Van Nuys Airport in L.A. and persuaded a baggage loader to release the singer's body to them. From Los Angeles they drove the coffin back to Joshua Tree. At the foot of Cap Rock, where four years before Gram had spent a memorably cosmic night with Richards, the Road Mangler honored his friend's wishes. He set fire to his body and watched it burn in the silent darkness. The smoldering remains of the body and the coffin were discovered by campers the next morning.

Postcards from Hollywood

At a meeting of Warner Communications heads in L.A. on August 9, 1973, Steve Ross told David Geffen that he wanted to merge Asylum Records with Elektra Records. Furthermore, he wanted the thirty-year-old Geffen to run it. The idea stemmed from Jac Holzman, who'd sold Elektra to Warner for $10 million in 1970 but was now attempting to ease his way out of the music business. Behind it lay the fact that the value of Geffen's Warner shares had slumped dramatically after the sale of Asylum.

"I got completely fucked on that deal," Geffen complained.

"At the same time my company had gone through the roof. I was very unhappy." Ross assuaged David's rage by agreeing to pay him the difference between the two valuations—more than $3 million—but only if he agreed to head Elektra-Asylum. Geffen was livid at being saddled with Holzman's label. His first instinct was to suggest that Atlantic Records combine with Elektra/Asylum and that he and Ahmet Ertegun run the conglomerate as cochairmen. "Everyone else is so stupid," he said to his old mentor. "Let's take over everything—films, music, the lot." Ahmet was receptive to the idea until Jerry Wexler exploded at the proposal. "Jerry Greenberg and I were given our orders from Ahmet and David, and we put together a plan," says Mel Posner, by that time a fifteen-year Elektra veteran. "Then Wexler refused to report to Geffen and that ended the whole thing. David and Jerry were 180 degrees from each other."

"I kind of postponed it, and David got very upset," Ertegun remembered. "But I think everyone thought he would come on too strong and be too disruptive." Geffen disputes that Ertegun cared about Wexler's or anybody else's feelings. "Jerry was never a consideration," he said, adding that "Ahmet is not that considerate of his employees." But Geffen's suggestion that Wexler report to him certainly incensed the man who had signed Ray Charles, Aretha Franklin, and Led Zeppelin. "One day," Wexler told Ertegun, "you'll cry tears of blood from this wonder boy of yours."*

Reluctantly, Geffen—bound to Warner by a five-year employment contract—agreed to become Elektra-Asylum chairman, moving Asylum into Elektra's offices at 962 North La Cienega Boulevard. "Like Asylum, the combined company will reflect my taste and the way I do business," he announced. "The best way to describe Asylum is the sound of serious artists and writers, and that's

---

*Tears of blood, no, but Ertegun certainly grew to despise Geffen. In Dorothy Wade's and Justine Picardie's book about him, *Music Man*, Atlantic producer Tom Dowd recalled a social visit to the home of Geffen and girlfriend Cher. "Look at that creep," Ahmet whispered to Dowd on seeing Geffen in tennis shoes and shorts. "How can he dress like that?" To Geffen, in a louder voice, he exclaimed, "David, what a lovely outfit!"

what the combined company will continue to be, and in that sense I don't think we're in competition with anybody." Almost out of pique, Geffen slashed the Elektra roster Holzman had built up so lovingly over two decades. Among the acts who went were Paul Butterfield, Delaney and Bonnie, and the Incredible String Band. "If you will," says Stan Cornyn, "he robbed the label of its vestigial character."

"Elektra was failing at the time," Geffen counters. "What made Elektra-Asylum exciting at that time was the fact that there were all these fabulous artists on Asylum. The only ones we inherited from Elektra at that time that really had a future were Queen and Carly Simon. The Doors were over, David Gates was pretty much over."

Geffen claimed Elektra had been "heading to oblivion," but the label's artists were dumbstruck by his ruthlessness. For Carly Simon it was as though Geffen had become her wicked stepfather. "I think an era died when Jac left," she later reflected. Judy Collins, long the jewel in Elektra's folk crown, felt so betrayed she refused to speak to Holzman. "I don't want to talk about Geffen," Holzman says now. "He knew and knows how to leverage every event to his advantage. Did it break my heart that Elektra became just another record label? Hey, when you leave a label you leave it." For his part, Geffen maintains that Elektra-Asylum was no more corporate or soulless than Asylum had been. "I thought it was no different," he says. "I thought we were more in control of our destiny when we had our own marketing and distribution, and I thought the company was better equipped to do the job after the merger."

For Elektra's surviving staff, the transition to the new merger environment was jolting. "We suddenly were in a different era," says Mel Posner, who became president of Elektra-Asylum in 1974. "Asylum was Jackson Browne and Linda Ronstadt and the Eagles. Everything broke loose, everything that David had envisioned as part of this thing. It was Laurel Canyon, it was California rock, it was a golden time." But with the bigger bucks came a more corporate approach to the business than Posner had known at Elektra. "We now had someone saying, 'What are you gonna do next quarter? What are your projections?'" he remembers. "I had this Wall Street guy come to me and say, 'How come you have Carly Simon down here for three hundred thousand records when you sold a million records last time?' I said, 'Because I don't know what this record's gonna do.' And he said, 'What kinda business you *got* here?!'"

Having whittled Elektra's roster down to just thirteen acts, Geffen was ever more brazen about his business style. "I was not a person who would say I was in this for the music," he said later. "I used to be offended by people who would tell me they were in it for the music who were just trying to make tons and tons of money. It's all self-serving crap, one way or the other."

Irving Azoff might have agreed. Stepping into the breach when Elliot Roberts fell sick and asked him to take over the Neil Young/Eagles tour, Azoff was making all kinds of bothersome noises about the Eagles' finances. Now that Asylum was yoked to Elektra, moreover, he saw his chance to strike a better deal for the band. He also saw that the Eagles were never going to be huge without having a sharper rock edge to their sound. With his background in the midwestern boogie belt—he'd booked bands such as the James Gang and REO Speedwagon—he suggested both a new producer and an additional guitarist. "The Eagles' problem was that they had a very non–rock and roll, nonthreatening posture," says Denny Bruce. "So now, instead of people saying, 'I really like your music because it's mellow,' the band took it a little step further. And you have to give Azoff credit that they brought in Bill Szymczyk and Don Felder."

When producer Szymczyk—whose credits included Joe Walsh and the J. Geils Band—came on board, the Eagles had already spent six weeks in London with Glyn Johns. All they had to show for another stint with the English producer were two ballads ("The Best of My Love" and "You Never Cry Like a Lover") written with J. D. Souther. "There'd always been disagreement with Glyn," says Bernie Leadon. "Randy Meisner had wanted to fire him after the first album and record the whole album over again. When *Desperado* didn't sell, we were all like, 'It's all Glyn's fault!'" With the very first track Szymczyk cut at the Record Plant—Jack Tempchin's driving, creamy-chorused "Already Gone"—the Eagles found their perfect rock-lite groove. A squealing solo by new guitarist Felder topped the song off perfectly. "'Already Gone'—that's me being happier," says Glenn Frey. "That's me being free." Complementing "Already Gone" and revved-up *Desperado* reject "James Dean" was "Best of My Love," purred by Don Henley. An airbrushed version of the Flying Burrito Brothers, "Best of My Love" was a No. 1 hit eight months later.

On the Border also featured "Ol' 55," a hymn to a vintage automobile by new Asylum signing Tom Waits. Waits was an anomaly on the label. His roots were in jazz and the beatnik era, and he'd gotten his break via the more eccentric L.A. scene nurtured by his manager, Herbie Cohen. But Waits had an influential fan in David Geffen, who checked out his act at the Troubadour several times. "The thing I noticed about Geffen was that I didn't notice anything," says Jerry Yester, who produced Waits's 1973 debut, *Closing Time*. "With Tom he let things evolve." Yester was intrigued by Waits's songs, which contrasted with the introverted poetics of Joni Mitchell or Jackson Browne. Instead Waits painted gritty pictures of people ("Rosie," "Martha"), places ("Virginia Avenue"), and drinking ("Closing Time"), singing them in a dyspeptic gurgle of a voice. Temperamentally he was closer to Tin Pan Alley than to Lookout Mountain Avenue.

"You sit in a room and write songs all day," Waits says. "Then you get these runners and you get the songs out to Ray Charles or Dusty Springfield. I mean, that's what Joni Mitchell was doing, too, it was just that the perception of yourself as a songwriter was changing. And I caught that wave of songwriters garnering understanding and sympathy and encouragement. For a while there, anybody who wrote and performed their own songs could get a deal. *Anybody*. So I came in on that."

"There were a lot of good writers we felt should have the chance to record," says Elliot Roberts, for whom David Blue played Waits's demos. "Waits was a little different, because he'd reinvented himself as a beatnik. He had the luxury of doing that in L.A. because it was an empty white canvas." A confirmed loner, Waits kept his distance from the Canyon in-crowd, preferring to hole up in the seedy Tropicana Motel at 8585 Santa Monica Boulevard. "It wasn't like I was adopted into a family and was gonna be *bathing* with these people," he reflects today. "The idea that you're on a label doesn't mean that we're breaking bread together every morning, and David Geffen's at the head of the table, praying. I'm sure a lot of them were good friends, and if they weren't they probably thought it was good to have it *appear* that they were good friends."

When the Eagles covered "Ol' 55," Waits was not impressed. He made no effort to curry favor with them or their acolytes. Of Messrs. Frey and Henley he later opined that "they're about as exciting as watching paint dry," adding that "they don't have cowshit on their boots—just dogshit from Laurel Canyon." He also took swipes at America, David Crosby, and Neil Young. "'I rode through the desert on a horse with no name,'" he said sneeringly to *ZigZag*. "How about '*I rode through the desert on a horse with no legs*'? That I can see, but the song is so ridiculous. '*I almost cut my hair*' . . . so what? Neil Young is another one who is embarrassing for displaying a third-grade mentality. '*Old man take a look at my life*' . . . that's real good."

"I was a young kid," Waits says with a sigh. "I was just corkin' off and bein' a prick. It was saying, 'Notice me' . . . followed by 'Leave me the fuck alone,' sometimes in the same sentence. I talked to Don Henley about that, and I apologized and I took it all back and we patched it up."

A kindred spirit of sorts was former Elektra star Tim Buckley, another product of the Herb Cohen school. By the time Buckley covered Waits's "Martha" on his 1973 album *Sefronia*, he'd toned down the experimentalism of *Starsailor* and was making more accessible R&B–based music. But he remained at odds with Southern California, as his 1972 album *Greetings from L.A.*—complete with a birds'-eye view of the city under a shroud of smog—heavily suggested. *Greetings* also was aggressively sexual, a long way from the effete and cerebral music that Buckley's singer-songwriter peers were making. Fueled by a diet of blaxploitation movies, songs such as "Get on Top" and "Move with Me" took aim not only at the acoustic bards of the day but also at Buckley's own former incarnation as curly-headed protest poet. "When I saw his L.A. set over a year ago," Chrissie Hynde wrote in *New Musical Express*, "I trotted dutifully to some bowling alley dive to see him and felt my brains drip outta my ears when the virginal innocent of my dreams got on stage and started belting out 'Get on top of me, darlin' woo-maan! Let me see what you learned!'"

Like Neil Young, Buckley argued that the 1960s dream was over, that folk's idealism had little relevance for the decadent 1970s. "It'll get more moronic," Tim told Hynde. "The '70s haven't been too optimistic, have they? But it's going to be great for the avant-garde.

Warhol's going nuts!" And like Tom Waits, he was out of step with the freewheeling L.A. spirit of the Eagles, dancing on the darker side of the California dream.

At Elektra-Asylum, nothing summed up the changes better than Geffen's determination to add Bob Dylan to his trophy cabinet. Cozying up to the Band's Robbie Robertson, David eagerly seized on the fact that Columbia was stalling on a new Dylan deal. He bought a beach house at Malibu, where Dylan now lived. Dylan duly signed to Asylum in late 1973, recording the patchy, undercooked *Planet Waves* shortly before undertaking a high-profile arena tour of the United States with the Band as his backing group. For Geffen, Dylan's signature was the ultimate status symbol. Yet for all the hype of "Tour '74," as the Dylan/Band extravaganza was known, Dylan was angry that *Planet Waves* fared poorly. Furthermore, he secretly despised Geffen. "[Dylan] thought Geffen was just interested in being a celebrity," one source told *Rolling Stone*. After the live double album *Before the Flood*, Dylan duly returned to Columbia. Stinging with rejection, Geffen lashed out at the singer, petulantly declaring that Dylan "should thank me" and adding later that Dylan had been "so mean, so jealous, so cheap, ego-ridden and petty, such an ingrate."

None of this stopped Geffen from crowing about Dylan—not least to his old adversary Jerry Wexler, who'd wanted Dylan himself for Atlantic. When Geffen and Wexler came face-to-face during a lunch at Joe Smith's Roxbury Drive house, the tension was palpable. At Geffen's first boastful remark about Dylan—perceived by Wexler as taunting—the older man retorted by accusing Geffen of paying too much for the artist. David said Jerry was past it, over the hill. At that, Wexler went for him, shrieking, "You'd jump into a pool of pus to come up with a nickel between your teeth!"

"I couldn't believe it," Geffen later said. "No one could. Jerry's face turned red. The veins on his neck looked like they were going to pop. I thought he was either going to have a heart attack or put a knife through my heart. He yelled at the top of his lungs with such violence and vitriol that everyone stopped what they were doing and just held their breath."

"Here was Wexler standing over Geffen, and Geffen has this little smile on his face but looks terrified," Smith remembers. "And

Steve Ross is standing and hollering, Mo Ostin is hollering, and I jump in on Jerry Wexler. Wexler's a strong guy and I'm pulling him back."

Afterward the assembled company sat around the dining room table in shocked silence. Smith's wife stood in the doorway and frantically signaled to her husband. He rose to see what she wanted. Loudly whispering in his ear, Donnie Smith told Joe, "I *told* you we shouldn't have had the cheese soufflé!"

9

After the Thrill Is Gone

Bodacious cowboys such as your friend
Will never be welcome here

—Steely Dan

Show Biz Kids

On March 11, 1974, two men and a woman entered the Troubadour, sat down at a table, and proceeded to work their way through a steady sequence of brandy Alexanders. Croaking a ragged version of Ann Peebles's "I Can't Stand the Rain," John Lennon and Harry Nilsson—with Lennon's companion May Pang between them—slowly became loud and abusive. As satirical comics the Smothers Brothers took the Troubadour's stage, Lennon and friend were in full alcoholic flow. When Rat Packer Peter Lawford asked them to quiet down, John and Harry jeered at him.

Things deteriorated still further when Tommy and Dick Smothers began their act. Nilsson primed the ex-Beatle with lewd remarks to direct at the stage. Matters escalated to the point where—for reasons best known to himself—Lennon taped a tampon to his forehead. When one of the Troubadour's waitresses suggested he shut up or leave, he asked if she knew who he was. "Yeah," the feisty young woman replied. "An asshole with a Kotex on his head." Robert Marchese was standing outside the club when Doug Weston asked him to eject the hecklers. "Soon as I walked in, the place went silent," the pugnacious Marchese recalls. "I put one hand on Lennon's wrist and the other on Nilsson's. I told Lennon he'd changed the world and said, 'Don't you feel like a stupid prick?' And then I took 'em out." Nursing his wounds the next morning at Lou Adler's Bel Air mansion, Lennon was contrite. "He sent Doug a bouquet of roses," says Marchese. "There was a note in it saying, 'Thank the gentleman in the football jersey for handling it so sensitively.'"

Rock stars in general were misbehaving in the Los Angeles of 1974. The city was teeming with drunks and cokeheads. "The really sordid people—the ghouls and the vampires—were the likes of Hoyt Axton," says Nick Kent. "Ringo Starr was always there being unpleasant—"I'm a Beatle and you're not." They'd stand around in bars and just be insulting to everybody else. 'We're the kings of this territory and if we wanna grab your girlfriend's breast we're gonna do it.'"

"By now the innocence had gone," says Danny Hutton, at whose Wonderland Avenue house Lennon and Nilsson regularly showed up. "You'd notice people turning up at your house and you had no idea who they were, and then they'd be over in the corner selling coke. Eventually people realized they weren't creating anymore."

The mood in America was flat. The year 1974 began with lines at gas pumps as the oil cartel flexed its muscles. Patty Hearst had been kidnapped by the Symbionese Liberation Army. The Watergate scandal was unfolding. In America's inner cities, drugs and crime grew to unprecedented levels. "The sixties" were finally over. The fact that most of the superstars of that explosive decade had turned thirty also was hard to avoid. *Rolling Stone* even ran a questionnaire on the topic. Among those interviewed were David Geffen ("If it's this good at 30 I can't wait to be 31."), Joni Mitchell ("This is a youth culture and few people in it know how to age gracefully."), and Randy Newman ("I think I've felt this old for a long time.").

Hollywood, fatigued and burned out, wallowed in the noir nostalgia of Roman Polanski's *Chinatown* and Robert Altman's *The Long*

Goodbye. Warren Beatty was shooting *Shampoo*, set on the eve of Richard Nixon's election victory in the turbulent year of 1968. Far from Laurel Canyon in the exclusive strip of coastline dwellings at Malibu, the glitzy 1970s were in full swing. This was where rock's new royalty dwelled, rubbing sandy shoulders with movie idols and moguls. "The music business had a whole anti-glamour thing for a while," Linda Ronstadt observed. "Now glamour is back in full style. It's starting to get like Hollywood stars again . . . it's suddenly very groovy to look like you're winning, to look like you're very rich."

"We were bedazzled," admits Ned Doheny. "You're with this actress and that producer, and all of a sudden it becomes kind of racy and fun. It becomes the same grinding-out-your-cigar-on-the-outstretched-palms-of-the-poor that you fought so desperately to deny yourself when you were starting."

The perfect sound track for the new milieu of Malibu was Joni Mitchell's *Court and Spark*, whose title track confessed that she "couldn't let go of L.A./city of the fallen angels." This masterful album featured such cool-blue ruminations on success and failure as "Trouble Child" and "People's Parties" plus—in the shape of "Free Man in Paris"—an homage to David Geffen. Uncomfortable with Joni's depiction of him as a man weary of "stoking the star maker machinery/behind the popular song"—perhaps because he preferred to remain out of view as a string-puller—Geffen asked her not to include the song on the album. He was appeased when "Free Man" hit No. 21 on the chart, later noting that *"Court and Spark* was a great achievement for Joni—it catapulted her into the forefront of recording stars."

Building on the expanded, jazzy palette of *For the Roses*, Mitchell on *Court and Spark* kissed good-bye to folk music for good. Sax and woodwind player Tom Scott became her de facto musical director, with his L.A. Express band of adroit, funky sidemen—including drummer John Guerin, her post-Souther squeeze—fleshing out nuanced, bittersweet chords. "I knew she was a heavyweight," Scott told *Rolling Stone*. "[Her] music was far beyond any so-called folk-rock person I'd ever heard."

"No section had been able to play my music," she says. "It was too intricate harmonically and rhythmically. I tried for four projects to

find a band, but it always squashed the music. Finally it was recommended to me that I look for jazz musicians. And I found the L.A.
Express and that worked well."

For those wedded to the idea of Joni as confessor—the maidenly
poet of introspection—*Court and Spark* came as a shock, even a
turnoff. "Joni reached a point where, to my mind, she was writing
about rich people," says Randy Newman. "And I lost interest."
Mitchell herself believed it was as valid to capture the ambience of
Bel Air and Malibu—of "Jack behind his joker/And stone-cold Grace
behind her fan"—as it had been to depict the earthier Laurel
Canyon dames she'd sketched four years earlier. "I can only say that
you write about that which you have access to," she says. "So if you go
from the hippie thing to more of a Gatsby community, so what? Life
is short and you have an opportunity to explore as much of it as
fortune and time allow." For some onlookers, though, Mitchell was
as much a participant in the Hollywood ritual as an observer. "She
was unbelievably snobbish," says Nick Kent. "She'd walk into a room,
and if she needed something she'd get some other rock star to ask
some mere mortal to get her a drink."

Mitchell was at once intoxicated by the elitist exclusivity of
the Geffen/Roxy/Malibu scene and intimidated by it, "coming to
people's parties/fumbling deaf, dumb, and blind." In "The Same
Situation," a womanizing star turns his gaze on Joni, "weighing
the beauty and the imperfection/To see if I'm worthy." In "Car on a
Hill" she waits for a lover who "makes friends easy/He's not like me/
I watch for judgment anxiously." The protagonist of "Trouble Child"
"breaks like the waves at Malibu." To her old Toronto friend, Israeli-
born singer Malka, Mitchell said that the loneliness and insecurity of
Court and Spark were mirrored in the rootless era that cultural commentators had already dubbed the "me decade." "This, I think, is an
especially lonely time to live in," she said. "So many people are
valueless and confused. I know a lot of guilty people who are living
a very open kind of free life who don't really believe that what they're
doing is right."

Joni's compatriot Neil Young also expressed his disillusion. Separated from Carrie Snodgress, whom he'd accused of infidelity, he
moved to an oceanfront redoubt at Zuma Beach and recorded the

stoned, mordant *On the Beach*. His new Danny Whitten was Cajun swamp rat Rusty Kershaw, an alcoholic fiddler/guitarist whose favorite occupation was mixing fried marijuana with honey. The album reflected Young's immobilizing depression at this period in his life. On the desolate blues of the title song he admitted he "needs a crowd of people" but "can't face them day to day." On "For the Turnstiles," accompanying himself on banjo at Broken Arrow, he observed a crowd leaving "bush league batters" to die on the diamond as they make for the exits. "Motion Pictures (for Carrie)" was a swipe at Snodgress, with Neil proclaiming that he "wouldn't buy, sell, borrow, or trade anything I have" to be a movie star. Only on the charged, Manson-inspired "Revolution Blues" did Young overcome his ennui, instead raging at his peers. "I've heard that Laurel Canyon is full of famous stars," he ranted: "Well, I hate them worse than lepers, and I'll kill them in their cars."

One of Young's favorite misanthropes, Jack Nitzsche, was now persona non grata at Zuma and Broken Arrow. Resembling an Amish version of Aleksandr Solzhenitsyn, Jack Nitzsche was in bad shape, drinking heavily and insulting old friends such as Young and the Rolling Stones in press interviews. Young, Nitzsche told *Crawdaddy*, "appeared to be a really hip, of-the-people guy, but it turned out to be bullshit." He added that Neil was "the biggest offender of all of them—his whole lifestyle is the millionaire who doesn't give a shit . . . about anybody but himself." Nitzsche hardly helped his own cause when he presented Mo Ostin with a 1974 solo album—$114,000 worth of session time, no less—that included a sneering put-down called "Little Al," complete with the line "Hey Mo, where you gonna go with that rock in your hip pocket?" Not surprisingly, Ostin declined to release the record. Nitzsche said that Ostin had liked it but added that that didn't mean anything "because he's got a tin ear anyway and he lets the assholes underneath him evaluate his music." He griped that "there's various ways a record company will decide what to push—'OK, this guy's got David Geffen as a manager and he's friends with the Stones.'"

For Nitzsche, Geffen represented the soulless greed of mid-1970s Los Angeles. Phil Spector had ripped him off, to be sure, but now Jack felt a nostalgia for the old-school, seat-of-your-pants biz of the early 1960s that Spector embodied. "It wasn't just entertainment any-more, it was big business," says Allison Caine. "And I think that was truly due to Geffen and Roberts and Azoff and those kinds of people. And it was a nasty business, too, because not everybody was on the same emo-tional, soulful, political plane. There were a lot of rip-offs going on."

"I would say that Elliot and I were in the music business, while David was in the finance business," says Ron Stone. "But it was my apprenticeship and it stood me in good stead. I really did learn about how all this worked—and how to take advantage of your artists."

Don't Interrupt the Sorrow

The year 1974 turned out to be a huge one for Geffen and Asylum. With *Court and Spark* bringing new success for Joni Mitchell, the label's other big acts also were in the ascendant: the Eagles with *On the Border*, Linda Ronstadt with *Heart Like a Wheel* (actually a last con-tractual obligation to Capital), Jackson Browne with *Late for the Sky*. If you factored in Elektra's success with Carly Simon's *Hotcakes*—an album Geffen claimed was the most expensive ever made—then it was a very good year indeed. *Time* magazine hailed Geffen as "the financial superstar of the $2 billion pop music industry."

"It was easily the most exciting time of all," says Mel Posner. "They were all making great music that was being accepted and becoming very popular. The Eagles didn't get to be arrogant until much later on. You had to love Jackson Browne for those songs." *Late for the Sky* was Browne's most assured album yet. With David Lindley's stinging lap-steel guitar behind him, and with backing vocals from the seraphic trio of Don Henley, J. D. Souther, and Dan Fogelberg, L.A.'s poet laureate sang powerfully of his continuing education "at love's pain and heartache school." Yet for all its weighty abstractions, hanging over *Late for the Sky* was a profound feeling of loss. "For a Dancer" grieved the loss of a friend. "Fountain of Sorrow" and the heart-melting title song grasped the inevitability of love's decline and the certainty of loneliness. The closing "Before the Deluge" was an apocalyptic lament for the 1960s dream and its failed Utopia. "I don't even know what I do and I don't quite know how it's supposed to be done," Browne admitted. "Generally it tends to be sort of looking in the rearview mirror. The songs are about a time that is past, or a resolve about the present that in some way relates to the past."

Perhaps the most gratifying success was that of Linda Ronstadt, who finally had the breakthrough LP she'd always wanted. With producer Peter Asher now in full control, *Heart Like a Wheel* was the perfect synthesis of country and California pop-rock. The album was heavy on cover versions of classics—Betty Everett and Hank Williams, Buddy Holly and the Everly Brothers—but also found room for newer songs by J. D. Souther, James Taylor, and Lowell George. It was a formula that would serve Ronstadt well till the end of the decade.

Although Souther played and harmonized on his own, aptly titled "Faithless Love," he was otherwise conspicuous by his absence on *Heart Like a Wheel*: he had, after all, jilted Linda for Joni Mitchell. In his place was guitarist Andrew Gold, who brought a more pop-oriented edge to Ronstadt's sound and would act as her bandleader for the next two years. With the album's success came accusations that Linda was merely a puppet in Asher's hands; it was the same old music-press sexism in a supposedly more enlightened era. The fact that she didn't write her own songs counted against her. "Anyone who's met Linda for ten seconds will know that I couldn't have been her Svengali," Asher remarks. "To me, she was everything feminism was about at a time when men still told women what to sing and what to wear."

Ronstadt's drive and determination to fashion a successful brand of country rock came at a cost, however. Lovers came and went in quick succession, often leaving her emotionally bruised. Longing for children, she knew that motherhood would have to be deferred while her career soared. "Linda had a goal and she got there, but I think she sacrificed a lot of things," says Nurit Wilde. "I think she desperately wanted to have a good relationship and to have children. She had relationships with a number of guys and they just didn't work out."

"It's only natural," Ronstadt told *Rolling Stone*, "[that] all during my twenties that I would be attracted to people that excelled at what I did, people like John David Souther, who I think is brilliant, you know, or Lowell George, whose musicianship is so wonderful. It's

only understandable that there would be fatal flaws in our relationship that would make it just very difficult to trust each other or to
surrender to each other, so to speak."

Ironically, the success for which she'd worked so hard over-
whelmed Ronstadt. "I think it was if anything harder for Linda to
deal with than failure," says David Geffen. Neither she nor Asher was
prepared for the fame that engulfed her in 1975. "I didn't know
what to think," Linda reflects. "People would act so strange, and
they'd come and bother you and have bad manners in public. And
that would cause *me* to respond with a lot of bad manners. Success
distorted personal relationships almost beyond recognition, in a way
that was very damaging." L.A. insiders also felt that Ronstadt had
forsaken her roots in the country rock scene. Among those who
frowned on her new sound was former sideman Chris Darrow. "The
essence of her organic ability got smoothed down too much," he
says. "Peter did her a service and a *dis*service. He made her a lot of
money and he made her a household name, but it might have been
just a little too slick."

If Ronstadt was too slick, where did that leave her old Troubadour buddies the Eagles? If the fruition of all those Troubadour
nights was the Eagles' saccharine "Best of My Love," it seemed tantamount to a sellout. When Bernie Leadon started to feel out of
place in the Eagles, the golden age of country rock was on the wane.
"It's hard to talk about the whole truth, because one doesn't want to
cast aspersions," Leadon says. "On a creative and a personal level,
Frey and I were very upfront with each other about being what he
called 'polar opposites.'" Another factor in Leadon's increasing
estrangement within the Eagles was his reluctance to partake any
longer in the band's round-the-clock drug consumption. "I stopped
doing cocaine, and I stopped smoking cigarettes, too," he says.
"We'd be on the way to the airport and I'd ask Glenn to roll down his
window, and he'd say, 'You roll down *your* window.' It just seemed like
every aspect of our relationship was opposed."

"I think Bernie and Randy felt left out, not just of the buzz but
of the hit songwriting," says J. D. Souther, who spent more time with
Frey and Henley than their fellow Eagles did. "It certainly wasn't
any plan to be exclusionary on my part. It just so happened that

Don and Glenn and I had punched our way out of those hoot nights at the Troub and we'd all survived." On the Eagles' tour plane, while Leadon, Meisner, and Don Felder stayed in the back, Frey, Henley, and Souther sat up front in a little cabin they dubbed "the Tuna Club."

For Leadon, the Eagles' sound was becoming too polished: "Don wanted things to be repeatably, predictably excellent. He didn't like it if, as a guitar player, you played a different lick to the one he was expecting to hear." The control and "predictable excellence" in the Eagles' sound was there for all to hear on *One of These Nights*, the 1975 album that pushed the group into the platinum stratosphere. The title track, a huge hit, was a slick slice of blue-eyed soul that sounded closer to the Stylistics than to the Flying Burrito Brothers. "As you get toward the mid-'70s you start to lose the intimacy of the music," says Domenic Priore. "Suddenly everything was silky strings and what *Rolling Stone* called 'the muffled flump-flump' of the L.A. drum sound. It became a part of that standardized, palatable rock sound so that these guys could take it from the fireplace to the rock arena."

"Lyin' Eyes," an equally big hit, was closer to Gram Parsons but was still a bleached version of Gram's country soul—the Burritos for Middle America. "'Take It Easy' was an amazing song, a road anthem that had a lot to say that was simple and was joyous," says Robert Plant. "But as soon as it got any more commercial and sugary, I checked out. It was too sedate: hippie rebel music coming of age, essentially." Frey and Henley could have cared less what the Led Zeppelin singer thought. They were now living high on the hog atop Bel Air's Briarcrest Lane, with panoramic views over the city whose airwaves they bossed. An endless procession of pneumatic women rolled up to tend to the Butch Cassidy and Sundance Kid of rock. "These were the horniest boys in town, living life without rules or limits," one anonymous ex-girlfriend said. "And still they loved to portray themselves in their music as the underdogs, the taken-advantage-of victims. We used to call that song 'Lyin' Guys.'"

But Henley, twenty-eight and still anxious, was only too aware of the price of success—of the way it insulated him against reality and risk. "Once you get comfortable," he told Crowe, ". . . your universe becomes defined into a little square. Eventually you get to where you don't know what the fuck's going on outside your own little rectangle." This jaded sense of insulation had much to do with Irving Azoff's aggressive form of management. The Eagles' manager took almost all the pressure off his charges, having formed what was now the most powerful rock stable in Los Angeles: Front Line Management. "Irving's 15% of everybody," J. D. Souther noted dryly, "turned out to be worth more than everyone's 85% of themselves."

Having felt let down by David Geffen, Frey and Henley were only too happy for Azoff to exact revenge. For his part, Geffen reluctantly accepted that he would have to play ball with Irving if Elektra-Asylum was to continue making millions out of the Eagles. "If he's ruthless, he learned at Geffen's feet," Henley said of Azoff. "He protected us and is the reason we're one of the few groups that actually made some money for itself rather than for everybody else."

That the Eagles were now the biggest band in America was astonishing to anyone who recalled their lowly beginnings in the Troubadour bar. The fact that their fellow Troub graduates Jackson Browne and Linda Ronstadt also had succeeded made it all the more remarkable. "It *was* extraordinary to think that all this had come out of that scene," says Tom Nolan. Yet for Nolan the changes weren't altogether healthy. "Before, you could just go up and talk to these people at the Troub. After, you had to go through the PR or the manager. It was all different." Success inevitably brought separation and distance, not only between the artists and their fans but also between artists who themselves had felt part of an intimate community. "There was a year or two where we all sort of scuffled and wound up meeting in the same sort of places," Jackson Browne reflects. "Then there was a year when we all made our first records. And then after that we saw each other less and less . . . mainly because we were all working really hard. We stopped passing songs around."

For Linda Ronstadt, "an empty sort of disillusioned hollowness" set in as friendships and creative partnerships dissipated. "To me it always seemed like there was a new wave of people coming in," she recalls. "And that was harmful because it made it feel like you didn't have to take particular care with this relationship, because there was something else that would come along." Los Angeles was the perfect place for the fragmenting of friendships: the fact that Angelenos spent much of their lives in their cars made a degree of alienation inevitable. Ronstadt herself confessed her love for her wheels, which were "a way of guaranteeing your privacy, so you always have that little private area to travel around in."

Success itself was the cause of many a crisis. "These people had been broke and had cared and had sung about it," says Judy James, who'd watched the scene evolve from hootenannys to sports stadiums. "And now they were twenty-four or twenty-five and they had a lot of money. What were they gonna sing about?"

The one member of Asylum's inner sanctum who hadn't made a lot of money was J. D. Souther, whose eponymous 1972 debut for the label had sunk without trace. There was a general feeling that it was time to rally round and make him a star in his own right. Yet one of his problems was that, for all the country-soulful sensitivity of his songs, his public front was arrogant and acerbic. He made little effort to endear himself to anyone outside the sacred circle of the Eagles and their labelmates. "J. D. was a pain in the ass," says Joe Smith, who would succeed David Geffen at the helm of Elektra-Asylum in December 1975. "We had him on tour once, and at the first stop in Boston he sees a store window with Dylan's album featured while his album is in the back. As a result he wouldn't do any interviews with radio stations that day—he stiffed our promotion guy. I said, 'J. D., you're on the label but nobody's gonna give a shit where you show up.'"

Behind the scenes, Geffen plotted to make something happen for Souther. In a throwback to the "supergroup" formation of Crosby, Stills, and Nash six years earlier, he schemed to create a new unit from the union of Souther and two legends who were currently out of a job. One of them was an ex-Byrd, the other a founding member of the Buffalo Springfield. Chris Hillman had quit his day job as a member of Manassas, while Richie Furay had finally given up hope that Poco would ever make it.

The transition into the Souther Hillman Furay Band was a messy one for Furay: though Poco was lured over to the Geffen-Roberts management stable in the fall of 1973, it quickly became obvious to

Richie's bandmates that Geffen's ulterior motive was to pry him apart from the group. "[Geffen] went to Richie and said, 'Listen, you're a star and these other guys are really holding you back,'" said Rusty Young, Poco's pedal steel player. "It was such a sort of unethical, low-type thing, the way he operates his business in general, that the people who were running his management company—John Hartmann and Harlan Goodman—freaked out. They said, 'We can't live our lives like this.'"

"It seemed like a good idea," Geffen said of the group's formation. "I knew them all well—Richie for six or seven years; Chris for almost that long. J. D. already recorded for me. I thought they'd sound great together so I talked them into it. I talked Richie into leaving Poco." On paper, Souther Hillman Furay *was* a good idea: two proven songwriting talents, one rock-solid musical anchorman, augmented by high-caliber players such as drummer Jim Gordon. In practice it was a catastrophe.

"Souther Hillman Furay was David Geffen's attempt to make me mainstream in the wake of the Eagles' success," reflects Souther. "I think he thought I would be the Neil of the group. It didn't work out because it was too much pressure too early on, and Richie and I were just oil and water." The tension between Souther and Furay was evident from the moment the group convened in snowbound Colorado to rehearse songs for their Asylum debut. Souther, a born loner, was incapable of the compromises required to make a rock and roll band work. Refusing to yield when it came to his own material, he greeted Furay's input with barely veiled contempt. "Souther I had to roust out of bed every morning while he cussed about having to sing on Richie's songs," says Phil Kaufman, executive-nannying the band as he had the Burritos and Stones before them. "It was, 'Fuck *him*! I ain't singin' on *his* song!'"

Geffen miscalculated badly when he invited the press to attend the rehearsal sessions. After one spat between J. D. and Richie, the latter announced he was quitting and stormed out of the room. "Who does he think he is?" Furay asked, gasping in disbelief to a writer from *Crawdaddy*. "Why did I leave Poco? For *this*?" As ever, Chris Hillman was caught in the middle. "SHF was Geffen deciding he could take three other guys and show up CSN," he said. "Our debut actually shipped gold and probably came back gold in returns." It was little surprise that the album was devoid of creative juice. Furay's cheery single "Fallin' in Love" cracked the Top 30, and the Asylum promo machine pushed *The Souther Hillman Furay Band* to No. 11. But nothing could disguise the blandness of the songs: this was lifeless country pop shading into homogenous album-oriented rock. The band was dead long before the release of 1975's tepid *Trouble in Paradise*. The SHF story remains a salutary lesson for any prospective supergroup Svengali. "They didn't get together on their own," Geffen conceded. "A lot of the problems came from the fact that this was a figment of *my* imagination." It was not a mistake he would make again.

The Smoker You Drink, The Player You Get

Throughout the early 1970s, the music that dominated the American singles chart was not the hip sound of the L.A. canyons. It was the pop music of Neil Diamond, Elton John, Olivia Newton-John, Barry Manilow, Helen Reddy, Dawn, Diana Ross, and the Jackson 5. The biggest singer-songwriter of the period was squeaky-clean John Denver. Even in the context of the L.A. scene, the top singles acts were the Carpenters and the unfashionable Three Dog Night. The latter, featuring Laurel Canyon legend Danny Hutton, chalked up no less than eleven Top 10 hits between 1969 and 1974.

"There was a real conflict going on at this time," says Mark Volman. "Joni and Jackson and Don Henley may have represented a new social order, but they only represented a minimal part of the real record industry. Probably the most commercially successful L.A. artists of the whole period were Bread and Three Dog Night. I *love* Jackson Browne but he never wrote an 'American Pie.'"

At the other end of the L.A. spectrum was a crop of talented young singer-songwriters who received no airplay at all. "What I most remember about the mid-'70s was that the music I cared about most wasn't getting played on the radio," says Browne. "I'm talking about the best songs by people like J. D. Souther, Eric Kaz, Karla Bonoff. Linda and others recorded them, but Linda had her huge hits with old Motown and Buddy Holly songs."

To Browne's list could be added his good friend Lowell George, who remained proudly out of step with the prevailing flavor of California rock. Like Linda Ronstadt, Browne worshiped George, to the point of asking him to tutor him in the ways of the slide guitar. By 1974 Little Feat were a long ways from the country-blues raunch of their early days. After adding guitarist Paul Barrère, bassist Kenny Gradney, and percussionist Sam Clayton to the lineup, the band was now a "sophisti-funk" powerhouse built around a potent combo of piano, congas, and slide guitar. The signature feel of 1973's *Dixie Chicken* wasn't Laurel Canyon but New Orleans, epitomizing L.A.'s tequila-soaked love affair with the rootsy, sensual South. With Bonnie Raitt and Bramlett on backing vocals, it was country funk chased with bayou soul.

"The Eagles, Jackson Browne and Linda Ronstadt have come to epitomize the L.A. sound and scene," noted local writer Don Snowden. "But Little Feat is perhaps the quintessential L.A. band, far more representative of the city's cultural diversity than the more homogenous styles of their better known compatriots." The Eagles, wrote Snowden, "roam the canyons and mansions as the balladeers of hip L.A." while Little Feat "chronicles life in the lower-rent districts of the City of Angels from the emotional perspective of the bluesman." *Dixie Chicken* did little to help the band's bank balance, however, and they struggled to repay Warner Brothers' faith in them. "The band was stop-start," says drummer Richie Hayward. "Plus there were personality clashes between Lowell and Billy [Payne] that made it uncomfortable but also contributed to the tension you hear on the records."

For *Feats Don't Fail Me Now* (1974), George holed up alone in a studio thousands of miles from California. Built in an industrial section of northern Baltimore, Blue Seas Recording gave George a new lease of life: the classic Feat tracks "Rock and Roll Doctor," "Oh Atlanta," and "Spanish Moon" were hatched there. The album even went gold after the band's managers begged Mo Ostin to push it harder than *Dixie Chicken*. Sadly, though, Feat's expanded lineup proved George's undoing: as time went on, the swampy soul of his songs increasingly lost out to the muso-fusion noodlings of his band. If George's heart lay in the Crescent City, Billy Payne emulated jazz-rock fusioneers Weather Report. Despite some legendary live performances, Little Feat was not a happy camp. Barring George's immortal ballad "Long Distance Love," *The Last Record Album*—with its spooky Neon Park depiction of a postapocalyptic Hollywood Boulevard—sounded tired. Moreover, drugs were decimating the band. "Lowell's hedonism had a lot to do with his losing authority within the group," says Richie Hayward. "He'd hide in the studio for days on end. It made him terribly unhappy."

Along with cocaine, tequila was affecting the canyon scene of the mid-1970s. George was in the studio with the hard-drinking Bonnie Raitt one night when they got in a squabble over who was going to play slide on the song they were recording. George's response was to smash her over the head with a bottle of José Cuervo.

Raitt was a recent addition to the Warner Brothers roster. Steeped in folk and blues, she was a feisty California redhead raised by radical actor parents who lived on Mullholland Drive. For her, Los Angeles was a city of jarring unreality. "It's just ironic," she told Ben Fong-Torres, "having been raised to understand what's wrong with this country and yet [to] live in this fantasy world where there's barely any black people." At fifteen, Raitt and a friend sang protest songs at a Troubadour hoot night. "I was like Miss Protest . . . the fat Joan Baez." But she spent her formative musical years on the coffeehouse circuit in Cambridge, Massachusetts. Two bluesy albums into her Warner career, she moved back to L.A. and began 1973's *Takin' My Time* with Lowell George in the producer's chair. "I was hanging out with Lowell and Van Dyke Parks," Raitt told John Tobler. "We ended up all living in Laurel Canyon at the time. Lowell and Van Dyke are very good friends, and I was a big fan. Warner Brothers has a whole mafia, I'm sure you're aware, and . . . I became ensconced in it."

The problem with being ensconced in the Warner-Reprise "mafia" was that it made Raitt uncertain of her musical direction. Juggling vintage blues with contemporary singer-songwriter covers, she was hard to market. "There are tons of women coming out now and we're all tapping the same source," she told writer Penny Valentine. "We write very little ourselves and we all do a little country, a little John David Souther, a little Eric Kaz."

L.A.'s love affair with the South also shone through on albums by

Randy Newman (*Good Old Boys*) and Ry Cooder (*Paradise and Lunch*), both released in 1974. *Good Old Boys* was a superb song suite about Dixie prejudice and Yankee hypocrisy, inspired by the Louisiana that Newman had experienced as a boy. "The North pretended to moral superiority in their racial behavior," Newman says of the song "Rednecks." "And thirty years later the North is *still* segregated. L.A. is segregated. *I* don't see black people in L.A." Playing guitar on *Good Old Boys* was Cooder, who—like Newman—combined a love of outmoded southern music with a jaundiced view of Southern California as the playground of privileged Caucasians. Coproduced by Lenny Waronker and Russ Titelman, *Paradise and Lunch* was as playful as it was soulful. Its droll and meticulous arrangements of blues and gospel obscurities underlined once again that Cooder was not a singer-songwriter. Five years later, at a time when by his own admission he was "mourning past styles," he decried "this white, middle-class, introspective stuff—people elevating their neuroses to mythic heights."

If Newman and Cooder were examples of California artists who felt guilt and anger over the injustices and inequalities of life in L.A., out-of-towners Steely Dan contributed their own running commentary on the city they'd adopted as a musical base. From "Show Biz Kids" (1973) to "Babylon Sisters" (1980), Donald Fagen and Walter Becker laid waste to la-la land in songs of peerless wit and sophistication. "For subject matter L.A. was certainly a lot of laughs, as it has been for many a satirist," says Fagen. "Neither of us really liked it, because we just weren't L.A.-type people. Nobody seemed to understand us there."

"To say that we were on the fringes of the scene would be to exaggerate our closeness to it," admits Becker. "We had our own little private rolling bubble of *schlock* that insulated us from the canyon cowboy thing." Like Randy Newman, Becker and Fagen liked to write in character, placing odious or politically suspect sentiments in mouths other than their own. Like Newman, too, they set sinister notions to bewitching hooks and grooves, in this case sung in a voice—Fagen's—that was more Stephen Sondheim than Don Henley.

Steely Dan's nod to African American music (jazz, R&B, funk) was part of rock's mid-1970s drift toward more urban sounds, including disco. Symptomatic of this shift was the second album by J. D. Souther. Produced by Peter Asher, *Black Rose* (1976) was a big-budget affair boasting the country-soul gems "Faithless Love" and "If You Have Crying Eyes," but it also featured the vanilla funk of "Midnight Prowl"—with Lowell George on slide guitar—and "Black Rose" itself. (Good as the record was, it failed to yield a hit. "Geffen and I fought about it," Souther admits. "I spent as much time and money as anybody else and then didn't really bust my ass to make him singles.")

"Music started to become very urban-oriented," Don Henley told *Rolling Stone*'s Anthony DeCurtis. "[It was] a reflection of the concrete and the steel and the pace. So we didn't, to paraphrase Joni Mitchell, get back to the garden." At the start of 1975, significantly, Mo Ostin hired Blue Thumb's Bob Krasnow to head up the black music division that Warner had never had. When Krasnow brought in a slew of black music greats—George Benson and Chaka Khan, Funkadelic and Bootsy Collins—it was clear that Burbank was no longer just about white singer-songwriters. Black music even penetrated Elektra-Asylum. When Joe Smith took over from David Geffen at 962 North La Cienega, he expressed concern that his blackest artist was Joni Mitchell. "I inherited that whole Geffen roster—Jackson, Joni, Linda, the Eagles, J. D. Souther," Smith says. "When they put Elektra and Asylum together, it had the Southern California/Laurel Canyon thing sewn up." Smith went to Steve Ross and pleaded his case for broadening the Elektra-Asylum catchment. "Geffen and Holzman never wanted black music on Elektra," he says, "but my mandate was to grow the company because nobody made records. I mean, Jackson Browne made a record every time Halley's Comet came over."

One night Smith had dinner with Ross and told him Elektra-Asylum needed to adapt. He added that it would cost a lot of money. "Steve said, 'It's your company—do it.'"

Paradise in Trouble

Bizarrely, given his lack of movie-studio credentials, David Geffen left Elektra-Asylum to become vice chairman of the Warner film division, reporting to his old boss Ted Ashley. *Variety* described

Geffen's role as "an executive perspective . . . the sort of billet that a crown prince might occupy."

"David wanted to carry on with Asylum but he became Ted Ashley's assistant and then executive VP of Warner Communications," says Elliot Roberts. "What he really wanted to do was take over Warner Communications, but Steve Ross was too formidable at that time." Geffen's desire to depart the rock and roll business had more than a little to do with Messrs. Crosby, Stills, Nash, and Young. The quartet had made him millions of dollars but had tested his patience to the limit.

The last straw was the band's reunion tour in the summer of 1974. "Every one of us had had some degree of success alone," Stephen Stills said of the decision to reunite, "but none of us had come across as a playing unit with the solidity that we had together." When the four members discussed it with Geffen and Roberts it was decided, in Stills's words, to "take it to the max, the nth degree." What that meant was something no band had attempted before—a summer tour of outside stadia, to be promoted by San Francisco veteran Bill Graham. Accusations that the quartet were only in it for the money weren't helped by an offhand quip Stills made to Cameron Crowe. "We did one for the art and the music, one for the chicks," he said. "This one's for the cash."

The scale of the operation shocked even insiders such as Carl Gottlieb. "Suddenly the money was just huge," he recalls. "Life was pretty extraordinary for those at the top of the food chain. Touring became an exercise in indulgence." Carrying an entourage of eighty-four people, the tour was a grotesque exercise in conspicuous consumption—of drugs, food, fuel, women, and any other perks of the profession that were available. For Stephen Stills in particular it was designed to prove that CSNY were bigger than Dylan, the Stones, or Led Zeppelin. "CSNY wrote the plan," he later boasted. "And no one has done anything since to equal what we set down in 1974."

The "Doom Tour," as David Crosby called it, also was designed to make money. Unfortunately, most of the cash was squandered on the road. Graham Nash calculated that out of the $11 million the dates grossed, each member of the quartet wound up with no more than

$300,000. "[The tour] brought in the largest grosses and probably least returns to the artists of any tour that has ever gone out," road manager Mac Holbert told Carl Gottlieb. "Everything that everybody thinks about rock and roll actually happened on that tour, and the amazing thing is that a lot of that excess was not utilized by the principals or even the band." Maybe, but Holbert recalls being summoned to one of Crosby's hotel suites and having to talk with the singer while girlfriend Nancy Brown fellated him. Crosby joked with Cameron Crowe that he planned to write a book called *A Thousand and One Ways for a Musician to Lose His Way and Forget What He Was Doing*.

Crosby's and Stills's coke-fueled megalomania was too much for Geffen. Stills, wearing football jerseys and still prey to drugged delusions that he'd served in Vietnam, wound up in a fistfight with Elliot Roberts and was obliged to seek new management. A year later, when he'd parted company not only from Roberts but also from Atlantic Records, he tried to justify his behavior to journalist Barbara Charone: "Sometimes I get a little drunk, sometimes I get a little out of it, sometimes I get out of tune onstage, but that's something that shouldn't be dissected. Sure I've got a little bit of that fuck-you attitude, it's my militaristic background."

On the 1974 tour, all four principal members of CSNY lived inside their own private cocoons. Neil Young, sunk in his *On the Beach* depression and hiding between a giant pair of aviator shades, declined to travel on the band's jet and instead motored from venue to venue in an old camper van. "[The tour] was a huge money trip," he later stated, "the exact antithesis of what all those people are idealistically trying to see in their heads when they come to see us play." Onstage there was little musical cohesion, just the expected sparring between Stills and Young and a relentless need by each member to assert himself above the others. This usually meant turning up the volume controls on their guitar amplifiers.

Although Stills and Young included smatterings of new solo work—Stephen's from his forthcoming *Stills*, Neil's from the as-yet-unreleased *Tonight's the Night*—when Young asked the audience at Long Island's Nassau Veterans Memorial Coliseum if they wanted to hear a new or an old song, a unanimous roar of "Old song!" rang out. Backstage, after Neil had ripped into the incendiary "Revolution Blues," Crosby politely suggested he dispense with his "dark shit numbers."

By the time the Doom Tour wound up at London's Wembley Stadium in mid-September, CSNY were in bad shape. Joni Mitchell, the chief support act for her old lovers, recalled that people were doing so much cocaine they walked onstage with nosebleeds. Bassist Tim Drummond sported a baseball shirt emblazoned with the stipulation "NO HEAD, NO BACKSTAGE PASS." Young fleetingly excelled—particularly with an electrifying "Don't Be Denied"—but Stills was in posturing guitar-hero overdrive for almost the entire set.*

Back in California there was much licking of wounds. Plans were made to start work on a third Crosby, Stills, Nash, and Young album. In mid-December Neil Young was en route to join the others at Sausalito's Record Plant studio when he made an abrupt about-turn and drove home, never to return. CSN were dumbfounded and enraged in equal measures. "Neil utilized CSN as a springboard for his own career," Graham Nash grouched to Dave Zimmer. "As soon as CSN didn't suit him he sloughed us off like an old snakeskin."

But Nash and Crosby had also had enough of Stills, who got into a heated argument with Nash over a harmony part for a Stills song called "Guardian Angel." Another fight, over Nash's song "Wind on the Water," led to Stills cutting the song's master tape with a razor blade. One night, with both men on short fuses, Nash kicked Stills out of his house. By early 1975 he and Crosby had decided to carry on as a duo, recording the *Wind on the Water* album in the early summer.

Each member of CSNY was dealing in his own way with the problems afflicting every major band of the period. The constant friction of insecure, drug-damaged musicians trying to keep things together had undone the Beatles, as it would undo many other groups. "It's not easy when you take someone who's basically right

---

*"Carry On" was dedicated to the memory of Mama Cass Elliott, who had suffered a fatal heart attack in London only weeks before, on July 29. She was thirty-two.

out of puberty and who becomes a millionaire responsible to no one," says Carl Gottlieb. "I mean, it's tough enough when you learn the lesson in middle age, but these guys got that experience very early on."

For Neil Young the 1974 tour seemed inadvertently to kick-start his emergence from the long depression of 1973–1974. Early in 1975 Carrie Snodgress was asked to leave the Broken Arrow ranch, with Young's mother, of all people, overseeing her expulsion. *Homegrown*, an unreleased album in the *Harvest* vein, exorcised the pain of life with her. Instead of releasing it, however, Young decided that now was the time to let loose the ragged glory of *Tonight's the Night*. With the album out—its disheveled intensity splitting fans down the middle—Young once again saddled up with the Horse, replacing Danny Whitten with new rhythm guitarist Frank "Poncho" Sampedro. "We're playing in a place where we're getting together to make up for what is gone and try to make ourselves stronger and continue," Young told Bud Scoppa. Purchasing a new Malibu home on Sea Level Drive, Young shook off the heavy gloom of the previous two years. "Somehow I feel like I've surfaced out of some kind of murk," he told Cameron Crowe. For Horse bassist Billy Talbot this was "an idyllic time." Neil, he said, was "just sparkling."

The aural result of these festive months was *Zuma*, an album of sometimes gleeful unburdening released in November 1975. "Don't cry no tears for me," Neil almost jeered on the opening track. On "Danger Bird," "Drive Back," and the molten "Cortez the Killer" one heard his playing at its splintered, squalling best, carving like a blade through the dense stomp of the Talbot/Ralph Molina rhythm section. If *Zuma* suggested bright daylight after the slumped small hours of *Tonight's the Night*, the feel was just as loose and spontaneous. "There are all kinds of different ways to work," says Linda Ronstadt. "Some people are oil painters and some people are sketch artists. Sketch artists like Neil have gotten a lot of the credit in this culture."

If *Zuma* was about rebirth, the L.A. music scene was mostly in the grip of drugs and disillusion—an end-of-an-era emptiness that infected virtually everybody. In three short years, drugs had killed Danny Whitten, Gram Parsons, the Association's Brian Cole, and the

GTOs' Miss Christine. When twenty-eight-year-old Tim Buckley died of a heroin overdose on June 29, 1975, it was as though the era of hoot nights and coffeehouse troubadours had gone forever. The nadir year was 1975—twelve months of flatulent music and bloated self-indulgence following on the heels of military meltdown and political sleaze. "For me the '60s really ended with the fall of Saigon," says Carl Gottlieb. "The '60s was sort of 1967 to 1975."

In *Long Time Gone*, the autobiography he cowrote with Gottlieb, David Crosby remarked that "the idea that rock and roll would be an ongoing lifetime pursuit hadn't really sunk in." Nobody had thought this far ahead, and now they weren't sure where music was going. If rock was the sound track of disenfranchised, rebellious youth, what did it mean to be a pampered millionaire in your early thirties? Perhaps it was at this point that the world stopped looking to musicians for answers and instead started to live vicariously through their heroes' hedonism. "What happened then was the forerunner of what it is now," says Jan Henderson, who'd roadied for Neil Young and others. "It was *me me me* and I'll stomp the shit out of you if I don't get it."

Nothing said Me Decade better than cocaine, a drug that turned the dweebiest music-biz nebbish into an übermensch. "Cocaine," says Linda Ronstadt, "made people deaf, it made people dead, and it made people real obnoxious." Waddy Wachtel, who replaced Andrew Gold as Ronstadt's guitarist/bandleader, says he never took a day off unless he couldn't score: "I thought that was how it was sup-posed to be. You get up in the morning and you fuckin' find a bump, and you keep lookin'. By nighttime, you don't *want* any food—who gives a shit about dinner? You wanna find more blow."

Nor was it just musicians who were at it. All of the major record labels in L.A. were crawling with coke fiends. "I remember when it started really taking over," says Bud Scoppa, then working for A&M Records. "By the end of 1975 there'd be a weekly marketing meeting in a big conference room, and people would get up and leave the room all the way through the meeting. *Everybody* was doing it. I thought it was devastating." Cocaine was no stranger to Asylum or Geffen-Roberts Management, either. Artists and staffers alike seemed to be wired around the clock. "For a while no one could say a bad thing about it," says Elliot Roberts. "No one realized that it was *totally* addictive, that it ate your cells away and made your nose fall off. Everyone was like, 'Wanna bump?' It was so *mainstream*."

"Drugs did decimate this business," says Ron Stone. "It sent lifestyle shock waves through the whole system. Someone like Crosby was clearly having a lot more fun than you were supposed to, and he paid a very heavy price for it. David *ate* life—wine, women, and song. And some of it didn't agree with him." Crosby himself was now a shadow of the scenemaker who'd inspired so many musicians in the L.A. of the mid-to-late 1960s. The motormouth of 1969–1970 missed the supergroup status of CSNY and began slipping into full-scale addiction. On "Homeward through the Haze" he sang of "my first hollow echo/In the halls of praise" and took veiled swipes at Young ("Samson") and Stills ("Little Caesar").

Drugs were merely part of the fallout from the CSNY tour, which took so much out of Elliot Roberts that he decided, early in 1975, to scale back his involvement in management. "We'd tried to be an agency," Roberts recalled. "That turned out to be a very bad idea. It took all of my life and my first marriage." At the height of his artists' careers Roberts chose to break up the company, keeping only his original clients Neil Young and Joni Mitchell and renaming his business Lookout Management. The rest of the Geffen-Roberts pie was sliced up with Geffen's blessing. America went with Harlan Goodman and the already axed John Hartmann. Crosby and Nash, who released *Wind on the Water* in October 1975, turned their affairs over to Leslie Morris, who'd assisted Geffen and Roberts from the early days at 9130 Sunset. Meanwhile, the Eagles' fortunes remained in the hands of Irving Azoff. "I don't think David or Elliot realized quite *how* big the Eagles would be," says Ron Stone. "Otherwise they'd have been more upset when Azoff walked off with them. When Irving called up to say he was leaving and taking the Eagles with him, Elliot is reputed to have sneered, 'Who are the Eagles?'"

"I was like, 'Shit, this changes everything,'" says Bernie Leadon. "I remember going to Elliot and saying, 'Dude, you're on top of the world. Why are you doing this?' And he basically said, 'When you've got enough, you've got enough.' He just wanted a quieter lifestyle." Leadon, who maintained a low profile in Topanga, wondered if he didn't secretly want the same thing. As weary of Learjets as he was of Glenn Frey's coked-out braggadocio, he sometimes yearned for the old country-rock days of easy-rolling poverty. Randy Meisner, too, chose to spend whatever time he could with his family back home in his native Nebraska.

Even new boy Don Felder preferred to stay out of the Eagles' limelight. "I'm glad that Don and Glenn project a lot of the band's L.A./Hollywood charisma," the guitarist told Cameron Crowe. "Even though Glenn's from Detroit and Don's from Texas, they really know and live the L.A. scene. Personally I don't feel comfortable living there." As was so often the case in bands, lack of communication undermined what little camaraderie had existed between Frey and Henley on one hand and Leadon and Meisner on the other. Things came to a head during the recording of *One of These Nights*. When Leadon presented the band with a song he'd cowritten with his girlfriend, Frey and Henley greeted it coolly. The fact that the woman in question was Patti Davis, daughter of Ronald Reagan, gave apparent validity to their suspicion of her. On December 20, 1975, Leadon officially quit the Eagles, to be replaced with indecent haste by Azoff client Joe Walsh. It was the final piece of Irving's puzzle: how to turn the Eagles from a country rock group into a stadium-busting guitar band. Though he'd begun his own solo career two years before, former James Gang axman Walsh was the perfect fit.

"Bernie wasn't ruthless, unlike Frey and Henley," says Chris Darrow. "It didn't surprise me that he was the first guy to leave, nor that he just sort of disappeared for a while and became somebody else." Similarly deficient in ruthlessness was Bernie's old bandmate Gene Clark, who had been dropped by A&M Records after the failure of *White Light*. Torn between his self-destructive urges and the deep spiritual yearning that pushed him to flee L.A. for the coastal northern California town of Mendocino, Clark found himself back inside the Asylum circle after his involvement in the Byrds' reunion album. Perhaps because his songs were the only substantial things on that record, David Geffen decided to offer him a solo deal.

Clark had a bunch of remarkable new tracks ready—songs he'd written up in Mendocino in an almost meditative state of reflection. Inspired by his readings of key Zen texts, they were long and mystical pieces, some of them bearing scant relation to Clark's usual country-folk style. Emanating from *No Other* was the comparative calm of life with his wife, Carlie, and son, Kelly. "There's a lot of bull-shit about Gene writing those songs in a cocaine haze," says his biographer John Einarson. "He was actually very spiritual and reflec-tive at that point in his life, and enjoying family life in Mendocino." Even the gorgeous "From a Silver Phial," a song that stayed true to Clark's country-folk style, turned out not to be a blatant cocaine reference.

Things changed, however, once Clark was installed at L.A.'s Village Recorders in March 1974. With Geffen's money to burn and manic producer Thomas Jefferson Kaye at his side, Clark made one of the most ambitious albums to come out of California in the mid-1970s, as rich with detail as *White Light* had been pared and minimal. A host of stellar sidemen—the Section players included—built the tracks into orchestral mood suites.

"No Other," the album's title track, seemed to derive from blax-ploitation funk of the time, benefiting from the wailing gospel-style chorus of Claudia Lennear, Cindy Bullens, and Ronnie Barron. "Strength of Strings" and "Lady of the North" were epics of haunt-ing beauty. "Silver Raven" was a hymn to cosmic transcendence and renewal. Though Clark cited the influence of the Rolling Stones' *Goat's Head Soup*, this was music out of synch with almost everything happening in rock in 1974.

A hundred thousand dollars later, Clark presented *No Other* to David Geffen at the Elektra-Asylum offices on North La Cienega Boulevard. To the singer's mortification, Geffen was horrified that his investment had bought him a mere eight tracks. "What can I do with eight songs that are six minutes long?" Geffen yelled at Clark. "Make a proper fucking *album*!" A crestfallen Clark watched as Gef-fen petulantly dropped the acetate in his bin. Gene tried to explain that there were five tracks that he and Kaye hadn't been able to fin-ish, but Geffen was in no mood to pump more money into the proj-ect. Clark never quite recovered from blowing his big shot at a comeback. He failed to land another major-label deal, and his drink-ing began to get worse. As Linda Ronstadt and the Eagles ascended on L.A.'s escalator, Gene slowly descended with the other mavericks who didn't fit the record industry's round holes. "He became an increasingly tragic figure, just because he lasted longer than the other guys," says Bud Scoppa. "He didn't leave as handsome a corpse."

Another cult artist on Asylum, Jimmy Webb, was at least marginally less self-destructive than Clark. But he was still struggling to shake off the MOR (middle of the road) tag that hung around his neck, even after Joni Mitchell made guest appearances on *Letters* (1972) and on *Land's End* (1974), his debut for Asylum. "I was instinctively drawn to people like Joni, because I knew she was a real artist," he says. "But I wasn't welcomed with open arms. You had to prove that you were a dyed-in-the-wool left-winger and that you'd been to the barricades. I'd achieved fame with very outspoken middle-of-the-roaders like Glen Campbell, who'd had John Wayne on his television show. So I came into this world of exquisite artists that I really wanted to be on intimate terms with, having to explain that I, too, used drugs and was really very hip."

"There was this whole idea that you had to be hip in order to do okay," says Linda Ronstadt, another fan of Webb's. "Jimmy achieved a great deal of success but was way, way out of the popular mainstream and was shunned and castigated for what was perceived as his lack of hipness."

Hipness wasn't an issue for Joni Mitchell, but critics turned on her when she released 1975's *The Hissing of Summer Lawns*. This masterful record, a more than worthy follow-up to *Court and Spark*, was derided for its supposed pretensions, both musical and literary. The influence of Tom Scott and the L.A. Express was deemed to be too far-reaching. It niggled reviewers that Joni employed synthesizers and Burundi drummers on the sinister "Jungle Line." There was unease that she was photographed on the album's inner sleeve in a swimming pool, implicitly an image of privilege. Turning her withering gaze on the bourgeois malaise of the suburbs ("The Hissing of Summer Lawns," "Harry's House") and the general dependency of women ("Edith and the Kingpin"), Mitchell also took a poke at the hypocritical complicity of artists in "The Boho Dance"—a dissection of the phony bohemianism of the L.A. scene. The poetry was stunning, the music sleek and diaphanous. "*Court and Spark* was about as

popular as it got," she reflects. "After that everything was compared unfavorably to it. *Hissing of Summer Lawns* was too jazzy, generally."

"Joni was coming off the heels of *Court and Spark*," says Ron Stone. "She turned left without signaling and the audience went straight on. And I think it hurt her feelings, her sense of who she was creatively." For Stone this was "an extraordinary moment," a turning point that Mitchell experienced as a wounding betrayal. "From that moment forward," he says, "the very special admiration that her audience came to her with changed. I think Joni has challenged people as much as Neil Young has, but it's less appreciated."

Asylum's oddest man out, Tom Waits, burrowed still deeper into the persona he'd created of a booze-sozzled Beat Generation hepcat. Both *The Heart of Saturday Night* (1974) and the live *Nighthawks at the Diner* (1975) chronicled the low lives of barflies, con artists, and fast women. Both albums kept a defiant distance from the world of denim cowboys and anguished confessors. "David Geffen rang me up one day and told me about Tom," says producer Bones Howe. "He said Jerry Yester had tried to cut him as a sort of folk artist, which he wasn't. He said, 'I think he's got a lot of jazz and beat influences.' And that was the beginning of eight years of really good friendship." Howe says his working relationship with Waits mainly came down to talking. "Preproduction always took place in some dumpy restaurant, talking about songs and music and people." *Nighthawks*, specifically, stemmed from Waits's concept of parodying beat-era poets who'd read their verse in front of jazz bands.

Waits by now was a permanent resident of the Tropicana Motel. Here he surrounded himself with a circle of cronies who included local legend Chuck E. Weiss. "Tom's whole act was Ratso Rizzo from *Midnight Cowboy*," says Robert Marchese, whom Waits name-checked on 1976's *Small Change*. "And he alienated himself from that Troubadour/Asylum scene. He didn't hang around them, but he liked being in the spotlight."

The glory days of the Troubadour were over anyway. In the words of Eve Babitz, who'd propped up its bar for the best part of a decade, the club was "a shell of its former self" whose thunder had been stolen by the Roxy on Sunset. On June 12, 1975, Doug Weston closed the club to rebuild and refurbish it. "I'd lost the basic lines of communication to the industry," Weston said. "I needed to come back into my club myself."

Three months later, the alumni of the Troubadour's heyday convened to play a show at the vast Anaheim Stadium. In a kind of denim apotheosis, a climax to the entire Laurel Canyon era— the Eagles, Linda Ronstadt, Jackson Browne, and J. D. Souther took the stage together on September 28, 1975, and harmonized sweetly for fifty-five thousand sun-kissed fans. It didn't get much bigger than this.

"How do you get from Longbranch Pennywhistle to Learjets and cocaine psychosis?" asks Jac Holzman, who'd known Browne as a fresh-faced kid from Orange County. "Money. That's how you get there. It's just the money, and everybody goes crazy."

Holzman pauses to recall a line from Graham Nash's song "On the Line." "Graham sang, 'Is the money you make worth the price that you pay?' The answer is there in the question. He had it in that song."

10

Go Your Own Way

Music lasts . . . a lot longer than relationships do.

—Neil Young

The Last Waltz

When Linda Ronstadt first met Warren Zevon, he stood before her mumbling and scratching his head. She thought he was a psychopath. In fact he had been on the L.A. music scene—as a keyboard player and occasional song supplier—for almost a decade.

The product of an improbable and unhappy union between a Russian Jewish father and a Scots-Welsh Mormon mother, Zevon had gotten a toehold in mid-1960s L.A. as half of folk-pop duo lyme & cybelle and as the writer of nonhits for the Turtles. "Warren was a good friend of ours," says the group's Mark Volman. "He was signed to our label and we did songs of his such as 'Outside Chance' and 'Like the Seasons.' He lived in a really small apartment in the center of Hollywood and we were tied together with him through some really introspective and experimental evenings . . . all wrapped around drugs."

A stint as bandleader for the Everly Brothers followed the release of the unrepresentative, Kim Fowley–produced *Wanted Dead or Alive* (1970). Though he held it together onstage, Zevon was a heavy drinker. "The road, booze and I became an inseparable item," he told *Rolling Stone*. In the context of Los Angeles, though, he was intellectual and acerbically funny. "As I got to know Warren I realized how clever he was," says Peter Asher, who produced Linda Ronstadt's version of Zevon's "Hasten Down the Wind." "He was writing about a different L.A., plus his songs were more literary. J. D. Souther was well read, too, but his songs were written more from an emotional perspective."

In 1972 Jackson Browne, who'd first encountered him at Barry Friedman's Laurel Canyon house in 1968, bagged Zevon a publishing deal with David Geffen's Companion Music. But the contract lapsed a year later and Warren drifted north to San Francisco. Returning to L.A. in 1975, Zevon was arrested for drunk driving in front of the Troubadour. With his second wife, Crystal, he moved to Spain, only to be summoned back in the early fall by the promise of a recording deal with Asylum.

Produced by Browne between October 1975 and February 1976, *Warren Zevon* was markedly different from the music of his Asylum peers. Like Tom Waits, Zevon visited unglamorous parts of L.A. that Joni Mitchell and the Eagles barely acknowledged. The antihero of "Carmelita" was "strung out on heroin/On the outskirts of town," meeting his dealer downtown on Alvarado Street. The voice of "Join Me in L.A." name-checked the Tropicana "on a dark and sultry day." The morose boozer of "Desperadoes under the Eaves" was holed up in the shabby Hollywood Hawaiian Motel on Yucca and Grace, oppressed by the very sun that drew the world to Southern California. Closer to the Sunset Strip vortex, "Poor, Poor Pitiful Me" lampooned the self-obsessed, sex-addicted L.A. rock star of the day, cruising the Rainbow Bar and doing the dirty with a masochistic chick at the Hyatt. In the immaculate "French Inhaler," with its sweet Frey/Henley backing vocals, Zevon hung with "these phonies in this Hollywood bar."

It was as if a Laurel Canyon version of Elvis Costello had suddenly surfaced in the midst of Asylum's pervasive complacency.

"The people who inhabit the commercial context in which Zevon makes his music," wrote Greil Marcus, "aren't merely integrated into the system . . . they *are* the system." A bridge between the singer-songwriter era and the new age of punk's Angry Young Men, *Warren Zevon* uncovered the sleaze and dread that lurked in Hollywood Babylon. "I don't know whether L.A.'s changed or whether I have," Zevon said. "I'm an Angeleno, having spent the bulk of my life here. I'm living in a cave right now—this hotel suite with no windows— [and] it's not untypical of the way I am."

Early in 1976, Jackson Browne was himself preparing to record an album that would give vent to the ennui and despair fueling Zevon's best songs. It was no coincidence that Asylum's favorite son had just married Phyllis Major, the blond beauty he'd stolen from Bobby Neuwirth. "Phyllis was very pretty, very sweet, and very suicidal," says Nurit Wilde. "I don't think she *knew* she was suicidal, but she told me once that she'd tried to kill herself by taking overdoses of LSD." Browne had barely begun work on *The Pretender* when, on March 25, 1976, Major OD'd on barbiturates and died. Left to raise his fourteen-month-old son, Ethan, on his own, Browne was devastated. Yet certain songs on *The Pretender*—"Your Bright Baby Blues," "Here Come Those Tears Again"—make clear that relations between the couple were already fraught.

Notwithstanding Jon Landau's thumping disco-rock production, *The Pretender* was understandably suffused by grief and loss. The sense of time passing and life fading from one's grasp—passing under "sleep's dark and silent gate"—was harrowing. A song for Ethan, "The Only Child," was unbearably tender in its imprecations to "take care of your mother." On the title track Jackson revisited the capitulation of *For Everyman*'s "Before the Deluge," surrendering to a state of happy idiocy as he forsook the illusion of "true love." "I didn't want to say the things that I went ahead and said after all," Browne confessed when *The Pretender* was released. To the *New Musical Express* he admitted that the album was "just about being totally lost." Browne also attested to Zevon's influence on the record. "He really influenced my thinking," he told Paul Nelson. "That line, 'I'm going to be a happy idiot' . . . that's not exactly the Browne touch, is it?" Years later, the *Village Voice* would describe Zevon as Browne's bad conscience. "I think it was hard for Jackson," says Craig Doerge, who played piano on "The Pretender." "Everybody always kept wanting 'Late for the Sky' over and over and over."

Six years later, British writer Richard Cook described *The Pretender* as "the apotheosis of Browne's art . . . the summary and summit of post-Woodstock despair." Despair was ubiquitous in Los Angeles in 1976. In this centennial year in America's short history, the first epoch of rock and roll was drawing to a close. An inertia had set in just as a new generation was rising up to slay its musical fathers. When, on Thanksgiving Day, Neil Young and Joni Mitchell joined Bob Dylan, Van Morrison, and others in the glorified wake that was the Band's "Last Waltz," it was as though they were waving good-bye to rock's golden age.

"The whole scene got a lot more desperate," said Ned Doheny. "You can hear a lot of it on the Eagles' records. There's a lot of bile in those records, a lot of arrogance." With perfect timing, Glenn Frey and Don Henley created their magnum opus around the concept of California itself—specifically "our interpretation of the high life of Los Angeles." *Hotel California*, released in late 1976 on the back of a huge-selling greatest-hits album, was both a flaunting and a self-flagellation, an album that found room for "Life in the Fast Lane" *and* "The Last Resort" ("where the pretty people play, hungry for power"). "This is a concept album, there's no way to hide it," Henley said. "But it's not set in the old West, the cowboy thing, you know. It's more urban this time." While Frey reveled in his fame and money, the neurotic Henley was consumed by the longing for credibility. He was desperate to show that he had a political conscience, that he could write songs worthy of Jackson Browne or such L.A. satirists as Randy Newman and Steely Dan. Yet curiously Henley also argued that it was the Eagles' job "to get people off, not to get them crazy and militant." He claimed that people were "concerned with their own individual lives, and getting their own personal trips together, and that's what we write about."

Neil Young, interestingly, numbered himself among the Eagles' fans. "If only for perfectly capturing the feel of L.A.," he opined in 1975, "the Eagles are the one band that's carried on the spirit of the

Buffalo Springfield." The group's slickest album to date, *Hotel California* was dominated by its bewitching title track. Born of a cod-reggae guitar riff cooked up by Don Felder, "Hotel California" was as creepy as it was catchy. The hotel in question stood as a metaphor for Hollywood itself, a place haunted by the ghosts of movie idols. "We never glorified California," Henley said in 1989. "We were running it down from the beginning."

An equally big hit from *Hotel California*, the brilliant "New Kid in Town," was a more veiled swipe at the L.A. dream. Substantially the work of J. D. Souther, it never mentioned the music business per se yet encapsulated the paranoia of stars who felt that at any moment their thunder might be stolen by the Next Big Thing. "We were in a solid gold shitter," Souther says. "You only got to pass through this as an artist if you were willing to see the surroundings from the perspective of *some* degree of reality. That's what "New Kid" was about. We were writing about our own replacements."

In the case of the Eagles, the replacement in question was Bruce Springsteen, the New Jersey boy whose 1975 album *Born to Run* was being hailed by dozens of critics as the savior of music. When Springsteen stormed the Roxy in October 1975, the Eagles' stage act of "loitering onstage" suddenly looked self-satisfied. For a music press that regarded Springsteen as the harbinger of rock's second wind, the Eagles embodied everything that was complacent about Southern California and its fast-lane attitude.

Yet for American youth of the mid-1970s, the Eagles were the dream of rock and roll incarnate. *Hotel California* became a state of mind—the land of blue jeans and cocaine, mirror shades reflecting palm trees, blond hair flowing from convertibles on freeways that led to the ocean. "It's very romantic," Don Henley told Tom Nolan. "It gets a hold on you. You love it and you hate it. It's a whore, but it's a fertile mother. L.A., to me, is what America is all about." Living the fast-lane life with Don and Glenn was Irving Azoff, who encouraged their hedonism both on and off the road. Glenn Frey's contemptuous, coked-out arrogance was part of what Azoff was selling.

"There was a certain intensity," Glenn Frey said in the late 1980s. "Perhaps a lot of it was bluff, because we were really just a bunch of skinny little guys with long hair and patched denim pants and turquoise." Azoff wasn't bluffing, however, when he took David Geffen and Warner Brothers to court to regain control of the Eagles' publishing. Alleging conflict of interest, he sought $10 million in damages, along with a retroactive royalty increase from the first album onward. Geffen claimed the suit was a "bullshit" issue designed to extract a new deal out of Warners, adding that he'd given Don Henley "the half he owned in the first place" after buying out his contract from Jimmy Bowen. But two years later Warners settled out of court and the Eagles retrieved their copyrights.

"Irving Azoff went about his career in a way that I didn't approve of," says Geffen. "He thought it was good to create distance between the clients and the record companies. He created a sense of paranoia. And I've always resented the fact that he was responsible for two of the only three lawsuits I ever had in my entire life—one with the Eagles and one with Don Henley."

Azoff also had to deal with the escalating tensions within the band. The relationship between Frey and Henley itself became so volatile that Henley left Briarcrest Lane and moved into Azoff's home in Benedict Canyon. "There were always tremendous difficulties with the Eagles' songwriting," says Geffen. "About who was more important and who was less important—things that happen in groups generally. I had a number of difficult times with them that were unpleasant for me, and I'm sure it was unpleasant for them, too."

Frey and Henley disagreed on several key issues: Frey was a supporter of Joe Walsh, for example, while Henley rooted for Don Felder. At least both men were united in their growing dislike of Randy Meisner, who'd long been a moody outsider. From Meisner's perspective—that of a man who'd been present at the dawn of country rock—the Eagles were now a cold-blooded cash cow, run by Azoff like a minicorporation. When the *Hotel California* tour kicked off in January 1977, the hostility between band members became unbearable. A fistfight broke out backstage between Frey and Meisner at a show in Knoxville, Tennessee. Back in L.A. at tour's end, Meisner was axed from the Eagles. With exquisite irony his replacement was the more affable Timothy Schmidt, who'd taken over the bass player's spot when Meisner left Poco.

Meisner, though, was doing well next to Gene Clark, one of the Eagles' original country-rock inspirations. After being dropped by Asylum, the haunted folk genius again lost his way. He landed a deal with Robert Stigwood's RSO label, but *Two Sides to Every Story* (1977) was a limp letdown after *No Other*. Roger McGuinn, by now a born-again Christian, took pity on his old bandmate and allowed him to stay at his house. Recovering from the nightmare of Souther Hillman Furay, Chris Hillman joined them to make it a trio. Notwithstanding the ignominious failure of the 1973 Byrds reunion, McGuinn, Clark, and Hillman started with high hopes and even pop aspirations. But the trio was fated not to last. During sessions for their 1979 debut album in Miami, Clark and McGuinn fell out and stopped speaking. During the recording of the trio's second album, Clark started using heroin. At a Roxy show by McGuinn and Hillman, Gene rolled up soused and gate-crashed the stage to sing the Byrds' "Feel a Whole Lot Better." The duo glowered at him. "Last time I saw Gene he was way out of his mind," says Robert Marchese. "I wouldn't let him into the Troubadour. I had to tackle him about six times. He kept running up and I kept tackling him and putting him down. I had to call the cops."

In the early 1980s, in a reprise of his years in Mendocino, Clark left Los Angeles to clean up in Hawaii. But even clean, he was a wreck. A cash-in 1985 tour to commemorate the twentieth anniversary of the Byrds—featuring neither McGuinn, Hillman, nor Crosby—was a disaster. "Gene was not in good shape," recalled John York, who played bass on the tour. "His stomach was really hurting him from all his past abuses and he could sometimes drift off into a mood."

In 1977, during a show at London's Hammersmith Odeon, McGuinn asked Clark, "Do you wanna be a rock and roll star?" Clark turned his head toward McGuinn and uttered the single word "No." The Tambourine Man had had enough.

Bombs Away, Dream Babies

If *Hotel California* and *Their Greatest Hits 1971–1975* confirmed that the Eagles were the biggest band in America, a challenge now came from an unlikely source. A radically revamped version of British blues-boom stalwarts Fleetwood Mac was reinventing the L.A. sound after incorporating native Californians Lindsey Buckingham and Stevie Nicks into its lineup.

Buckingham was a guitarist who'd played with Warren Zevon in the Everly Brothers' touring band. Nicks, his girlfriend, was an ethereal blonde who'd scraped by in L.A. as a waitress and cleaner. When Fleetwood Mac's cofounder, Mick Fleetwood, heard the couple's 1973 album *Buckingham-Nicks*, he was impressed and suggested they amalgamate with his band. Already signed to Reprise, the new Fleetwood Mac quickly hit big with 1975's self-titled album. Tracks such as "Landslide" and the Top 20 hit "Rhiannon" established Nicks's bewitching style of AOR folk-pop, laying the groundwork for "Dreams," "Sara," and a clutch of other classics.

Late in 1975, Nicks received an unexpected call from Don Henley, who'd just ended a tempestuous relationship with interior designer Loree Rudkin. Having just broken up with Buckingham, Stevie was easily seduced. To *Rolling Stone* she gushed that Henley and Frey were "the Errol Flynns and Tyrone Powers" of the 1970s. "Don taught me how to spend money," she told Courtney Love years later. "I just watched him. He was okay with, say, buying a house like *that*, or sending a Learjet to pick you up." Henley's Learjet pickups became so legendary in the business that he himself later coined the phrase "Love 'em and Lear 'em." Nicks must have felt the bittersweet irony of that phrase when she became pregnant by Henley and found herself pressured into having an abortion. "Sara," her heartbreaking song about the aborted child, became a Top 10 hit for Fleetwood Mac in late 1979.

Rumours, the follow-up to *Fleetwood Mac*, was a vinyl soap opera about the hurt, betrayal, and partner-swapping within and outside the group. With two couples—John and Christine McVie, Lindsey Buckingham and Stevie Nicks—splitting up, and Mick Fleetwood and his wife, Jenny Boyd, also on the outs, Fleetwood Mac was not a happy camp. "One of the things that gave the group this tension was you had these two couples who were 75 percent of the way to being broken up, and the group just accelerated what was happening anyway," Buckingham recalled. "Stevie and I and John and Christine broke up in the middle of *Rumours*. We were doing something important; we had the tiger by the tail, and you had to categorize your emotions to make that work."

In 1977, *Rumours* outstripped the sales of even *Hotel California*, holding the No. 1 position in America for an astonishing thirty-one weeks. "It was party time," remembered Mick Fleetwood. "It was a roller coaster to the nth degree, full hog. Ferraris, jets everywhere. We were living the life, and people didn't talk about the music, just twelve million albums, then eighteen million albums."

"That was the music business at its decadent zenith," Glenn Frey told Anthony DeCurtis of the annus mirabilis that was 1977. "I remember Don had a birthday in Cincinnati and they flew in cases of Château Lafite-Rothschild. I seem to remember that the wine was the best and the drugs were good and the women were beautiful and, man, we seemed to have an endless amount of energy."

Not everybody was so entranced. For Linda Ronstadt, whose own sales continued to skyrocket with *Prisoner in Disguise* (1975) and *Hasten down the Wind* (1976), the scale of the success wasn't necessarily conducive to music of quality and distinction. The sometime darling of the Troubadour was especially unhappy playing the "sheds" on the summer tour circuit. "I didn't feel coliseums were appropriate places for music," she says. "I liked the money, but it wasn't musically satisfying." Like Neil Young and Joni Mitchell before her, Ronstadt experienced deep depression even as her success escalated. High-profile boyfriends—Mick Jagger, Albert Brooks, California governor Jerry Brown—came and went. Her weight constantly fluctuated as she ate to soothe her anxieties. She saw therapists and jogged on Malibu Beach.

For Ronstadt, the success of the 1970s was marred by cocaine. "There was a direction that friendships could have gone in with people like Waddy that was enormously complicated by drugs," she says. "It made us all less responsible." Los Angeles was finally losing its allure for Linda. "L.A. is real comfortable," she said, "but on the B side of that is that things tend to get a little too laid-back and mellow." Unlike many of her contemporaries, she had one eye on the musical rebellion fomenting on the East Coast and on the other side of the Atlantic.

When punk rock finally showed up in L.A., it was too close to home for the exalted stars of Elektra-Asylum. The mainstream L.A. record business, for whom the Roxy was home away from home, barely acknowledged the Ramones, let alone local punk bands such as the Germs.

"Corporate rock became the name of the game in the mid- to late '70s," says Lenny Waronker. "The business became very sexy—a cash-cow business. And when you become a good business, *look out*." The days of soullessly formulaic AOR—of Boston, Journey, Foreigner, REO Speedwagon—were just around the corner. While he had cash cows of his own—James Taylor, Gordon Lightfoot—Waronker and production partner Russ Titelman persisted with less commercial artists. In 1977 they even managed to coax a smash hit, the withering and much-misunderstood "Short People," out of Randy Newman. The song was partly a swipe at Irving Azoff, who'd overaggressively pursued Newman in an effort to add him to his Front Line collection.

Waronker and Titelman also coproduced a new artist signed to Warner Brothers in 1978. Rickie Lee Jones had been in L.A. since 1973, where she'd settled after a rootless, restless upbringing in Chicago and Phoenix. A born bohemian, she fell in with a new family of outsiders who included Tom Waits and Chuck E. Weiss. By late 1977 Jones was stepping out with Waits—a passionate relationship fermented by alcohol—and performing in small clubs around town. She had a nasal little-girl voice and used it to sing jazzy songs about shady street people, close cousins to her boyfriend's characters. Lowell George fell in love with her "Easy Money" after hearing her perform it in Topanga. Former Warner staffer Sal Valentino played it for Waronker. "She came in with massive attitude, to the point where you were kind of intimidated," Lenny remembers of their first meeting."

Jones's breakthrough hit was born of hanging out at the Tropicana Motel. "Chuck E.'s in Love" was a sassy sketch of the bumbling Weiss, who'd never imagined that he would inspire a hit record. *Rickie Lee Jones* (1979) wasn't all flip boho cool, though. There was delicate nostalgia in "On Saturday Afternoons in 1963," torchy intensity in "Company" and "Coolsville." "Rickie in some ways filled the hole left by Joni," says Ron Stone, who later managed her. "What they had in common was their sheer artistry."

Rickie Lee Jones was altogether slicker than the latest offerings from her beau. For Tom Waits, *Small Change* (1976) had been a significant leap forward—the move from noir pastiche to great art. Grittier and less sentimental, the album marked a switch in his approach that was sustained through *Foreign Affairs* (1977) and *Blue Valentine* (1978). "*Small Change* was really the beginning of the poetry," says Bones Howe, the album's producer. "We sort of moved away from the idea of *songs*."

Waits was small potatoes to Joe Smith, whose performance as head of Elektra-Asylum relied to an unhealthy degree on the Eagles. Unfortunately for Joe, the follow-up to *Hotel California* would be a long time coming. Leveraging the band's power, Irving Azoff tantalized Smith, dangling the prospect of the album before him and then yanking it away as he pried more money and points out of Elektra-Asylum. Desperate to meet his projections for 1978, Smith pressured Warner to settle the Geffen lawsuit and offered a million-dollar bonus if the band delivered the album for the Christmas market.

It didn't help Smith that the chemistry within the Eagles had become toxic. Worst of all, Frey and Henley started to dislike and distrust each other, finding it hard to write as a result. Underneath everything, the pressure of trying to match or top *Hotel California* was crippling them. When the aptly named *The Long Run* finally saw daylight in September 1979, only two of its tracks were credited solely to the Frey-Henley partnership. On the Eagles' world tour of 1980, the bickering between Frey and Henley continued. In mid-October of that year they put the band out of its multimillion-dollar misery.

On November 21, Henley was arrested after paramedics treated a naked sixteen-year-old girl suffering from drug intoxication at his house. It was life imitating Randy Newman's "It's Money That I Love." Henley was charged with unlawful possession of marijuana, cocaine, and quaaludes and contributing to the delinquency of a minor.

Almost a decade later, he cowrote "The End of the Innocence," a pained elegy for love before it becomes corrupted by money and status. "The dream was unfulfilled," he told Anthony DeCurtis that year. "We turned from a society that was concerned with our brothers and our fellow man into a society that was very self-centered, self-concerned, about money and power." "The Heart of the Matter," another track on *The End of the Innocence*, was a magnificent articulation of life postdivorce cowritten by Henley and J. D. Souther, both waking up to the wreckage of their love lives. The song's key line was the perfect rebuttal to the whole greed-is-good ethos of the 1980s. "How can love survive," Henley asked, "in such a graceless age?"

End of the Innocents

Despite being recorded later, Rickie Lee Jones's own version of "Easy Money" appeared before the version Lowell George included on his 1979 solo album *Thanks, I'll Eat It Here*. Given the state the Little Feat singer was in, this wasn't entirely surprising. Among the problems cocaine caused him, the drug made Lowell obsessively perfectionistic in the studio. "He was really a tortured person," says Billy Payne. "If we hadn't brought Teddy Templeman back in for *Time Loves a Hero* I think Little Feat might have collapsed."

"There was a picture of me and the band on the sleeve of *Time Loves a Hero*," Templeman says. "Lowell has his hands down in it, and they're covering about five grams of coke. Michael McDonald came in the studio one day and watched Lowell snort a whole gram in one nostril. He went, 'Jesus Christ, I can't believe what I just saw!'" *Time Loves a Hero* (1977) was a poor album by anybody's standards: the dearth of songwriting inspiration was there for all to hear. For its only halfway decent track, "Rocket in My Pocket," Templeman was forced to bring Bonnie Raitt into the studio to play a slide solo. It was a ploy that worked: Lowell promptly hauled himself out of bed and drove to the studio to prove he could do better.

George's health was plummeting, especially with the onset of chronic drugs-related hepatitis. Living up in Topanga with his beleaguered second wife, Elizabeth, and daughter Anara, he was increasingly becoming a burden. "I think he was blind to the support he'd had," says his friend Martin Kibbee. "He was pretty callous and self-centered in those last months." When Billy Payne and Paul

Barrère went on the road with singer Nicolette Larson—a girlfriend of Neil Young's who'd just scored a Top 10 hit with a version of his "Lotta Love"—Little Feat was effectively finished.

Featuring the usual West Coast session suspects, George's solo *Thanks, I'll Eat It Here* was a typical L.A. album of the time: lots of horns and gospelly organ, backing vox galore, all very Boz Scaggs. Best of all was the piningly lovely "20 Million Things," the equal of any of Lowell's other great ballads. *Thanks* never cracked the Top 50 but it did get the Fat Man back on the road in the summer of 1979. Martin Kibbee thinks George was consciously leaving his old friends behind. But just before he left, Lowell visited Billy Payne. "He came out to my house in the Valley on his motorcycle," Payne recalls. "It was the middle of the night, and his eyes were as big and black as saucers. He came to the door and started to say something, but he just couldn't say it. His eyes started to brim with tears, and then he just walked away. That was the last time I ever saw him."

When *Musician*'s Bill Flanagan interviewed him on June 18, 1979, the thirty-four-year-old Lowell George was very sick. He weighed almost three hundred pounds, he was suffering from bronchitis, and he was doing vast amounts of coke. Eleven days later, after performing in Washington, D.C., he suffered a fatal heart attack in his hotel room. His wife and his road manager were at his bedside waiting for paramedics to arrive.

Back in L.A., Lowell's friends couldn't believe he'd gone. Many tears were shed at his funeral, and then again at a tribute concert where Linda Ronstadt, Jackson Browne, and J. D. Souther harmonized heartbreakingly on a song called "Peace Divine." A total of $250,000 was raised for Lowell's widow and daughter. "It was like everybody foresaw their own doom," says Souther. "Nobody was exempt. You started to see rock and roll as such a transient thing, a fragile little membrane holding us aloft above the spikes and barbs of all of this absurdly decadent experience."

Less publicly lamented was the death of Souther's former paramour Judee Sill. What exactly happened to that brilliant singer-songwriter in the years after her second album, *Heart Food* (1973), remains vague. Sessions for a third album, *Dreams Come True*, took place at Mike Nesmith's studio in Van Nuys but were only released (in a mix by Jim O'Rourke) in 2005. "I heard many years later that she despaired of her relationship with David Geffen and went back to drugs," says Jim Pons, who'd produced her first album. A series of car accidents, one involving being rear-ended in Hollywood by none other than Danny Kaye, necessitated a series of excruciating operations on her back and the use of heavy painkillers. Because of her criminal record, doctors would not prescribe her legal opiates. It was only a matter of time before she was scoring again on the street. Sill was found dead at her North Hollywood home on November 23, 1979, the cause of death given as "acute cocaine and codeine intoxication." Many of her old musical associates did not find out till the following year.

Three years later, on December 2, 1982, Sill's former Asylum labelmate David Blue died of a heart attack in New York while jogging around Washington Square. His body lay in a morgue for three days before anyone thought to look for him.

Drugs, death, disillusion: it wasn't as though Los Angeles had a monopoly on these matters. But because it remained the unholy grail for every fame-hungry dreamer in America, the City of the Angels boasted more than its fair share of people falling from grace and plunging into a spiritual void. Where once the Sunset Strip and Laurel Canyon had represented the movement for change and social justice, now they were merely part of the entertainment vortex of money and celebrity.

Some artists struggled more than others with this loss of meaning. The most trenchant account of the hollowness at the heart of late 1970s rock came in the shape of Jackson Browne's *Running on Empty*. Recorded on the road during Browne's summer tour of 1977, the album was about being a rock star—about sex, drugs, and tour buses, and the intermittent feeling that rock and roll had become an empty ritual. On the title song he yelped, "I don't know about anyone but *me!*"—a disarming postscript to the era of self-realization.

Recorded in a Holiday Inn room in Illinois, with David Lindley scraping away on an acrid fiddle, the track "Cocaine" was an update of the Reverend Gary Davis blues song with "additional lyrics" by Browne and Glenn Frey. The sound of Jackson snorting a line and then giggling with Lindley could be clearly heard after they finished the song.

In the late 1970s and early 1980s, however, Browne was one of the few major stars to stay true to the 1960s commitment to social and political change. His close involvement with movements such as MUSE [Musicians United for Safe Energy] showed that "Mr. L.A." could think beyond self. "A lot of people subscribe to the Oscar Wilde notion that it's not enough to succeed if one's friends don't fail," says J. D. Souther. "I think Jackson is one of those people, like Bonnie Raitt, who's genuinely thrilled when their friends do well."

Browne also continued to be generous with his time, putting his own recording career on hold as he set to work on the second album by Warren Zevon. The songs on 1978's *Excitable Boy*—"Accidentally Like a Martyr," "Lawyers, Guns, and Money," and more—were as savage as anything on Steely Dan's *Gaucho* or Randy Newman's *Little Criminals*. "With a cold eye, a boozer's humor, and a reprobate's sense of fate," Greil Marcus wrote, "this California rounder put Los Angeles back on the rock and roll map and nearly blew the Malibu singer-songwriter crowd right off it." Featuring the one-hit-wonder novelty "Werewolves of London," Zevon's sophomore work was coproduced by Browne and Waddy Wachtel. "Jackson figured that the way Warren and I related to each other would really help him," Wachtel says. "With that album, Henley would be there one night, Frey and Souther the next. It was the thing to do: drop by Warren's session. We were drunk out of our asses all the time."

But Zevon's drinking wasn't a laughing matter, especially since he and his wife, Crystal, now had a baby daughter. "Much of 1977 was a nightmare," he confessed to *Rolling Stone*'s Paul Nelson. "Crystal and I lived apart for several months, and I was seriously into the noir life—vodka, drugs, sex. Somehow I got the songs written for *Excitable Boy*. I thought my days were numbered in fractions." The success of *Excitable Boy*, which went Top 10 in the spring of 1978, only made matters worse. During a show in Chicago, Zevon was so drunk he fell offstage and spent the rest of the tour either on crutches or in a wheelchair. In the late summer, Warren, Crystal, and Ariel Zevon moved north to the plush coastal city of Santa Barbara in an effort to distance him from said noir life. The ploy didn't work. After getting embarrassingly drunk at his own housewarming party, Zevon repaired to the four-track studio he'd built in the guest cottage and started firing a .44 Magnum at the portrait of himself on the cover of *Excitable Boy*.

The incident got Zevon into rehab in Santa Barbara, with Jackson Browne and Paul Nelson driving up for an intervention. But the following year Warren was drinking again, and his marriage ended. When Nelson visited him in Santa Barbara he brought along one of Warren's heroes—the great crime writer Ross MacDonald, a long-time resident of the city. It was as though Lew Archer, MacDonald's compassionate private investigator, had himself arrived on a mercy mission. "I went to the door and Lew Archer was there, come to save my life," Zevon told Tom Nolan.

If Jackson Browne was alarmed by Zevon's alcoholism, he was horrified by the state of his old mentor David Crosby. The fact that he shared so many political ideals with Crosby made it even more painful to watch the walrus-mustached one—in the company of his similarly addicted girlfriend Jan Dance—degenerate into chronic cocaine addiction. Waddy Wachtel, who'd first seen the drug up close in Crosby's company, now witnessed the full denouement of the cocaine adventure. At a Crosby recording session, the ex-Byrd sat in his vocal booth with a freebase pipe, refusing to share his drugs with anyone. "I opened the door and it stunk of ether," Wachtel remembers. "I said, 'Can I steal a little bump?' And he went, 'I dunno, man, I don't have enough.' I said, 'Excuse me? There's a small mountain here!' He said no. I said, 'Okay, let's both remember this.'"

Crosby's escalating drug use ran in parallel with his disillusion at the failure of the hippie revolution he'd helped to foment. "[There is] the unrealized shame of having failed the world and not knowing what to do about it," he'd told *New Musical Express*'s Steve Turner in 1976. He felt profoundly threatened by the end of the singer-songwriter era, buoying himself with fantasies of its revival. "This year," he said, "is going to be the year of the singer-songwriter again because Mitchell's going to come out again, Paul Simon's going to come out again. . . . James is going to come out again."

The hardest thing for Crosby to accept was that CSNY was over. If he and Graham Nash still harbored hopes that the supergroup would come together properly again, a reunion at Miami's Criteria studio in the spring of 1976 soon dashed them. Stephen Stills and

Neil Young had been working at Criteria since January, having revived "the spirit of Buffalo Springfield"—Stephen's words—at a Stills gig in Stanford, California, the previous November. The ongoing love/hate relationship between Stills and Young baffled many onlookers. They seemed unable to go their separate ways, as if addicted to their own power struggle.

When Stills-Young became CSNY redux, all went tolerably well until Crosby and Nash returned to Los Angeles in May. But the moment their backs were turned, Stills and Young made the bilateral decision to revert to their duo project and wiped their colleagues' vocals from the tapes. Crosby and Nash were shattered, and made no secret of their feelings in the press. "How many times," Nash said, "can you keep going up and saying, 'Okay, I'll stand here while you hit me again, but just don't hit me as hard as you did last time'?"

"I could see the control that Neil wanted to exert over everybody, and it was an unpleasant thing to see," says Nurit Wilde, the photographer who'd known Neil since his first days in L.A. "When he had that little cabin at the top of Laurel Canyon he was vulnerable and needy and he would ask for advice and unburden himself to you. Boy, that disappeared very quickly. I don't think Neil has much of a soul. Maybe he saves it for his music."

"I just left a trail of destruction behind me," Young admitted with a faint hint of pride. "On the other hand, what I would have had to do to *talk* to all those people and go *through* all that would've replaced three or four of those records in energy." He also used the phrase "trail of destruction" in Jim Jarmusch's 1997 documentary *Year of the Horse*, adding that the resulting "guilt" was "the hardest part" of his survival as a rock star.

If Stephen Stills thought he had Young to himself in 1976 he was sorely mistaken. Sixteen shows into the Stills-Young Band tour that summer, the Canadian bailed. "Dear Stephen," he wrote in a note to his erstwhile confrere, "funny how some things that start spontaneously end that way. Eat a peach, Neil." Joe Vitale, who drummed on the tour, remembers Young's sudden departure as mystifying. "It's like when you look at a happy marriage and everything just seems peachy keen," he says. "And then suddenly there's a divorce." Two weeks after Neil's exit, actual divorce papers were served to Stills by Veronique. These were dark days for the former prime mover in Buffalo Springfield.

Shortly before Christmas of that year, Crosby, Stills, and Nash booked into L.A.'s Record Plant studio to start work on what would be 1977's *CSN* album. When recording sessions continued in Miami the atmosphere was happy and healthy. Stills's and Crosby's demons were temporarily at bay; Stills even laid off the booze. For all three men it was tantamount to picking up where they'd left off before the entrance of Neil Young.

By now Young's about-faces were becoming almost predictable. With three hundred thousand copies of his three-album retrospective *Decade* ready to be shipped in 1977, he asked Mo Ostin to hold off on releasing it for another year. After 1978's mellow (and very successful) *Comes a Time* he became wildly enthusiastic about punk rock. Always swift to align himself with the latest incoming threat, he instinctively knew that the only way not to become a dinosaur was to attack his fellow stegosauruses. "I'm like a dinosaur with a large tail," he told Richard Cook. "I look around, there's not many dinosaurs left, just a lot of smaller animals moving very fast. And it's their vibrant energy that I need to stay alive."

Punk attracted Young almost to the degree that it aggravated the likes of David Crosby and Stephen Stills. "As soon as I heard them saying, 'God, what the fuck is *this*?!,'" Young said, "I knew it was a sure sign right there that they're going to bite it if they don't watch it.'" In "Thrasher," a song on 1979's *Rust Never Sleeps*, he described CSN as "lost in crystal canyons," adding cold-bloodedly that they were "just deadweight to me."

Rust Never Sleeps was not only a collection of great songs ("My My, Hey Hey," "Pocahontas," "Powderfinger") but also implicitly a statement about what rock and roll meant after twenty-five years. The point was made even more unequivocally in the concert film of the same name shot at San Francisco's Cow Palace in October 1978. With its giant amplifiers, hooded roadies, and use of announcements from the sound track to *Woodstock*, *Rust Never Sleeps* questioned the legacy of rock culture even as it enacted its ongoing role as tribal theater.

When *Rolling Stone* named Young "Artist of the 1970s," it was not hyperbole. More than any of the other iconic 1960s artists who'd followed through in the subsequent decade (Dylan, Lennon, the Stones), Young had best caught the turbulence of the time, the pain of the comedown, and the intensity of the burnout. As the decade turned, he looked forward with a strange uneasiness. "The '80s are here," he told Cameron Crowe. "I've got to just tear down whatever has happened to me and build something new. You can only have it for so long before you don't have it anymore. You become an old-timer . . . which . . . I could be . . . I don't know."

"It's better to burn out than fade away," Neil sang searingly on "Hey Hey, My My" (and "My My, Hey Hey"). Yet he himself chose the love of his wife and two sons—both of whom suffered from cerebral palsy—over the suffering for art that incinerated so many of his restless fellow seekers. For Young, that meant "shutting the door on my music" for most of the 1980s, hiding behind disguises and reactionary stances.

Crosby, Stills, Nash, and Young weren't quite extinguished, however. When, against all the odds, David Crosby cleaned up his act after serving jail time, the overblown *American Dream* (1988) was pieced together at Young's Broken Arrow ranch in northern California. Even then, David Geffen was still involved in their careers and playing them off against each other. "Crosby, Stills, and Nash are *old fat farts!*" he screamed when Ahmet Ertegun declined to pay Young 50 percent of the album's royalties. "The only one with any *talent* is Neil Young!" Again the reunion fizzled out. This time it was Stills who was ensnared in freebase hell. "Do I think cocaine destroyed CSNY?" Young asked. "Absolutely. Cocaine and ego."

Joni Mitchell—Young's compatriot and the sometime lover of Crosby, Stills, and Nash—took a different route out of the mid-1970s. After the press turned on *The Hissing of Summer Lawns* she made the parched *Hejira* (1976), a travelog of an album written as she drove alone across America and featuring the sinewy playing of bassist Jaco Pastorius. "*Hejira* was not understood until years later," she says. "That was a really well-written record, but it was kind of kissed off. People that take it traveling, it really gets to them. Listening to

'Amelia' while driving across the desert can be a very emotional experience." That song, in which Mitchell compared her journey to that of the vanished Amelia Earhart, was as much a self-portrait as a haunting meditation on the fearless 1920s airwoman; a message, she said, "from one solo pilot to another . . . sort of reflecting on the cost of being a woman and having something that you must do."

Flying so high, Mitchell slowly alienated herself not only from her audience but also from her friends: the word *hejira* was an Arabic term for the breaking of ties. On Bob Dylan's Rolling Thunder tour of 1975 she clashed with Joan Baez and challenged the radical chic of Dylan's campaign to free boxer Rubin "Hurricane" Carter. In Memphis she inadvertently caused offense to aging Beale Street bluesman Furry Lewis when he misunderstood a remark about the open tunings they shared. If *Hejira* demanded more from the listener than *Court and Spark* had done, the self-indulgent double LP *Don Juan's Reckless Daughter* (1977) left Mitchell fans bemused. And she went still farther with *Mingus* (1979), her homage to a dying jazz giant. "Somebody asked me how I'd allowed Joni to make *Mingus*," recalls Joe Smith. "I said, 'You don't *allow* Joni Mitchell. If Joni Mitchell wants to make a Mingus album she makes it. If she's not happy that it doesn't sell, she'll make a more commercial album next time.'" Come the 1980s, Joni did exactly that. Her first release of the decade was 1982's *Wild Things Run Fast*, as close to a pop album as she has ever made.

Along with her friends Neil Young and Don Henley, Mitchell was now signed to a new label called Geffen Records. The label's namesake had himself all but quit the entertainment industry in late 1976. Hating the Warner movie division, David left his job as vice chairman on November 10. He learned quickly how fickle friendships were in Hollywood, and how unpopular his arrogance had made him. At Clive Davis's post-Grammys breakfast at the Beverly Hills Hotel, music-business lawyer Brian Rohan physically attacked him and was widely applauded for it.

To say that Geffen was burned out would be an overstatement, but when in August 1977 he was diagnosed with bladder cancer—mistakenly, as it turned out—he decided it was time to slow down. "I had had enough at that moment," he says. "I'd had too much of the music business, and I needed to get away from it for a while." For three years, based in New York, he taught and lectured on business. By night he cavorted with Calvin Klein and the Studio 54 crowd. But in 1980 he was ready to make a comeback.

Handsomely backed by Steve Ross and Mo Ostin, Geffen Records took off slowly, with flops by Elton John and Donna Summer. But Geffen parlayed his friendship with John Lennon into a deal that paid off handsomely after the ex-Beatle was shot dead in December 1980. With former Warner vice president Eddie Rosenblatt as his president, he brought in a formidable A&R staff. "By then I had a very different approach to the record business than I'd had with Asylum," he says. "I wasn't starting off with that deep personal involvement with the artists. I also figured out that I was no longer the guy who could be the A&R person and pick the music."

"At some point David said, 'I'm not really the finder of talent anymore,'" says Mel Posner, who headed Geffen's international department. "He said, 'Let me get the best people.' And that's what he did. He got John Kalodner and Gary Gersh and Tom Zutaut, and they became stars in their own right." Over the ensuing decade, that troika of talent-finders would bring a host of multiplatinum artists— from Cher and Aerosmith to Guns N' Roses and Nirvana—to Geffen. Yet the man himself managed to antagonize the very Reprise/Asylum artists (Young, Mitchell, Henley) who'd brought him such success in the 1970s. Any notion that he would re-create the "boutique" ambience of Asylum in the new decade was quickly dispelled when Young's and Mitchell's albums failed to sell. "David started feeling real pressure," Elliot Roberts recalled. "[He felt] that he wasn't as good as Mo."

Infamously, Geffen in 1983 took the unprecedented step of suing Young for making "musically uncharacteristic" records. At a time when his label was notching up bland hits by Asia and Quarterflash, he accused Young of making deliberately uncommercial albums, such as the electronic *Trans* (1982). This time he made a foe not only of Young but also of Roberts, his oldest ally. "We stopped hanging out at that point," Roberts said. "I couldn't trust him anymore, and he couldn't trust me anymore. Horrible. It ended our friendship."

Meanwhile, Mitchell blamed her commercial failure on Geffen, alleging that he'd failed to pay her publishing royalties. On at least one occasion the former Bel Air housemates got into a screaming match in Geffen's office, with Joni demanding to be released from her contract. In 1994 she returned to Reprise and Mo Ostin. "If I didn't talk to her for the rest of my life," Geffen bluntly told his biographer Tom King, "I wouldn't miss her for a minute."

CODA

Like a Setting Sun

Something may come out of the '70s.
Either it's a transition or a demise.

—Donald Fagen

In the fall of 1977, as the Eagles and Linda Ronstadt played to vast crowds in coliseums, their old watering hole the Troubadour was in trouble—so much so that Doug Weston was forced to ask Jackson Browne to play a twenty-fifth anniversary benefit show to help it survive. "The bartenders there were all fucked up on pills and coke," says Robert Marchese. "It became an ugly scene, and that was one of the reasons Doug eventually had to close it the first time. At the anniversary show, Jackson came but a lot of the others didn't. And they should have."

Adapting to the times, Weston even sanctioned the booking of punk bands at the Troubadour. But after fans of the Bags rampaged through the club, overturning tables, the club's waitresses petitioned Doug to ban such rowdy sounds from the former oasis of singer-songwriters and country rock. The Troubadour did survive, thanks in part to power pop and heavy metal, but it was a sad place, haunted by the ghosts of its glory years. In "The Sad Café," the elegiac finale to *The Long Run*, the Eagles mourned the club where they'd first convened but typically wondered whether those whose "dreams came true" were really any more fortunate than those who stayed behind.

If it was any consolation to Weston, the Roxy also struggled in the late 1970s. But then the whole lifestyle represented by the two clubs was drawing to a close. The acts that had defined them were too big to play them now, while the acts that did play them had few ties to the canyon music communities. Laurel Canyon itself was no longer the rock sanctuary it had been for twenty-odd years. "The people who were successful got away from the lousy streets and the homes that leaked the wind through the boards," says Stan Cornyn.

When Joni and friends moved to Bel Air and Beverly Hills—and bought their plush beach homes in Malibu—it was less out of love for pseudo-rural living than out of a growing need for exclusivity. For all the egalitarianism they'd espoused in the 1960s, they were now distant stars like the silver-screen idols whose old mansions they were buying. "The real impetus of this movement to the hills is no longer love of the great outdoors or frontier rusticity," Mike Davis wrote in *Ecology of Fear*, "but, as critic Reyner Banham recognized in the 1960s, the search for absolute 'thickets of privacy' outside the dense fabric of common citizenship and urban life."

"Before we all had nice houses we lived in crummy apartments and it was so depressing that we all went out to clubs every night," Linda Ronstadt reflected in 1980. "And the clubs provided a surrogate family. But then we all got record deals and money and big houses and that surrogate family changed. [The family] became the staff—you know, the people who help run your life—because our lives became so complicated with all the traveling."

Laurel Canyon is still comparatively funky and unmanicured, but real-estate values have shot up to the point where only rich bohemians and SUV-driving yuppies can afford to live there. The canyon's life as a rock and roll haven may have ended symbolically when Frank Zappa's old cabin burned down on Halloween night in 1981. "By then any notion of community had passed," says Ron Stone.

Impoverished musicians now dwell in Silverlake and Echo Park—the very neighborhoods where Souther and friends first lived in the late 1960s and early 1970s. Yet the musical legacy remains in Laurel Canyon. "I hate calling it magic, because that's crazy hippie talk," says Tim Mosher, punk rocker turned TV composer. "But the '60s culture definitely had a lasting effect. Laurel Canyon is an inspiration."

Such sentiments echo the original inspiration canyon dwellers felt when they moved into houses on Kirkwood Drive and Lookout Mountain Avenue in the mid-1960s. "If you look at *MTV Cribs*," says Chris Darrow, "they're all living in these big houses and they're all real proud of their gated communities and it's all chrome and clean white walls. And it's the *exact antithesis* of what happened in that particular period of time."

"My sense is that it was magical, and that people felt that at the time," says Joel Bernstein, photographer and confidant of Neil Young and Joni Mitchell. "To be in the California sun and air with that kind of pot, and with this large influx of people, particularly from the urban Northeast, made New York seem like Mammon."

No doubt the gentrification of Laurel Canyon was as inevitable as the commodifying of rock and roll itself. Talk to any survivors from those halcyon days of life on Lookout Mountain Avenue and their sadness is palpable. "I'm not in step with any music that's being made right now that I hear," J. D. Souther said in 1998 as he lamented the loss of "a context, when Jackson and Bonnie and I would all be going to the studio . . . and Lowell and Linda and the Eagles and Zevon and Waddy . . . a context that was shared to some extent even though within it we were each very individual voices."

By the late 1990s the great artists of the Warner/Reprise/Elektra/ Asylum enclave barely sold records anymore. MTV, ageism, and niche radio combined to squeeze them out of the market. Only giant nostalgia tours by the Eagles brought the baby boomers out of their suburban cul-de-sacs. "There's no corporate room for the likes of Joni Mitchell or Randy Newman anymore," says David Anderle. "And they become hostile because of that." Few have become quite as hostile as Mitchell. "Everybody's a singer-songwriter now, but not everybody should be," she complained in 1998. "And that's why I think music has gone downhill . . . the standards have dropped severely."

For his part, Newman shakes his head at the lack of artist development in today's industry. "Lenny Waronker was artist-friendly but an artist like me couldn't get started now in the business," he says with a sigh. "There are few record companies now which would give you the time I was given to develop, to where *Sail Away* sold respectably, or who give you that long *afterwards*."

Newman lasted for just one album—1999's *Bad Love*—on the DreamWorks label where Waronker now worked. He claims that he spent more on his drummer for that album than the label spent on promoting it. "I think I heard something out of Mo's or Lenny's mouth to the effect that, 'Well, [*Bad Love*] just didn't sell,'" he says. "I'd never heard that from them before."

In October 2003 I sat in Waronker's office in Beverly Hills and asked him about Randy and Rickie Lee Jones, as well as his latest singer-songwriter protégé Rufus Wainwright. For several years Lenny and Mo had been trying to keep the Reprise ethos alive at DreamWorks Records, a company partly bankrolled by none other than David Geffen. It hadn't worked, and DreamWorks was about to be sold to Universal. If Neil or Joni or Randy or Rickie Lee had been around today, I asked Waronker, would we even have heard their second or third albums?

"I remember having a conversation with Rickie Lee once," he said in response. "She was upset about comparatively low sales and I said, 'This isn't about selling a million records. This is about coming out, getting rave reviews, and selling fifty or sixty thousand albums. And that'll allow us to go to the next one and the next one. And somewhere in there it's gonna blow up.' But now it's so different. The costs of marketing the records are so high, and the way the business has gone, based on the corporatization of all this stuff, forces you to worry about a report card every three months. The risk-taking isn't the same."

Waronker's old Warner colleague Joe Smith says the changes started in the 1980s, when he became president of Capitol Records. "When I took over at Capitol I knew it was a different ball game," he says. "I wasn't running a label, I was running a corporation. When I left Capitol I did an interview with Robert Hilburn at the *L.A. Times* and I said, 'This is what's gonna happen. These corporations have sucked it up and they're gonna consolidate. The music division is just one division that has to show quarterly profits and it will cut down on the ability to reinvest or believe in an artist.' And that's exactly what *did* happen."

"You have to appreciate that the '60s and early '70s were a unique time," says Mel Posner. "We could take chances and the penalties were not as severe as they are today. We could make mistakes and *learn* from our mistakes. It was a rare kind of luxury."

There are those who suggest it's mawkish to lionize the likes of Holzman, Ostin, and Waronker—that their day was done and that they failed to see that pop music was now a business of instant success. Trying to develop singer-songwriters in the age of hip hop, boy bands, and R&B divas simply showed how out of touch they were.

Still, it was hard not to mourn the passing of the great rock executives, maverick facilitators of talent who'd provided platforms for the leading lights of the Southern California scene. Even David Geffen, for some the bête noire of the story, waxes nostalgic for the singer-songwriter era. "It was the greatest ride that one could possibly imagine," he says. "Artistically, financially, fulfilling dreams and aspirations and making friends with incredibly talented people and watching them grow and succeed, it was thrilling. The '80s, which were considerably more successful for me, weren't nearly as magical."

It was also difficult not to see the business, and the way it exploded from the mid-1970s to the mid-1980s, as inherently self-corrupting. "There was this old hippie who told me how when he first heard Bob Dylan he knew for a fact that money was shit," says Fred Goodman, author of that sobering study *The Mansion on the Hill*. "Then he said he looked around later on and wasn't so sure. He said he'd thought about what those of us who were there with our hearts threw away—and about the sharp-eyed ones who came along later and picked it up."

"I don't think anyone sets out *not* to have limousines," says J. D. Souther. "But I think that at some point your conscience—if you can keep it awake—sees that if a corporate executive is making a thousand times as much per year as his line workers, he's clearly lost touch with a certain aspect of his humanity."

Ned Doheny, whose independent wealth gave him a singular perspective on those illustrious friends who struck it lucky, remains dismayed by the impact of money on their lives. As one of the participants in the 1967 Elektra Ranch experiment that helped inaugurate the Laurel Canyon era, Doheny saw its beginning, middle, and bloated end. "Let's say hypothetically that somewhere down the line you make $500 million, what good does that do you when you've sold your soul in the bargain?" he says. "I don't really know anybody who's benefited from success. While you're busy being dazzled by the kaleidoscope of fractured light and advantage, part of you is also being drained away. And you don't even see it.'"

In selling their souls for fame and riches, the stars of the 1960s and 1970s helped create a world where passive consumerism replaced emotional engagement and political commitment. The apathy of twentysomethings over the environment and Iraq is shocking when one harks back to the civil rights and Vietnam War protests of the 1960s.

"The understanding of history for this new generation seems to come down to *Star Wars*," says David Anderle. "Nobody is writing songs about what Bush is doing. And you get to thinking, 'Maybe the power of music is over.'"

He pauses and proffers a sad smile. "Maybe I should go downstairs and not worry about it," he says. "But I keep saying to my son, *'Don't you guys get it?'*"

Notes

1 Expecting to Fly

2 *"The Ash Grove was where"*   Jackson Browne, author interview, October 18, 1993.

3 *"The whole scene"*   Linda Ronstadt, author interview, February 7, 1995.

3 *"The scene was just tiny"*   Ry Cooder, author interview, May 9, 2005.

3 *"L.A. was less the promised land"*   Jac Holzman, author interview, October 22, 2003.

4 *"Billy was a wonderful guy"*   Barry Friedman (Frazier Mohawk), author interview, October 13, 2003.

4 *"The Beatles validated rock and roll"*   Lou Adler, author interview, June 18, 1993.

4 *"What started happening"*   Henry Diltz, author interview, October 12, 2003.

5 *"They'd sit there"*   Jerry Yester, author interview, November 1, 2003.

5 *"At some point"*   Diltz, op. cit.

5 *"It was kinda like"*   Yester, op. cit.

5 *"Chris told me"*   David Jackson, author interview, October 31, 2003.

5 *"You mainly just went"*   Browne, op. cit.

5 *"We all came over and went"*   Ronstadt in Anthony Fawcett and Henry Diltz, *California Rock, California Sound*, p. 114.

6 *"The influx of"*   Adler, op. cit.

7 *"The company had learned"*   Stan Cornyn, author interview, October 20, 2003.

7 *"We got on the London express"*   Joe Smith, author interview, October 2, 2003.

7 *"It's amazing how little"*   Waronker, author interview, October 20, 2003.

7 *"We were a kind of poor man's"*   Randy Newman, author interview, November 6, 1995.

8   *"We used to crank out"*   David Gates, author interview, June 24, 1996.

8   *"Dylan exploded"*   Browne, op. cit.

8   *"I had 2½ percent"*   Derek Taylor, author interview, August 21, 1992.

8   *"New York itself"*   Smith, op. cit.

9   *"Stephen ended up"*   Friedman, op. cit.

9   *"Stephen was definitely talented"*   Nurit Wilde, author interview, October 9, 2003.

10   *"We wanted hits"*   Waronker in Gene Sculatti, liner notes for *Feelin' Groovy: The Best of Harper's Bizarre*, Warner Archives, 1997.

10   *"We never made profit"*   Smith, op. cit.

11   *"My goal"*   Waronker, author interview, October 20, 2003.

11   *"I'm sitting"*   Denny Doherty, author interview, October 23, 2003.

11   *"I didn't know what"*   Young in Jimmy McDonough, *Shakey*, p. 150.

12   *"Neil was a very sweet fellow"*   Wilde, op. cit.

12   *"The whole thing was"*   Young in Scott Young, *Neil and Me: The Neil Young Story* (Toronto: McClelland & Stewart, 1984).

12   *"People thought Neil"*   Friedman, op. cit.

12   *"the easiest to like"*   Young in *World Countdown News*, 1967.

12   *"Our living room"*   Mark Volman, author interview, October 8, 2003.

12   *"The Springfield live"*   Diltz, op. cit.

13   *"There was a severe"*   Van Dyke Parks, author interview, June 19, 1993.

13   *"People like that"*   Friedman, op. cit.

13   *"I thought"*   Waronker, author interview, October 20, 2003.

13   *"I needed weight"*   Ibid.

13   *"Jack really loved Neil"*   Judy Henske, author interview, October 8, 2003.

14   *"There were a lot of problems"*   Young in Cameron Crowe, "So Hard to Make Arrangements for Yourself: The *Rolling Stone* Interview with Neil Young," *Rolling Stone*, August, 14, 1975.

14   *"We know each other"*   Stills in Ritchie Yorke, "Stephen Stills: An Interview in England—Part 2," *Circus*, September 1970.

15   *"David was a bit"*   Billy James, author interview, October 24, 2004.

15   *"In the beginning, David"*   Dickson in Dave Zimmer, *Crosby, Stills and Nash*, p. 28.

15   *"After 'Eight Miles High'"*   Clark in interview with Monty Smith, *Omaha Rainbow*, December 1977.

16   *"I can't do it"*   Clark story based on quotes from author interview with Denny Bruce, October 6, 2003.

16   *"a fussy schoolmarm attitude"*   Taylor, op. cit.

16   *"I remember hearing"*   Stills quote in Zimmer, op. cit., p. 48.

16   *"David was charming"*   Nurit Wilde, author interview, October 9, 2003.

17   *"They drove up"*   Crosby in B. Mitchel Reed radio interview, 1971.

17   *"[Smack] was always"*   Crosby in David Crosby with Carl Gottlieb, *Long Time Gone*.

17   *"He was the main cultural luminary"*   Browne, op. cit.

17   *"The Byrds were"*   Ron Stone, author interview, June 25, 1993.

18   *"The San Francisco groups"*   Adler, op. cit.

18 *"I saw everything"*   Judy James, author interview, November 3, 2003.
18 *"The industry totally changed"*   Tom Wilkes, author interview, October 25, 2003.

2 Back to the Garden

19 *"The canyon was old"*   Lenny Waronker, author interview, October 20, 2003.
20 *"You'd go up Laurel Canyon"*   Henry Diltz, author interview, October 3, 2003.
20 *"That you can actually"*   Cholodenko in Michael Walker, "Still Hazy after All These Years," *Los Angeles Times Magazine*, June 1, 2003.
20 *"There are canyons"*   Chris Darrow, author interview, October 4, 2003.
20 *"It was more like"*   June Walters, author interview, Los Angeles, October 24, 2003.
21 *"Laurel Canyon was darker"*   Jill Robinson, author interview, May 19, 2004.
21 *"The first espresso machines"*   Walters, op. cit.
21 *"Every Monday night"*   Robinson, op. cit.
21 *"People would swoop down"*   Barry Friedman, author interview, October 13, 2003.
21 *"The canyon was part"*   Carl Gottlieb, author interview, October 4, 2003.
21 *"It was so exciting"*   Jerry Yester, author interview, November 1, 2003.
22 *"When I was a kid"*   Mickey Dolenz, author interview, October 14, 2003.
22 *"It was a tough adjustment"*   Ibid.
22 *"Jim Morrison"*   Arthur Lee, author interview, June 24, 1993.
23 *"I remember Jim"*   Linda Ronstadt, author interview, February 7, 1995.
23 *"Paul really believed"*   Gottlieb, op. cit.
23 *"People like Paul"*   Jac Holzman, author interview, October 22, 2003.
23 *"It was always open house"*   Jackson Browne, author interview, October 18, 1993.
23 *"They kept coming over"*   Browne in Cameron Crowe, "A Child's Garden of Jackson Browne," *Rolling Stone*, May 23, 1974.
23 *"Barry was off the scale"*   Holzman, op. cit.
23 *"Jac would make his royal visits"*   Haeny in Jac Holzman and Gavan Daws, *Follow the Music*, p. 22.
23 *"L.A. was all about hanging"*   David Anderle, author interview, June 26, 1993.
24 *"Billy got very heavily"*   David Anderle, author interview, October 9, 2003.
24 *"Columbia never gave"*   Michael Ochs, author interview, June 14, 1993.
24 *"At the time"*   Judy James, author interview, November 3, 2003.
24 *"I wasn't the first"*   James from Jerry Hopkins, "Scenes: Los Angeles," *Rolling Stone*, June 22, 1968.
25 *"Billy's house"*   Tom Nolan, author interview, October 21, 2003.
25 *"We would go to hoot nights"*   James, op. cit.
25 *"Billy was sort of"*   Browne in Holzman/Daws, op. cit., p. 224.
25 *"Jackson was very talented"*   James, op. cit.
25 *"Billy was extremely bright"*   Holzman, op. cit.

25   *"Jackson was not"*   Friedman, op. cit.

26   *"For those who"*   Richard Meltzer, "Young Jackson Browne's Old Days," *Rolling Stone*, June 22, 1972.

26   *"Jackson and I"*   Ned Doheny, author interview, February 23, 2004.

27   *"In those days"*   Ibid.

27   *"We persuaded Jac Holzman"*   Browne, author interview, op. cit.

28   *"kind of like bringing in"*   Browne in Holzman/Daws, op. cit., p. 234.

28   *"In terms of girls"*   Friedman, op. cit.

28   *"It was certainly dysfunctional"*   Ibid.

28   *"By the time I got up"*   Anderle, op. cit.

28   *"I refused to be corrupted"*   Doheny, op. cit.

29   *"They came back from Paxton"*   James, op. cit.

29   *"My stopping smoking dope"*   Browne in Holzman/Daws, op. cit., p. 251.

29   *"You cannot discount"*   James, op. cit.

29   *"Slowly but surely"*   Ibid.

30   *"Laurel Canyon just seemed"*   Bruce Langhorne, author interview, September 21, 2004.

30   *"John began that song"*   Denny Doherty, author interview, October 23, 2003.

30   *"Cass was Elsa Maxwell"*   Ibid.

30   *"Cass was a major catalyst"*   Diltz, op. cit.

30   *"I don't have the psychology"*   Elliott in Richard Goldstein, *Goldstein's Greatest Hits* (Englewood Cliffs, N.J.: Prentice-Hall, 1970), p. 61.

30   *"There were a couple of good-looking guys"*   Denny Bruce, author interview, October 6, 2003.

31   *"They were under"*   John York, author interview, November 2, 2003.

31   *"By this time"*   Lou Adler, author interview, June 18, 1993.

31   *"The public relates"*   Phillips in Michael Thomas, "The Wolfking as Lord Byron," *Rolling Stone*, November 12, 1970.

31   *"America always re-creates"*   Gottlieb in Crosby/Gottlieb, *Long Time Gone*, p. 126.

31   *"A lot of the music"*   Darrow, op. cit.

32   *"One of the reasons"*   Dan Bourgoise, author interview, June 23, 1993.

32   *"What came in"*   Mark Volman, author interview, October 8, 2003.

32   *"I really think"*   Ibid.

32   *"I genuinely felt"*   Webb in Ben Edmonds, liner notes for *The Moon's a Harsh Mistress* (Rhino Records, 2004).

32   *"It was the right time"*   DeShannon in Parke Puterbaugh, liner notes for *The Best of Jackie DeShannon* (Rhino Records, 1991).

32   *"We just felt"*   Stan Cornyn, author interview, October 20, 2003.

33   *"Mo had had"*   Joe Boyd, author interview, July 3, 2003.

33   *"Mo would hang"*   Cornyn, op. cit.

33   *"In those days"*   Ian Whitcomb, author interview, June 16, 1993.

33   *"a Reprise lode of gold"*   Cornyn in Stan Cornyn with Paul Scanlon, *Exploding*, p. 71.

33   *"In my head"*   Cornyn, author interview, op. cit.

33   *"Andy knew about things"*   Joe Smith, author interview, October 20, 2003.

3   New Kids in Town

35   *"Elliot pitched"*   Mitchell from 2003 documentary *Joni Mitchell—Woman of Heart and Mind: A Life Story*, released by Eagle Vision.

36   *"It was almost like"*   Malka Marom, ibid.

36   *"I was really a folk singer"*   Joni Mitchell, author interview, September 14, 1994.

36   *"Elliot became wildly excited"*   Geffen in *Woman of Heart and Mind*, op. cit.

36   *"When she first came out"*   Roberts in *Woman of Heart and Mind*, op. cit.

36   *"Right away I thought"*   Crosby in *Woman of Heart and Mind*, op. cit.

37   *"We went back to L.A."*   Crosby in Crowe, "Crosby, Stills, Nash, and Young Carry On," *Crawdaddy*, October 1974.

37   *"These were two very willful people"*   Joel Bernstein, author interview, October 30, 2003.

37   *"Everything about Joni"*   Elliot Roberts, author interview, June 18, 1993.

37   *"Driving around"*   Mitchell, author interview, September 14, 1994.

38   *"Elliot would sleep"*   Ron Stone, author interview, June 25, 1993.

38   *"Because Crosby 'hangs out'"*   Jerry Hopkins, "Scenes: Los Angeles," *Rolling Stone*, June 22, 1968.

38   *"Right away"*   Bernstein, op. cit.

38   *"In his heart"*   Elliot Roberts, author interview, June 18, 1993.

38   *"David was very enthusiastic"*   Mitchell, op. cit.

39   *"They each described"*   Bernstein, op. cit.

40   *"Joni invented everything"*   Taylor in *Woman of Heart and Mind*, op. cit.

40   *"David says"*   Gottlieb, author interview, October 4, 2003.

40   *"Cass had organized"*   Henry Diltz, author interview, October 3, 2003.

41   *"She got me on the phone"*   Joe Smith, author interview, October 2, 2003.

41   *"Like Neil"*   Diltz, op. cit.

41   *"the high-frequency rock'n'roar"*   Shelton in Richie Unterberger, *Eight Miles High*, p. 80.

41   *"As if an aural backlash"*   Happy Traum, "The Swan Song of Folk Music," *Rolling Stone*, May 17, 1969.

42   *"Groups had broken up"*   Ellen Sander, *Trips*.

42   *"Neil was painfully shy"*   Linda McCartney in McDonough, *Shakey*, op. cit., p. 202.

42   *"I know that baby"*   Young/Stills story in Denny Bruce, author interview, October 6, 2003.

43   *"The Springfield had started"*   Roberts, author interview, June 18, 1993.

43   *"Oh, he'd plotted it all"*   Roberts in Steve Erickson, "Neil Young on a Good Day," *New York Times Magazine*, July 30, 2000.

43   *"Everyone thought of the group"*   Davis in Fred Goodman, *The Mansion on the Hill*, p. 80.

43   *"I think Neil always"*   Furay in Zimmer, *Crosby, Stills and Nash*, op. cit., p. 47.

43   *"I just had too much energy"*   Young in Cameron Crowe, "The Last American Hero," *Rolling Stone*, February 8, 1979.

43   *"I'd never met anybody like him"*   Nash in Dave Zimmer, "Graham Nash: The Winds of Change," *BAM*, February 1980.

44 *"Cass showed me"*   Nash in Zimmer, *Crosby, Stills and Nash*, op. cit., p. 42.

44 *"Joni's place"*   Mark Volman, author interview, October 8, 2003.

44 *"I was in there on top"*   Nash in B. Mitchel Reed radio interview, 1971.

45 *"I can only liken it"*   Nash in *Woman of Heart and Mind*, op. cit.

45 *"There really was an ethic"*   Roberts, author interview, June 18, 1993.

45 *"England was boring me"*   Nash in Ritchie Yorke, "Crosby Stills Nash & Young: In the Reaches of Laurel Canyon," *Fusion*, November 28, 1969.

45 *"It's hard to define that period"*   Roberts, author interview, June 18, 1993.

45 *"Warner Brothers"*   Young quote in McDonough, op. cit.

45 *"Warners was a big standard-bearer"*   Bob Merlis, author interview, June 11, 1993.

45 *"Neil and Joni were coming at it"*   Waronker, author interview, October 20, 2003.

46 *"I told Lenny"*   Randy Newman, author interview, November 6, 1995.

46 *"Randy and some others"*   Waronker, op. cit.

46 *"There was marijuana"*   Randy Newman, author interview, July 26, 2003.

46 *"Randy was sadder"*   Van Dyke Parks, author interview, June 19, 1993.

46 *"I was trying to ask questions"*   Ibid.

47 *"Warners was comfortable"*   Russ Titelman, author interview, June 30, 1993.

47 *"Jack's mother"*   Judy Henske, author interview, October 8, 2003.

47 *"That was quite a summer"*   Denny Bruce, author interview, October 6, 2003.

48 *"Neil wasn't as social"*   Diltz, op. cit.

49 *"When I was very young"*   Nurit Wilde, author interview, October 9, 2003.

49 *"I knew he could get this done"*   Roberts, author interview, June 18, 1993.

50 *"From the day I arrived"*   David Geffen, author interview, December 8, 2004.

50 *"Stay with people"*   Brandt in Fred Goodman, *The Mansion on the Hill*, op. cit., p. 120.

50 *"She was a very strange girl"*   Geffen in Joe Smith with Mitchell Fink, *Off the Record*, p. 304.

50 *"a window into something"*   Crosby in Michelle Kort, *Soul Picnic*, p. 47.

50 *"People said"*   Henske, op. cit.

51 *"[David] credited Sander"*   Tom King in *David Geffen*, p. 96.

51 *"David was an opportunist"*   Smith, op. cit.

51 *"He never stopped"*   Essra Mohawk, author interview, February 2, 2004.

52 *"I knew [Jerry's] accomplishments"*   Geffen in Jerry Wexler with David Ritz, *Rhythm and the Blues*, pp. 223–224.

52 *"I saw in him"*   Ertegun in Dorothy Wade and Justine Picardie, *Music Man*, p. 221.

52 *"the most sophisticated"*   Geffen in Wexler/Ritz, loc. cit.

52 *"Later I saw [Geffen's] devotion"*   Ibid.

52 *"There was so much going on"*   Geffen, author interview, op. cit.

53 *"David stopped the car"*   Roberts, author interview, June 18, 1993.

53 *"The word got around"*   Jackson Browne, author interview, October 18, 1993.

53 *"[David] had a description"* Bones Howe in Goodman, *The Mansion on the Hill*, op. cit., p. 143.

53 *"By 'significant artists'"* Geffen, author interview, December 8, 2004.

53 *"We were both very involved"* Ibid.

53 *"Elliot in some strange way"* Stone, op. cit.

53 *"In the Laurel Canyon and Topanga areas"* Bernstein, op. cit.

54 *"Elliot Roberts is a good dude"* Crosby in Ben Fong-Torres, "David Crosby: The *Rolling Stone* Interview," *Rolling Stone*, July 23, 1970.

54 *"David may have wanted"* Browne, op. cit.

4   Horses, Kids, and Forgotten Women

56 *"John [Phillips] and Denny [Doherty]"* Michelle Phillips in unpublished interview with Mick Brown, summer 2003.

56 *"He was an odd guy"* David Jackson, author interview, October 31, 2003.

57 *"Most of us that came out of bluegrass"* Chris Darrow, author interview, October 4, 2003.

57 *"Everybody went, 'Oh, my God'"* Jackson, op. cit.

57 *"Doug became"* Ibid.

58 *"The wave hit L.A."* Cooder in Grundy and Tobler, *The Guitar Greats* (London: BBC Books, 1983), p. 110.

58 *"We were fooling around"* Sneaky Pete Kleinow, author interview, July 13, 2004.

58 *"[Hearts and Flowers] were"* Messina in John Einarson, *Desperados*, op. cit., p. 37.

59 *"I hated it"* Linda Ronstadt, author interview, February 7, 1995.

59 *"Linda was young"* Nurit Wilde, author interview, October 9, 2003.

59 *"Linda says to me"* Judy Henske, author interview, October 8, 2003.

59 *"Everybody's going to the country"* Ronstadt in interview in *Country Song Roundup*, October 1970.

59 *"I think it was unconsciously"* Bernie Leadon, author interview, October 23, 2003.

60 *"It broke the city open"* Kurt Wagner, author interview, February 1, 2004.

60 *"I wanted to do a sort of modern folk thing"* Nik Venet, author interview, June 25, 1993.

60 *"I think Neil Young and I"* Stills in Ritchie Yorke, "Stephen Stills: An Interview in England—Part 1," *Circus*, August 1970.

61 *"Gram was a good kid"* Chris Hillman, author interview, November 4, 1997.

61 *"Gram and Nancy"* Eve Babitz, author interview, November 5, 1997.

62 *"It took me two years"* Parsons in Judith Sims, "Ex-Byrd Gram Parsons Solos: He's No Longer in a Hurry," *Rolling Stone*, March 1, 1973.

62 *"My main recollections"* Suzi Jane Hokom, author interview, November 5, 1997.

62 *"Lee was older"* Ibid.

62 *"There were probably twenty"* Chris Darrow, author interview, November 4, 1997.

63 *"I knew very little about Gram"* Hillman, op. cit.

63 *"We were simply looking"* Roger McGuinn, author interview, November 4, 1997.

63 *"Our fans were heartbroken"* McGuinn in Rob Hughes and Nigel Williamson, "God's Own Singer: Gram Parsons," *Uncut*, October 2003.

63 *"He was a rich kid"* McGuinn, author interview, op. cit.

64 *"Gene was nervous"* Gosdin in Sid Griffin, "Dr. Byrd . . . and Mr. Hyde," *Mojo*, August 1998.

64 *"He watched the show"* Pamela Des Barres, author interview, October 21, 2003.

65 *"Doug and I"* Leadon, op. cit.

65 *"Doug and Gene"* Hillman in Einarson, *Desperados*, op. cit., p. 129.

65 *"A&M wanted to become hip"* Tom Wilkes, author interview, October 25, 2003.

66 *"I was around"* Darrow, op. cit.

66 *"That was pretty much the end"* Leadon, op. cit.

66 *"The Eagles will tell you"* Domenic Priore, author interview, October 10, 2003.

66 *"Gene always seemed unhappy"* Berline in Einarson, *Desperados*, op. cit., p. 165.

67 *"a hillbilly Shakespeare"* John York, author interview, November 2, 2003.

67 *"The Sunset Strip"* Priore, op. cit.

67 *"When the Troub came along"* Ronstadt, author interview, February 7, 1995.

67 *"If you sold out the Troubadour"* Tom Waits, author interview, January 28, 1999.

68 *"There was Big Tit Sue"* Robert Marchese, author interview, October 22, 2003.

68 *"It was such a sexual experience"* Michael Ochs, author interview, June 14, 1993.

68 *"too much posturing and moving around"* Jac Holzman, author interview, October 22, 2003.

68 *"Weston would sign"* McLean from Troubadour notes supplied by Johnny Black of *Rocksource*.

69 *"The bar was the place"* Judy James, author interview, November 3, 2003.

69 *"The Troub was the only place"* Jackson Browne, author interview, October 18, 1993.

69 *"the people who had grown their hair"* Perkins in John Einarson, *Desperados*, op. cit., p. 8.

69 *"There was a sort of music community"* Browne, op. cit.

69 *"There'd been a long period"* Ronstadt, author interview, February 7, 1995.

70 *"In those days"* Ibid.

70 *"Linda was the most underrated"* Chris Darrow, author interview, October 4, 2003.

71 *"Linda was relentless"* Leadon, op. cit.

71   *"It's like the musician pool"*   Ronstadt in Janet Maslin, "Linda Ronstadt: The Image vs. the Woman," *Rolling Stone*, May 9, 1974.

71   *"I think I knew exactly"*   J. D. Souther, author interview, October 13, 2004.

71   *"I saw copies of* Surfer *magazine"*   Frey in Fawcett/Diltz, *California Rock, California Sound*, p. 127.

72   *"I came out here"*   Frey in Judith Sims, "The Eagles Take It Easy and Soar," *Rolling Stone*, August 17, 1972.

73   *"A couple of times"*   Browne in Pete Frame, Paul Kendall, and John Tobler, "Happy-Go-Lucky Me! Jackson Browne," *ZigZag*, January 1977.

73   *"J. D. once told me"*   Eve Babitz, author interview, June 17, 1993.

73   *"There is no room for compassion here"*   Liza Williams in "Monday Night, Troubadour Bar, Time—Now," *Los Angeles Free Press*, August 30, 1970. Included in Williams, *Up the City of Angels*, (New York: G. P. Putnam's Sons, 1971), p. 90.

73   *"[It] was and always will be"*   Frey in Cameron Crowe, "The Eagles: Chips off the Old Buffalo," *Rolling Stone*, September 25, 1975.

73   *"Glenn had very long hair"*   Wilde, op. cit.

74   *"scorch the bar with his eyes"*   Eve Babitz, "Honky Tonk Nights: The Good Old Days at L.A.'s Troubadour," *Rolling Stone*, August 23, 1979.

74   *"Southern California"*   Ned Doheny, author interview, February 23, 2004.

74   *"I didn't think about Longbranch Pennywhistle"*   Ibid.

74   *"The first night I walked in"*   Henley in Joe Smith, *Off the Record*, op. cit., p. 351.

74   *"It was a total complete flop"*   Henley in Judith Sims, op. cit.

75   *"The guys in the South"*   Darrow, author interview, October 4, 2003.

75   *"The sound may have originated"*   Ron Stone, author interview, October 14, 2003.

5   Escape from Sin City

77   *"When Linda Ronstadt"*   Judy Henske, author interview, October 8, 2003.

77   *"Topanga really was"*   Joel Bernstein, author interview, October 30, 2003.

78   *"a haven for dusty cowboy boots"*   Jerry Hopkins, "It's Happening in Los Angeles," *World Countdown News*, Spring 1968.

78   *"That was when Topanga"*   Michael Ochs, author interview, June 14, 1993.

78   *"The movie industry"*   Lenny Waronker, author interview, October 20, 2003.

79   *"Neil hung around Topanga"*   Barry Hansen, author interview, June 21, 1993.

79   *"He was always very self-contained"*   Henry Diltz, author interview, October 3, 2003.

79   *"People were always"*   Elliott Roberts, author interview, June 18, 1993.

80   *"Right in the middle"*   Denny Bruce, author interview, October 6, 2003.

80   *"Neil was always dominated"*   Roberts in Jimmy McDonough, *Shakey*, op. cit., p. 289.

80   *"Charles Manson used to"*   Hansen, ibid.

80   *"Keith Richards came in"*   Phil Kaufman, author interview, November 7, 2003.

81 *"The Stones were willing participants"* Bud Scoppa, author interview, October 9, 2003.

81 *"They used him"* Seiter in Judson Klinger and Greg Mitchell, "Gram Finale: The Profoundly Sick Life and Mysteriously Perverse Death of the Prince of Country-Rock," *Crawdaddy*, October 1976.

81 *"We were good friends"* Linda Ronstadt, author interview, February 7, 1995.

81 *"To me that kind of living"* Ibid.

82 *"Chris lived down the street"* Tom Wilkes, author interview, October 25, 2003.

82 *"We said, 'This is country rock'"* Ibid.

83 *"I had everybody out there"* Ted Markland, author interview, October 25, 2003.

83 *"There's a kind of wistful"* Ned Doheny, author interview, February 23, 2004.

83 *"Sid said there's this place"* Kaufman, op. cit.

84 *"It seemed like an endless night"* Keith Richards, author interview, September 23, 1997.

84 *"We had binoculars"* Anita Pallenberg, author interview, October 28, 1997.

84 *"He used to go out there"* Kaufman, op. cit.

84 *"Everyone was convinced"* Frank Mazzola, author interview, October 29, 2003.

84 *"The Burritos turned up at the Troub hoot"* Bernie Leadon, author interview, October 23, 2003.

85 *"There was a slow progression"* Pamela Des Barres, author interview, October 21, 2003.

85 *"There was a lot of rock action"* Kim Fowley, author interview, June 12, 1993.

85 *"The pictures I took that day"* Eve Babitz, author interview, November 5, 1997.

85 *"I couldn't understand why"* Michael Ochs, author interview, June 14, 1993.

85 *"The people that embraced the Burritos"* Ronstadt, op. cit.

86 *"Henley and Frey"* Leadon, op. cit.

86 *"We're talking about five years"* Scoppa, op. cit.

86 *"We were all aware"* John York, author interview, November 2, 2003.

86 *"Just playing with Clarence"* Ibid.

86 *"They wanted to show"* Ibid.

87 *"On Saturday nights"* Gates in Joe Smith, *Off the Record*, op. cit., p. 329.

87 *"Delaney and Bonnie"* David Anderle, author interview, June 26, 1993.

88 *"Van Morrison was a huge influence"* Anderle, author interview, October 9, 2003.

88 *"Lenny and Randy"* Ted Templeman, author interview, October 30, 2003.

88 *"Ry was the youngest"* Waronker, op. cit.

88 *"He was doing something"* Ibid.

88 *"I made a lot of weird records"* Ry Cooder, author interview, May 9, 2005.

89 *"The Factory lived"* Jan Henderson, author interview, October 5, 2003.

89 *"Somehow a demo"* George in Andy Childs, "Huge Stars, Big Hearts, and Little Feat," *ZigZag*, 1973.

89 *"They were going to sign"* Russ Titelman, author interview, June 30, 1993.

89 *"He came to me"* Parks in Bud Scoppa's liner notes for the Little Feat box set *Hotcakes and Outtakes* (Rhino Records, 2000).

90 *"That was the time"* Paul Barrére, in Scoppa, liner notes for *Hotcakes and Outtakes*.

90 *"It was like Frank"* Pamela Des Barres, author interview, June 22, 1993.

90 *"I live in the middle"* Zappa in Barry Miles, *Zappa* (New York: Grove Press, 2004), p. 122.

90 *"the predecessor"* Zappa in Richie Unterberger, *Eight Miles High*, p. 290.

90 *"Frank's music"* Mark Volman, author interview, October 8, 2003.

90 *"Frank was never really* scathing" Ibid.

91 *"Frank was so far ahead"* Ibid.

91 *"I always felt"* Anderle, author interview, June 26, 1993.

91 *"Frank just finally fired Lowell"* Des Barres, op. cit.

92 *"I don't know if Tim"* Jerry Yester, author interview, November 1, 2003.

92 *"Help the Raven"* Story from Frank Zappa with Peter Occhiogrosso, *The Real Frank Zappa Book* (London: Picador, 1989), pp. 102–103.

92 *"[Frank] was afraid of the very thing"* Payne quote from Scoppa, liner notes for *Hotcakes and Outtakes*, op. cit.

92 *"There were a lot of weird people"* Joni Mitchell, author interview, September 14, 1994.

93 *"a mystical flirtation"* Didion, *The White Album*, p. 41.

93 *"Everybody was experimenting"* Mazzola, op. cit.

93 *"What had tied"* Chester Crill, author interview, October 4, 2003.

93 *"The Sunset Strip got really ugly"* Henderson, op. cit.

93 *"L.A. was a dangerous environment"* Kaufman, op. cit.

94 *"With really intelligent people"* Phillips in Michael Thomas, "The Wolfking as Lord Byron," *Rolling Stone*, November 12, 1970.

94 *"At the beginning"* Nurit Wilde, author interview, October 9, 2003.

94 *"I enjoyed working with Terry"* York, op. cit.

94 *"Terry Melcher told me"* Doheny, op. cit.

95 *"Manson lucked into a situation"* Des Barres, op. cit.

95 *"Charlie got pissed off"* Denny Doherty, author interview, October 23, 2003.

95 *"I've met so many"* Ibid.

95 *"the fat life of the delectable canyons"* Banham, *Los Angeles*.

96 *"It just destroyed us"* Lou Adler, author interview, June 18, 1993.

96 *"a collective sin"* Van Dyke Parks, author interview, June 19, 1993.

96 *"There was something swarming"* Dalton in "Altamont: An Eyewitness Account," *Gadfly*, November 1999.

96 *"two ends of the same mucky stick"* Rock Scully with David Dalton, *Living with the Dead: Twenty Years on the Bus with Garcia and the Grateful Dead* (Boston: Little, Brown, 1996), p. 185.

6 A Case of Me

99 *"You couldn't get these guys"* Allison Caine, author interview, October 29, 2003.

100   *"Graham ended up"*   Mitchell in the documentary *Woman of Heart and Mind: A Life Story*, 2003.

100   *"This really was a moment"*   James in Holzman/Daws, *Follow the Music*, p. 227.

100   *"Stephen was really a great musical anchor"*   Derek Taylor, author interview, August 21, 1992.

100   *"[Stephen] craved success"*   Ellen Sander, *Trips*.

101   *"Crosby had never really"*   Ibid.

101   *"Graham was—and still is"*   Ron Stone, author interview, October 14, 2003.

101   *"Cocaine was this* elixir"   Jonh Ingham, author interview, May 26, 2004.

102   *"Crosby brought Stills over"*   Waddy Wachtel, author interview, October 17, 2003.

102   *"Everything is an art"*   Crosby in Sander, op. cit.

102   *"The disagreements"*   Domenic Priore, author interview, October 10, 2003.

102   *"When we first came"*   Nash in Robert Sandall, "Crosby, Stills and Nash: My, How You've Grown!," *Q*, June 1992.

102   *"I've seen Crosby, Stills, and Nash"*   Hendrix in Zimmer, *Crosby, Stills and Nash*, p. 90.

102   *"There were too many people dying"*   Robert Marchese, author interview, October 22, 2003.

103   *"It all started to become"*   Tom Nolan, author interview, October 21, 2003.

103   *"The first major change"*   David Anderle, author interview, October 9, 2003.

103   *"When I worked for Elliot"*   Caine, op. cit.

103   *"The association"*   Gottlieb in Crosby/Gottlieb, *Long Time Gone*, p. 145.

103   *"I think he loved the music"*   Caine, op. cit.

103   *"Even though we knew"*   Crosby in Zimmer, op cit., pp. 79–80.

104   *"Elliot was shrewd"*   Caine, op. cit.

104   *"I quickly figured out"*   David Geffen in David Rensin, *The Mailroom*, p. 121.

104   *"There are two schools"*   Gottlieb, author interview, October 4, 2003.

104   *"David was extremely intense"*   Ibid.

104   *"I never felt I was too protective"*   Geffen, author interview, December 8, 2004.

104   *"That was the beginning"*   Rothchild in Fred Goodman, *The Mansion on the Hill*, p. 142.

105   *"It was an intense time of"*   Nash in Joni Mitchell documentary *Woman of Heart and Mind*, 2003.

105   *"Joni had the confidence"*   Stone, op. cit.

106   *"When [her] first album came out"*   McCaslin from Richie Unterberger, *Eight Miles High*, p. 126.

106   *"It was difficult for a woman"*   Mitchell, author interview, September 14, 1994.

106   *"I didn't think about"*   Linda Ronstadt, author interview, February 7, 1995.

106   *"A lot of them were secretaries"*   Denny Bruce, author interview, October 6, 2003.

106   *"I used to go up to Laurel Canyon"*   Des Barres, author interview, October 21, 2003.

106 *"See, it wasn't* that *long ago"*   Nurit Wilde, author interview, October 9, 2003.

106 *"the great outpouring"*   Robbins in Monte Beauchamp, ed., *The Life and Times of R. Crumb* (New York: St. Martin's Press, Griffin Books), 1998.

106 *"We liked to think"*   Stone, op. cit.

107 *"Unfortunately"*   Chris Darrow, author interview, October 4, 2003.

107 *"the problem of people thinking"*   Ronstadt in Katherine Orloff, *Rock 'n' Roll Woman*, p. 130.

107 *"The world had become"*   Mitchell in Alan Jackson, "Portrait of the Artist," *NME*, November 30, 1985.

107 *"the daring of youth"*   Warren in Mark Kurlansky, *1968*, p. 186.

107 *"Politics is bullshit"*   Dylan in Timothy White, *James Taylor: Long Ago and Far Away* (London: Omnibus Press, 2002), p. 167.

107 *"The time was right"*   Maslin, "Singer/Songwriters," in Jim Miller, ed., *The Rolling Stone Illustrated History of Rock & Roll* (New York: Random House/Rolling Stone Press, 1980), p. 339.

108 *"My style at that time"*   Taylor in Giles Smith, "The Man Whose Drug Intake Worried John Belushi," *Q*, August 1993.

108 *"I brought James over here"*   Peter Asher, author interview, October 18, 2003.

108 *"Peter and I settled a deal"*   Joe Smith, author interview, October 2, 2003.

108 *"The fact that Warners"*   Asher, op. cit.

109 *"What was really new to me"*   Ibid.

109 *"James seemed like the perfect guy"*   Kortchmar in Timothy White, op. cit., p. 157.

109 *"We loved that James Taylor record"*   Ned Doheny, author interview, February 23, 2004.

109 *"I never thought"*   Chris Darrow, op. cit.

109 *"At the time"*   Taylor in Joe Smith, *Off the Record*, p. 308.

110 *"Lou had made so much money"*   Matthew Greenwald, author interview, October 4, 2003.

110 *"Lou really had a production deal"*   David Geffen, author interview, December 8, 2004.

110 *"Her brain changed"*   Asher, op. cit.

110 *"Carole moved to the canyon"*   Lou Adler, author interview, June 18, 1993.

111 *"L.A. is a more relaxed environment"*   King in Miles, "The Definitive Carole King Story," 1976.

111 *"I want songs of hope"*   Ibid.

111 *"The rhythm sections"*   Adler, op. cit.

111 *"Carole was squeezing my hand"*   Ibid.

111 *"Funnily enough"*   Ibid.

111 *"My production values"*   King in Bob Chorush, "Carole King, with New LP, Arrives," *Rolling Stone*, December 23, 1971.

112 *"Laurel Canyon"*   Newman in Jay Ruby interview, January 1970, in Pauline Rivelli and Robert Levin, *The Rock Giants* (New York: World, 1970), p. 78.

112 *"I never believed"*   Randy Newman, author interview, November 6, 1995.

112 *"I wrote 'Suzanne'"*   Newman, author interview, July 26, 2003.

112 *"Dylan and others"* Ibid.

113 *"At* Rolling Stone" Ben Fong-Torres, author interview, October 23, 2003.

113 *"Being made a vice president"* Lenny Waronker, author interview, October 20, 2003.

113 *"Warners hired people"* Barry Hansen, author interview, June 21, 1993.

113 *"None of us had long hair"* Waronker, op. cit.

113 *"We didn't know"* Van Dyke Parks, author interview, June 19, 1993.

114 *"I had a family"* Newman, author interview, July 26, 2003.

114 *"By 1970"* Mark Volman, author interview, October 8, 2003.

114 *"I think you could say"* Ibid.

114 *"A lot of the confessional stuff"* Judy Henske, author interview, October 8, 2003.

115 *"After* Sweet Baby James" Taylor in Timothy White, op. cit., p. 185.

115 *"I'm getting a little tired"* Spector in *The Rolling Stone Interviews: 1967–1980: Talking with the Legend of Rock and Roll* (repr., New York: St. Martin's Press, 1989).

115 *"It still always shocks me"* Roberts in McDonough, *Shakey*, p. 321.

115 *"With CSNY"* Fong-Torres, op. cit.

116 *"Everybody was tryin' to do their own thing"* Young in McDonough, op. cit., p. 316.

116 *"Taylor was ousted from the band"* Taylor interviewed by Chris Salewicz, *Let It Rock* magazine.

116 *"I'm not going to say"* Young in Ritchie Yorke, "Crosby, Stills, Nash, and Young: In The Reaches of Laurel Canyon," *Fusion*, November 28, 1969.

116 *"I picked up the* New York Times" Geffen in Joni Mitchell documentary *Woman of Heart and Mind.*

116 *"The producers were either"* Geffen in Crosby/Gottlieb, op. cit., pp. 162–163.

117 *"That's what got them out of touch"* Wilde, op. cit.

117 *"When we did the first CSN record"* Nash in Sandall, op. cit.

117 *"The conflicts then"* Crosby in Crosby/Gottlieb, op. cit., pp. 194–195.

117 *"What we've got to do"* Young in Ben Fong-Torres, "Crosby, Stills, Nash, Young, Taylor, and Reeves," *Rolling Stone*, December 27, 1969.

117 *"Nash had to work so hard"* Bruce, op. cit.

118 *"Neil's insatiable need"* Nash in McDonough, op. cit., p. 324.

118 *"After Christine died"* Roberts in Crosby/Gottlieb, op. cit., p. 184.

118 *"Heroin was more prevalent"* Essra Mohawk, author interview, February 2, 2004.

119 *"The whole idea"* Joel Bernstein, author interview, October 30, 2003.

119 *"A lot of times"* Young in McDonough, op. cit., p. 319.

119 *"People tended"* Mitchell in William Ruhlmann, "Joni Mitchell: From Blue to Indigo," in Stacey Luftig, ed., *The Joni Mitchell Companion: Four Decades of Commentary* (New York: Schirmer Books, 2000), p. 36.

119 *"The first album"* Crosby in B. Mitchell Reed radio interview, 1971.

120 *"What the trick is with us"* Crosby in Ben Fong-Torres, "David Crosby: The *Rolling Stone* Interview," *Rolling Stone*, July 23, 1970.

120   *"We were now applauding"*   White in Bill Graham with Robert Greenfield, *Bill Graham Presents: My Life Inside Rock and Out* (New York: Doubleday, 1992).

120   *"In my experience"*   Geffen in Crosby/Gottlieb, op. cit., p. 146.

120   *"It was my instinct"*   Stills in Michael Wale, "Talking to Stephen Stills," *ZigZag*, December 1972.

120   *"I photographed Crazy Horse"*   Bernstein, op. cit.

121   *"My job was to sit"*   Jan Henderson, author interview, October 5, 2003.

121   *"One second [Jack]"*   Lofgren in Chris Briggs, "Crazy Horse, Neil Young, Grin, and All That Mob," *ZigZag*, December 1973.

121   *"When Neil came out"*   Bruce, op. cit.

122   *"I feel very kindred to Neil"*   Mitchell in Vic Garbarini, "Joni Mitchell Is a Nervy Broad," *Musician*, January 1983.

122   *"[Joni] writes"*   Young in Cameron Crowe, "So Hard to Make Arrangements for Yourself: The *Rolling Stone* Interview with Neil Young," *Rolling Stone*, August 14, 1975.

122   *"a monster talent"*   Wilde, op. cit.

122   *"Graham is a sweetheart"*   Mitchell to Dave DiMartino in *Mojo*, August 1998.

122   *"I remember the week"*   Carl Gottlieb, author interview, October 4, 2003.

123   *"Joni and Graham"*   Henry Diltz, author interview, October 3, 2003.

123   *"I want my music"*   Mitchell in Jerry Gilbert, "Joni Still Feels the Pull of the Country," *Melody Maker*, January 10, 1970.

124   *"Joan was never one"*   Elliot Roberts, author interview, June 18, 1993.

124   *"I liked small clubs"*   Joni Mitchell, author interview, op. cit.

124   *"I was pretty unconscious around then"*   Taylor in Giles Smith, op. cit.

124   *"James and Joni"*   Asher, op. cit.

125   *"I was at my most defenseless"*   Mitchell in Karen O'Brien, *Shadows and Light*, p. 135.

125   *"You had to take your hat off"*   Caine, op. cit.

125   *"Joni's music"*   Taylor in Stuart Werbin, "The *Rolling Stone* Interview: James Taylor and Carly Simon," *Rolling Stone*, January 4, 1973.

125   *"It turned forever"*   Flanagan in *Joni Mitchell—Woman of Heart and Mind* documentary, 2003.

125   *"The ultimate irony"*   Penny Stallings, *Rock 'n' Roll Confidential* (London: Vermillion, 1984), p. 167.

125   *"I was really mad"*   Mitchell, author interview, op. cit.

126   *"She built"*   Stone, op. cit.

7   With a Little Help from Our Friends

127   *"Geffen was* always *at the Troub"*   Bill Straw, author interview, May 20, 2004.

128   *"You could walk into that office"*   Henry Diltz, author interview, October 3, 2003.

128   *"We were very fortunate"*   Elliot Roberts, author interview, June 18, 1993.

128   *"David was quite brilliant"*   Ron Stone, author interview, October 14, 2003.

128 *"Elliot actually had a mind"* Peter Asher, author interview, October 18, 2003.

128 *"Geffen-Roberts definitely"* John York, author interview, November 2, 2003.

128 *"You have to remember"* Stone, op. cit.

129 *"I met David"* Tony Dimitriades, author interview, October 15, 2003.

129 *"It's not a big lie"* Nyro story told by Ellen Sander in Tom King, *David Geffen*, p. 136.

129 *"We got the break of our lives"* Joe Smith, author interview, October 2, 2003.

129 *"Geffen had helped"* Browne in Pete Frame, Paul Kendall, and John Tobler, "Happy-Go-Lucky Me! Jackson Browne," *ZigZag*, January 1977.

130 *"The letter said"* Geffen in R. Meltzer, "Young Jackson Browne's Old Days," *Rolling Stone*, June 22, 1972.

130 *"It was the only tape"* Roberts, op. cit.

130 *"Jackson was very pretty"* Geffen in Michelle Kort, *Soul Picnic: The Music and Passion of Laura Nyro*, p. 122.

130 *"He was a real soulmate"* Raitt from the DVD *Under the Covers: The Music, Artists, and Stories behind the Album Covers You Love*, 2002.

130 *"It was an astonishing deal"* Tom King, *David Geffen*, p. 141.

130 *"Geffen was eager, attentive"* Stan Cornyn, author interview, October 20, 2003.

131 *"I was devoted to her"* Geffen in Kort, op. cit., p. 150.

131 *"I know it broke his heart"* Sander, *Trips*.

131 *"We were looking at A&M"* Geffen, author interview, December 8, 2004.

131 *"They somehow created"* Ben Fong-Torres, author interview, October 23. 2003.

131 *"I was young and naive"* Geffen, author interview, December 8, 2004.

131 *"A bunch of hippies"* David Anderle, author interview, June 26, 1993.

132 *"This is one of the few places"* Geffen in Fred Goodman, *The Mansion on the Hill*, p. 143.

132 *"I took my relationships seriously"* Geffen in Crosby/Gottlieb, *Long Time Gone*, p. 220.

132 *"I remember David once"* Jackson Browne, author interview, October 18, 1993.

132 *"I met Jackson with Geffen"* Bud Scoppa, author interview, October 9, 2003.

132 *"We were all young"* Geffen, author interview, December 8, 2004.

133 *"The truth is"* Jimmy Webb, author interview, November 26, 2003.

133 *"There was this amazing scene"* Tackett in Bud Scoppa, liner notes for *Little Feat: Hotcakes and Outtakes*, Rhino Records box set, 2002.

133 *"You could have picked"* Straw, op. cit.

133 *"Jackson was Geffen's protégé"* Webb, op. cit.

133 *"David relied entirely"* Asher, op. cit.

134 *"That idea of artists"* Lenny Waronker, author interview, October 20, 2003.

134 *"Some people"* Browne from undated transcript of Crowe's interview for "A Child's Garden of Jackson Browne," *Rolling Stone*, May 23, 1974, quoted in Fred Goodman, *The Mansion on the Hill*, p. 150.

134 *"Glenn was our suggestion"* Linda Ronstadt, author interview, February 7, 1995.

134 *"John [Boylan] and Linda"* Henley to Cameron Crowe, "Chips off the Old Buffalo," *Rolling Stone*, September 25, 1975.

135 *"A lot of people in L.A."* Boylan from 1996 *Entertainment Weekly* interview quoted in Marc Eliot, *To the Limit*, p. 67.

135 *"Jackson said"* J. D. Souther, author interview, October 13, 2003.

135 *"It was about three or four months"* Bernie Leadon, author interview, October 23, 2003.

135 *"The Eagles weren't going to fail"* Geffen, author interview, December 8, 2004.

135 *"This was going to be our best shot"* Glenn Frey to Cameron Crowe, "Chips off the Old Buffalo," *Rolling Stone*, September 25, 1975.

135 *"We had lofty goals"* Leadon, op. cit.

136 *"We knew and committed to them"* John Hartmann in Fred Goodman, *The Mansion on the Hill*, p. 232.

136 *"What David did"* Holzman to John Tobler, "Jac Holzman Then and Now," *ZigZag*, Spring 1973.

136 *"I think David wanted me"* Ned Doheny, author interview, February 23, 2004.

136 *"David took the crème de la crème"* Eve Babitz, author interview, June 17, 1993.

136 *"I think he was far too smart"* Nurit Wilde, author interview, October 9, 2003.

136 *"I don't think David"* Souther, op. cit.

137 *"David hadn't come to terms"* Doheny, op. cit.

137 *"David was like a conduit"* Roberts, op. cit.

137 *"I found myself in dire straits"* Blue in John Tobler, "Rambling through with David Blue," *ZigZag*, April 1974.

137 *"Judee had been in Hollywood"* Mark Volman, author interview, October 8, 2003.

138 *"I remember her coming home"* Jim Pons e-mail, June 2004.

138 *"There's no one more important"* Souther, op. cit.

138 *"I remember going"* Straw, op. cit.

138 *"I knew very little about Judee"* Graham Nash e-mail, May 2004.

138 *"When I first met him"* Sill in Grover Lewis, "Judee Sill: Soldier of the Heart," *Rolling Stone*, April 13, 1972.

139 *"I always thought he was"* Derek Taylor, author interview, August 21, 1992.

139 *"He had girlfriends"* Judy Henske, author interview, October 8, 2003.

139 *"They were the best couple"* Chris Darrow, author interview, October 4, 2003.

139 *"Linda had great taste in songs"* Souther, op. cit.

139 *"All of us spent countless hours"* Ibid.

140 *"Asylum was definitely shelter"* Ibid.

140 *"They're not out there"* Roberts in Steve Chapple and Reebee Garofalo, *Rock 'n' Roll Is Here to Pay*, p. 284.

140 *"Asylum had one style"* Cornyn, op. cit.

140 *"The Asylum vibe"* Craig Doerge, author interview, October 8, 2003.

140 *"Asylum was a very pompous thing"*   Robert Marchese, author interview, October 22, 2003.

140 *"They've all become very successful"*   Geffen in Roy Carr, "Will CSNY Ever Reunite and Find True Happiness?: This Is David Geffen, by Gentleman's Agreement, Manager to the Superstars," *New Musical Express*, July 29, 1972.

141 *"David and Elliot were cunning"*   Doheny, op. cit.

141 *"Ahmet was extremely erudite"*   Ibid.

141 *"Elliot Roberts had a ritual"*   Denny Bruce, author interview, October 6, 2003.

141 *"Elliot was our personal Woody Allen"*   Souther, op. cit.

142 *"I asked them why"*   Essra Mohawk, author interview, February 2, 2004.

142 *"Joni knew who Judee was"*   Art Johnson in booklet accompanying Sill's *Dreams Come True*, Water Records, 2005.

142 *"We were sorry to lose Joni"*   Waronker, op. cit.

142 *"We were roommates"*   Geffen in *Joni Mitchell—Woman of Heart and Mind* documentary, 2003.

142 *"He must be talking to an artist"*   Ertegun in George W. S. Trow Jr., "Eclectic, Reminiscent, Amused, Fickle, Perverse (Ahmet Ertegun)," 1978 *New Yorker* profile.

143 *"I was watching [James's] career"*   Mitchell to Penny Valentine in *Sounds*, June 3, 1972.

143 *"I remember when she sang it to me"*   Geffen, author interview, December 8, 2004.

144 *"I don't have a large circle"*   Mitchell, op. cit.

144 *"Oh, it was a low blow"*   Mitchell, author interview, September 14, 2004.

144 *"Assumptions were made"*   Ibid.

144 *"I'm not trying to exonerate"*   Doheny, op. cit.

144 *"I guess what he meant"*   Mitchell, author interview, September 14, 2004.

144 *"Artists tend to be difficult"*   Geffen, author interview, December 8, 2004.

145 *"an extremely quiet and modest gentleman"*   Geffen in Roy Carr, op. cit.

145 *"It was the straw"*   Geffen, author interview, December 8, 2004.

145 *"Stephen kinda thought"*   Geffen in Carr, op. cit.

145 *"attendant managers"*   Stills in Dave Zimmer, *Crosby, Stills and Nash*, pp. 134–135.

146 *"Nash took Rita away"*   Crosby in Zimmer, p. 136.

146 *"people can't listen to a song"*   Nash in Ben Fong-Torres, "Far Out in a Loft with Graham Nash," *Rolling Stone*, August 19, 1971.

146 *"The trouble is"*   Crosby in Ben Fong-Torres, "David Crosby: The *Rolling Stone* Interview," *Rolling Stone*, July 23, 1970.

147 *"Don't worry"*   Story in Bruce, op. cit.

147 *"You never knew"*   Young in McDonough, *Shakey*, p. 353.

147 *"I was saying, 'OK'"*   Young in Nick Kent, "Neil Young and the Haphazard Highway That Leads to Unconditional Love," in *The Dark Stuff*, p. 317.

148 *"all but abdicated"*   John Mendelssohn, *Rolling Stone*, March 30, 1972.

149 *"Everybody said"*   Young in Bud Scoppa, "Tonight's the Night: Play It Loud and Stay in the Other Room!," *New Musical Express*, June 28, 1975.

149   *"[That] turned him against everything"*   Roberts in Cameron Crowe, "Neil Young: The Last American Hero," *Rolling Stone*, February 8, 1979.

149   *"The tour was torture"*   Nitzsche in David Talbot and Barbara Zheutlin, "Expecting to Fly: Jack Nitzsche," *Crawdaddy*, November 1974.

149   *"The ridicule Neil suffered"*   Snodgress to McDonough, *Shakey*, op. cit., p. 380.

149   *"Jack always felt"*   Bruce, op. cit.

149   *"At Warners"*   Ibid.

150   *"I thought what was happening"*   Young in McDonough, *Shakey*, op. cit., p. 379.

150   *"For the first time"*   Young in Cameron Crowe, "Chips Off the Old Buffalo," *Rolling Stone*, September 25, 1975.

150   *"The Eagles were* made *to sell"*   Roberts, author interview, June 18, 1993.

150   *"Being around Geffen"*   Frey in Joe Smith, *Off the Record*, p. 353.

151   *"'Take It Easy' was"*   Domenic Priore, author interview, October 10, 2003.

151   *"The way we actually broke"*   Roberts, author interview, June 18, 1993.

151   *"They sang 'Witchy Woman'"*   Diltz, op. cit.

152   *"I saw the Eagles'"*   Jonh Ingham, author interview, May 26, 2004.

152   *"The Eagles fine-tuned"*   Cotton to John Einarson, *Desperados*, p. 229.

152   *"The weird thing"*   Darrow, op. cit.

152   *"The singer-songwriter thing"*   Asher, author interview, June 25, 1993.

152   *"None of us were"*   Frey in Crowe, "Chips off the Old Buffalo," op. cit.

152   *"It's my assumption"*   Frey in Fred Goodman, *The Mansion on the Hill*, p. 234.

152   *"At the moment"*   Geffen in Carr, op. cit.

152   *"I looked at Asylum"*   Waronker, op. cit.

153   *"After I joined the Eagles"*   Leadon, op. cit.

153   *"Cass had given up"*   Denny Doherty, author interview, October 23, 2003.

153   *"I stayed up"*   Ibid.

154   *"Terry liked witty, funny people"*   Eve Babitz, author interview, November 5, 1997.

154   *"It must have been a week"*   Anita Pallenberg, author interview, October 28, 1997.

154   *"They told me, 'Okay'"*   Bergman in Judson Klinger and Greg Mitchell, "Gram Finale: The Profoundly Sick Life and Mysteriously Perverse Death of the Prince of Country-Rock," *Crawdaddy*, October 1976.

154   *"There's a history"*   Perry Richardson, author interview, October 28, 1997.

154   *"He blew up"*   Chris Hillman, author interview, November 4, 1997.

155   *"I went with my hat"*   Parsons in Loraine Alterman, "Parsons Knows," *Melody Maker*, April 7, 1973.

155   *"I think he felt"*   Richardson, op. cit.

155   *"I keep my love"*   Parsons in private letter, 1972.

155   *"Never"*   Gretchen Carpenter, author interview, November 5, 1997.

156   *"He'd flirted with decadence"*   Scoppa, op. cit.

156   *"He was the kind of person"*   Hillman, op. cit.

157   *"Gene and Jesse"*   Rick Clark in Sid Griffin, "Gene Clark: Dr. Byrd . . . and Mr. Hyde," *Mojo*, August 1998.

158 *"My real feelings"* McGuinn in Johnny Rogan, *Crosby, Stills, Nash and Young*, p. 64.

8 The Machinery vs. the Popular Song

187 *"Every record company"* Neal Preston, author interview, October 22, 2003.

187 *"The open boomtown quality"* Babitz in *Eve's Hollywood* (New York: Delacorte, 1974).

188 *"Warners' music sales were rising at an average of 28 percent a year"* Steve Chapple and Reebee Garofalo, *Rock 'n' Roll Is Here to Pay*, pp. 208–209.

188 *"The mood was pretty buoyant"* Barry Hansen, author interview, June 21, 1993.

188 *"we have developed a looseness"* Wickham memo from Mo Ostin archive, February 15, 1973.

188 *"I was much more gregarious"* Joe Smith, author interview, October 2, 2003.

189 *"I've felt often"* Simon in Stuart Werbin, "The *Rolling Stone* Interview: James Taylor and Carly Simon," *Rolling Stone*, January 4, 1973.

189 *"The scene of the two families"* Smith, op. cit.

189 *"All rock and roll heaven"* Ibid.

189 *"Randy was one of the funniest people"* Russ Titelman, author interview, June 30, 1993.

190 *"half of the time was spent," "kinda outside"* Waronker and Newman in David Felton, "Randy Newman, the Amazing Human: You've Got to Let This Fat Boy in Your Life," *Rolling Stone*, August 31, 1972.

190 *"If you have a Black Sabbath"* George in Steve Moore, "Little Feat: Still Out There among the Great Unknown Bands," *Rolling Stone*, August 2, 1973.

191 *"Lowell was so incredibly generous"* Tackett in Bud Scoppa, liner notes for *Little Feat: Hotcakes and Outtakes* (Rhino Records, 2000).

191 *"I had the party house"* Danny Hutton, author interview, June 10. 1993.

191 *"The Doobies were just"* Ted Templeman, author interview, October 30, 2003.

191 *"Lenny was the catalyst"* Ibid.

192 *"Many times I felt"* David Geffen, author interview, December 8, 2004.

192 *"What happens"* Ron Stone, author interview, October 14, 2003.

192 *"Asylum was an artist-oriented label"* Henley in Marc Eliot, *To the Limit*, p. 91.

192 *"I think Geffen stiffed everybody"* Ned Doheny, author interview, February 23, 2004.

192 *"When he first started out"* Jimmy Webb, author interview, March 23, 2005.

193 *"Manager-client relations"* Carl Gottlieb, author interview, October 4, 2003.

193 *"At the time I don't recall"* Geffen, op. cit.

193 *"After I decided to sell to Steve Ross"* Ibid.

193 *"Geffen sent them a ticket," "a little pea"* Dexter and Peek in David Rensin, "America: What This Band Needs Is a Hat Trick," *Rolling Stone*, November 8, 1973.

193 *"Clive had everything laid out"* Fogelberg in Paul Zollo, liner notes for *Portrait: The Music of Dan Fogelberg from 1972 to 1997* (Columbia Legacy, 1997).

194 *"bury the band"* Hartmann in Fred Goodman, *The Mansion on the Hill*, p. 242.

194 *"I immediately made"* Azoff in Joe Smith, *Off the Record*, p. 356.

194 *"Irving said"* Bernie Leadon, author interview, October 23, 2003.

194 *"I never liked Azoff"* Doheny, op. cit.

194 *"I went back"* Azoff in Joe Smith, op. cit.

195 *"Our life then was simpler"* Henley in the DVD *Under the Covers: The Music, Artists, and Stories behind the Album Covers You Love*, 2002.

195 *"We'd all been"* Frey in Cameron Crowe, "Conversations with Don Henley and Glenn Frey," liner notes for *The Very Best of the Eagles*, (Rhino Records, 2003).

195 *"Glenn was enamored"* Leadon, op. cit.

195 *"The metaphor was probably"* Henley in Marc Eliot, *To the Limit*, op. cit., p. 93.

195 *"the evils of fame and success"* Ibid.

196 *"I think we all have an affection"* Souther in interview with Debbie Kruger at www.debbiekruger.com.

196 *"The process of writing"* Browne in 1994 documentary *Jackson Browne: Going Home*.

196 *"Jackson seems equally divided"* Janet Maslin, review of *For Everyman*, *Rolling Stone*, November 22, 1973.

197 *"Lindley is perfect for me"* Browne in Fawcett/Diltz, *California Rock, California Sound*, p. 80.

197 *"We got together"* Lindley in interview in *Mix*, May 1990.

197 *"I think the reality"* Doheny, op. cit.

198 *"Like Jackson"* Lenny Waronker, author interview, October 20, 2003.

198 *"I thought Linda"* Geffen, op. cit.

198 *"Linda would hear a song"* David Jackson, author interview, October 31, 2003.

198 *"Linda went out with a lot of guys"* Denny Bruce, author interview, October 6, 2003.

199 *"Tough situation"* Souther in Fawcett/Diltz, op. cit.

199 *"We were like kids"* Ronstadt in Fong-Torres, "Heartbreak on Wheels," *Rolling Stone*, March 27, 1975.

199 *"Someone's got to cook"* Ronstadt in Nolan in "The Linda Ronstadt Coverup!," *Phonograph Record*, November 1974.

199 *"She had a number of producers"* Ben Fong-Torres, author interview, October 23, 2003.

199 *"J. D. and I used to go"* Linda Ronstadt, author interview, February 7, 1995.

199 *"He's reserved"* Taylor in Ben Fong-Torres, "Peter Asher Presents Platinum Diggers of '77, Starring James Taylor and Linda Ronstadt," *Rolling Stone*, December 29, 1977.

199 *"He knew what to do"* Waddy Wachtel, author interview, October 17, 2003.

200 *"Most guys had a tendency"* Ronstadt, op. cit.

200 *"Linda was my educator"* Peter Asher, author interview, October 18, 2003.

200 *"There's not a girl singer"* Ibid.

200 *"A lot of times"* Doheny, op. cit.

200 *"I went over that line"* Ronstadt in Jean Vallely, "The *Playboy* Interview," *Playboy*, April 1980.

201 *"It made me nervous"* Ronstadt, author interview, February 7, 1995.

201 *"She even confessed to Ben Fong-Torres that she'd tried heroin"* Ronstadt confession in Ben Fong-Torres, "Heartbreak on Wheels," op. cit.

201 *"I wrote some songs"* Mitchell in Sean O'Hagan, "Idol Talk: Joni Mitchell," *New Musical Express*, June 4, 1988.

201 *"The Roxy was a big threat"* Robert Marchese, author interview, October 22, 2003.

202 *"You had to have coke"* Bruce, op. cit.

202 *"There were a lot of feelings"* Ronstadt, author interview, February 7, 1995.

202 *"There was a period"* Geffen, op. cit.

202 *"conjured up images"* Sugerman in *Wonderland Avenue: Tales of Glamour and Excess* (London: Sidgwick & Jackson, 1989).

202 *"The very people"* Ronstadt, author interview, February 7, 1995.

202 *"Whatever gig you went to"* Jonh Ingham, author interview, May 26, 2004.

203 *"The Roxy and the Troub"* J. D. Souther, author interview, October 13, 2004.

203 *"The Byrds had just finished"* Nick Kent, author interview, July 14, 1993.

203 *"Everybody got really bored"* Greg Shaw, author interview, May 13, 1993.

203 *"Glenn Frey is"* Smith, author interview, October 2, 2003.

203 *"I remember seeing Frey"* Kent, op. cit.

203 *"The people who lived"* Robert Plant, author interview, September 18, 2003.

204 *"Robert desperately wanted"* Nancy Retchin, author interview, April 30, 2004.

204 *"The canyon scene"* Plant, op. cit.

204 *"The downfall of the '60s dream"* Pamela Des Barres, author interview, June 22, 1993.

204 *"The '60s are definitely not"* Young in McDonough, *Shakey*, pp. 409–410.

205 *"I short-circuited there"* Stills in Zimmer, *Crosby, Stills and Nash*, p. 162.

205 *"We'd been at each other's faces"* Crosby in Jaan Uhelszki, "Crosby & Nash: Rocky & Bullwinkle in Marin County," *Creem*, February 1976.

205 *"Neil didn't want"* Snodgress in McDonough, *Shakey*, op. cit., p. 402.

205 *"I don't want to talk about"* Young in Johnny Rogan, *Crosby, Stills, Nash and Young*, p. 65.

205 *"I know I've blown"* Stills in Rogan, ibid., p. 66.

205 *"Tragedy was written across"* Nash in Zimmer, *Crosby, Stills and Nash*, op. cit., p. 164.

205 *"I just didn't feel like"* Young in Bud Scoppa, "Tonight's the Night: Play It Loud and Stay in the Other Room!," *New Musical Express*, June 28, 1975.

206 *"He's had a lot of bad breaks"* Elliot Roberts, author interview, June 18, 1993.

206 *"He likes to surround himself"* Nils Lofgren in Andy Childs, "Rock 'n' Roll Gymnast," *Zigzag*, March 1977.

206 the canyon's *"dark side"* Andes in McDonough, *Shakey*, op. cit., p. 408.

206 *"Neil's always been very conscious"* Lofgren in Andy Childs, op. cit.

207 *"I took the Eagles"* Roberts, op. cit.

207 *"Neil had a unique place"* Leadon, op. cit.

207 *"Gram was real easy"* John Lomax III, author interview, November 1997.

207 *"A lot of it had to do"* John Delgatto, author interview, November 1997.

208 *"Death [is] something"* Parsons in Judson Klinger and Greg Mitchell, "Gram Finale: The Profoundly Sick Life and Mysteriously Perverse Death of the Prince of Country-Rock," *Crawdaddy*, October 1976.

208 *"The things I like of Gram's"* Ronstadt, author interview, February 7, 1995.

209 *"I've been to Vietnam"* Barbary in Klinger/Mitchell, op. cit.

209 *"He'd cleaned up"* Keith Richards, author interview, September 23, 1997.

209 *"I got completely fucked"* Geffen in Holzman/Daws, *Follow the Music*, p. 389.

210 *"Jerry Greenberg and I"* Mel Posner, author interview, October 14, 2003.

210 *"I kind of postponed it"* Ertegun in Wade and Picardie, *Music Man*, p. 227.

210 *"Jerry was never a consideration"* Geffen in ibid.

210 *"One day"* Jerry Wexler with David Ritz, *Rhythm and the Blues*, p. 254.

210 *"Like Asylum"* Geffen in "Founder Holzman Leaves Elektra; Geffen In," *Rolling Stone*, September 13, 1973.

210 *"Look at that creep"* Dowd in Wade and Picardie, *Music Man*, op. cit., pp. 229–230.

211 *"If you will"* Stan Cornyn, author interview, October 20, 2003.

211 *"Elektra was failing"* Geffen, author interview, December 8, 2004.

211 *"I think an era died"* Simon in Holzman/Daws, *Follow the Music*, op. cit., p. 393.

211 *"I don't want to talk about Geffen"* Jac Holzman, author interview, October 22, 2003.

211 *"I thought it was no different"* Geffen, op. cit.

211 *"We suddenly were in a different era"* Posner, op. cit.

211 *"We now had someone saying"* Ibid.

212 *"I was not a person"* Geffen in Holzman/Daws, *Follow the Music*, op. cit., p. 391.

212 *"The Eagles' problem"* Bruce, op. cit.

212 *"There'd always been disagreement"* Leadon, op. cit.

212 *"Already Gone'"* Frey in Cameron Crowe, "Conversations with Don Henley and Glenn Frey," op. cit.

213 *"The thing I noticed about Geffen"* Jerry Yester, author interview, November 1, 2003.

213 *"You sit in a room"* Tom Waits, author interview, January 28, 1999.

213 *"There were a lot of good writers"* Roberts, op. cit.

213 *"It wasn't like I was"* Waits, author interview, September 3, 2004.

214 *"they're about as exciting"* Waits in Fred Dellar, "Would You Say This Man Was Attempting to Convey an Impression of Sordid Bohemianism?" *New Musical Express*, June 5, 1976.

214 *"'I rode through the desert"* Waits in John Platt, "No Time for Cosmic Debris," *Zigzag*, June 1977.

214 *"I was a young kid"* Waits, author interview, September 3, 2004.

214 *"When I saw his L.A. set"* Hynde from her Tim Buckley feature "How a Hippie Hero Became a Sultry Sex Object . . . ," *New Musical Express*, June 1974.

214 *"It'll get more moronic"* Buckley in Hynde, ibid.

215 *"Dylan 'should thank me'"* Geffen in Fred Goodman, *The Mansion on the Hill*, op. cit., p. 251.

215 *"so mean, so jealous"* Geffen in Tom King, *David Geffen*, p. 252.

215 *"You'd jump into a pool of pus"* Wexler in *Rhythm and the Blues*, p. 253.

215 *"I couldn't believe it"* Geffen, ibid.

215 *"Here was Wexler"* Smith, author interview, October 2, 2003.

216 *"I told you"* Ibid.

9   After the Thrill Is Gone

218 *"Soon as I walked in"* Robert Marchese, author interview, October 22, 2003.

218 *"The really sordid people"* Nick Kent, author interview, July 14, 1993.

218 *"By now the innocence"* Danny Hutton, author interview, June 10, 1993.

218 *"If it's this good"* "34 Who Are 30," *Rolling Stone*, January 3, 1974.

219 *"The music business"* Janet Maslin, "Linda Ronstadt: The Image vs. the Woman," *Rolling Stone*, May 9, 1974.

219 *"We were bedazzled"* Fred Goodman, *The Mansion on the Hill*, p. 245.

219 *"I knew she was a heavyweight"* David Rensin, "Tom Scott: Joni's Spark," *Rolling Stone*, August 1, 1974.

219 *"No section had been able"* Joni Mitchell, author interview, September 14, 1994.

220 *"Joni reached a point"* Randy Newman, author interview, July 26, 2003.

220 *"I can only say"* Mitchell, op. cit.

220 *"She was unbelievably snobbish"* Kent, op. cit.

220 *"This, I think"* Mitchell in Malka, "Joni Mitchell: Self-Portrait of a Superstar," *Maclean's*, June 1974, in Luftig, *The Joni Mitchell Companion*, p. 71.

221 *"appeared to be a really hip"* Nitzsche in David Talbot and Barbara Zheutlin, "Expecting to Fly: Jack Nitzsche," *Crawdaddy*, November 1974.

221 *"because he's got a tin ear"* Ibid.

222 *"It wasn't just entertainment"* Allison Caine, author interview, October 29, 2003.

222 *"I would say that Elliot"* Ron Stone, author interview, June 25, 1993.

222 *"the financial superstar"* Quoted in Tom King, *David Geffen*, p. 227.

222 *"It was easily"* Mel Posner, author interview, October 14, 2003.

222 *"I don't even know"* Browne in Joe Smith and Michael Fink, *Off the Record*, p. 314.

223 *"Anyone who's met Linda"* Peter Asher, author interview, June 25, 1993.

223 *"Linda had a goal"* Nurit Wilde, author interview, October 9, 2003.

223 *"It's only natural"* Peter Herbst, "Rock's Venus Takes Control of Her Affairs: The *Rolling Stone* Interview," *Rolling Stone*, October 19, 1978.

224 *"I think it was if anything"* David Geffen, author interview, December 8, 2004.

224 *"I didn't know"* Linda Ronstadt, author interview, February 7, 1995.

224 *"The essence of her organic ability"* Chris Darrow, author interview, October 4, 2003.

224 *"It's hard to talk"* Bernie Leadon, author interview, October 23, 2003.

224 *"I stopped doing cocaine"* Ibid.

224 *"I think Bernie and Randy"* J. D. Souther, author interview, October 13, 2004.

225 *"Don wanted things"* Leadon, op. cit.

225 *"As you get toward"* Domenic Priore, author interview, October 10, 2003.

225 *"'Take It Easy' was an amazing song"* Robert Plant, author interview, September 18, 2003.

225 *"These were the horniest boys"* Marc Eliot, *To the Limit*, p. 117.

225 *"Once you get comfortable"* Henley in Cameron Crowe, "Chips off the Old Buffalo," *Rolling Stone*, September 25, 1975.

226 *"Irving's 15%"* Souther in Goodman, *The Mansion on the Hill*, op. cit., p. 247.

226 *"If he's ruthless"* Henley in Eliot, *To the Limit*, op. cit., p. 108.

226 *"It was extraordinary"* Tom Nolan, author interview, October 21, 2003.

226 *"There was a year or two"* Jackson Browne, author interview, October 18, 1993.

226 *"an empty sort of disillusioned hollowness"* Ronstadt in Herbst, op. cit.

226 *"To me it always seemed"* Ronstadt, author interview, February 7, 1995.

227 *"a way of guaranteeing your privacy"* Ronstadt in Fawcett/Diltz, *California Rock, California Sound*, p. 113.

227 *"These people had been broke"* Judy James, author interview, November 3, 2003.

227 *"J. D. was a pain in the ass"* Joe Smith, author interview, October 2, 2003.

228 *"[Geffen] went to Richie"* Young in *Omaha Rainbow* interview, Spring 1979.

228 *"It seemed like a good idea"* Geffen in Peter Knobler, "Souther, Hillman & Furay . . . and Geffen," *Crawdaddy*, July 1974.

228 *"Souther Hillman Furay"* Ibid.

228 *"Souther I had to roust"* Phil Kaufman, author interview, November 7, 2003.

228 *"Who does he think he is?"* Furay in Knobler, op. cit.

228 *"Our debut"* Hillman in Bill Wasserzieher, "This Byrd Has Flown: Chris Hillman Comes to the Coach House," *OC Weekly*, August 1997.

229 *"They didn't get together"* Geffen in Knobler, op. cit.

229 *"There was a real conflict"* Mark Volman, author interview, October 8, 2003.

229 *"What I most remember"* Browne, author interview, October 18, 1993.

230 *"The Eagles, Jackson Browne"* Don Snowden, "Little Feat: The Rock and Roll Doctors," *Rock around the World*, July 12, 1977.

230 *"The band was stop-start"* Richie Hayward, author interview, March 4, 1994.

231 *"Lowell's hedonism"* Ibid.

231 *"George's response"* Story from Denny Bruce, author interview, October 6, 2003.

231   *"It's just ironic"*   Raitt in Ben Fong-Torres, "Ain't Gonna Be Your Sugar Mama No More: Bonnie Raitt Sings a Woman's Blues to the Victims of a Man's World," *Rolling Stone*, December 18, 1975.

231   *"I was hanging out with Lowell"*   Raitt in John Tobler, "At Home with Bonnie Raitt," *ZigZag*, June 1976.

231   *"There are tons of women"*   Raitt to Penny Valentine, *Street Life*, May 1, 1976.

232   *"The North pretended"*   Newman, op. cit.

232   *"mourning past styles," "this white, middle-class"*   Cooder in Mikal Gilmore, "Ry Cooder: The Reluctant Curator," *Rolling Stone*, September 20, 1979.

232   *"For subject matter"*   Donald Fagen, author interview, March 5, 1993.

232   *"To say that we were"*   Walter Becker, author interview, December 9, 1999.

233   *"Geffen and I"*   Souther, author interview, October 13, 2004.

233   *"Music started to become"*   Henley in Anthony DeCurtis, "Hotel California," in Ashley Kahn, Holly George-Warren, and Shawn Dahl, eds., *Rolling Stone: The '70s* (New York: Little, Brown, 1998).

233   *"I inherited that whole"*   Smith, author interview, October 2, 2003.

233   *"Geffen and Holzman"*   Ibid.

233   *"Steve said"*   Ibid.

234   *"an executive perspective"*   "Random Notes," *Rolling Stone*, January 29, 1976.

234   *"David wanted to carry on"*   Elliot Roberts, author interview, June 18, 1993.

234   *"Every one of us"*   Dave Zimmer, *Crosby, Stills and Nash*, p. 171.

234   *"take it to the max"*   Ibid.

234   *"We did one for the art"*   Stills in Cameron Crowe, "Crosby, Stills, Nash, and Young Carry On," *Crawdaddy*, October 1974.

234   *"Suddenly the money"*   Carl Gottlieb, author interview, June 11, 1993.

234   *"CSNY wrote the plan"*   Stills in Zimmer, op. cit.

235   *"Everything that everybody"*   Holbert in Crosby/Gottlieb, *Long Time Gone*, p. 251.

235   *"Sometimes I get a little drunk"*   Stills in Barbara Charone, "Stills: From Fish Bowl to Pleasure Dome," *Sounds*, August 16, 1975.

235   *"[The tour] was"*   Young in Crowe, "Neil Young: The Last American Hero," *Rolling Stone*, February 8, 1979.

236   *"dark shit numbers"*   Roy Carr, "Crosby, Stills, Nash, Young, and Bert," *New Musical Express*, August 31, 1974.

236   *"Neil utilized CSN"*   Nash from Zimmer, *Crosby, Stills and Nash*, op. cit., p. 178.

236   *"It's not easy"*   Gottlieb, op. cit.

237   *"We're playing in a place"*   Young in Bud Scoppa, "Tonight's the Night: Play It Loud and Stay in the Other Room!," *New Musical Express*, June 28, 1975.

237   *"Somehow I feel like"*   Young in Cameron Crowe, "So Hard to Make Arrangements for Yourself: The *Rolling Stone* Interview with Neil Young," *Rolling Stone*, August 14, 1975.

237   *"an idyllic time," "just sparkling"*   Talbot in Crowe, "Neil Young: The Last American Hero," *Rolling Stone*, February 8, 1979.

237   *"There are all kinds"*   Ronstadt, author interview, February 7, 1995.

238   *"For me the '60s"*   Gottlieb, op. cit.

238 *"the idea that rock and roll"* Crosby in Crosby/Gottlieb, *Long Time Gone*, op. cit., p. 253.

238 *"What happened then"* Jan Henderson, author interview, October 5, 2003.

238 *"Cocaine"* Ronstadt, author interview, February 7, 1995.

238 *"I thought that was how"* Waddy Wachtel, author interview, October 17, 2003.

238 *"I remember when it started"* Bud Scoppa, author interview, October 9, 2003.

238 *"For a while no one"* Roberts, op. cit.

239 *"Drugs did decimate"* Stone, op. cit.

239 *"We'd tried to be an agency"* Roberts, op. cit.

239 *"I don't think David or Elliot"* Stone, op. cit.

239 *"I was like, 'Shit'"* Leadon, op. cit.

240 *"Even though Glenn's"* Felder in Cameron Crowe, "Chips off the Old Buffalo," op. cit.

240 *"Bernie wasn't ruthless"* Darrow, op. cit.

241 *"There's a lot of bullshit"* John Einarson, e-mail to author, October 25, 2003.

242 *"He became an increasingly"* Scoppa, op. cit.

242 *"I was instinctively drawn"* Jimmy Webb, author interview, March 23, 2005.

242 *"There was this whole idea"* Ronstadt, author interview, February 7, 1995.

242 "Court and Spark *was"* Joni Mitchell, author interview, September 14, 1994.

243 *"Joni was coming off"* Ron Stone, author interview, October 14, 2003.

243 *"David Geffen rang me up"* Bones Howe, author interview, June 22, 1993.

243 *"Preproduction always"* Ibid.

243 *"Tom's whole act"* Marchese, op. cit.

243 *"I'd lost the basic lines"* Weston in "L.A.'s Troubadour Closes—Maybe," *Rolling Stone,* July 17, 1975.

244 *"How do you get"* Jac Holzman, author interview, October 22, 2003.

244 *"Graham sang"* Ibid.

10 Go Your Own Way

245 *"Warren was a good friend"* Mark Volman, author interview, October 8, 2003.

246 *"The road, booze and I"* Zevon in Paul Nelson, "The Crackup and Resurrection of Warren Zevon," *Rolling Stone,* March 19, 1981.

246 *"As I got to know Warren"* Peter Asher, author interview, October 18, 2003.

247 *"The people who inhabit"* Greil Marcus, "Warren Zevon's Red Harvest," *Village Voice,* March 6, 1978.

247 *"I don't know whether L.A.'s changed"* Zevon in Fawcett/Diltz, *California Rock, California Sound,* p. 153.

247 *"Phyllis was very pretty"* Nurit Wilde, author interview, October 9, 2003.

247 *"I didn't want to say"* Steve Clarke, "Metaphysical Graffiti: An Interview with Jackson Browne," *New Musical Express,* December 18, 1976.

247 *"He really influenced"*   Paul Nelson, "We Are All on Tour: Are You Prepared for the Pretender—Jackson Browne?" *Rolling Stone*, December 16, 1976.

248 *"I think it was hard for Jackson"*   Craig Doerge, author interview, October 8, 2003.

248 *"the apotheosis of Browne's art"*   Richard Cook, "Ramblin' on Empty," *New Musical Express*, July 31, 1982.

248 *"The whole scene"*   Doheny in Fred Goodman, *The Mansion on the Hill*, p. 245.

248 *"This is a concept album"*   Henley in Constant Meijers, "Up to Date with the Eagles," *ZigZag*, December 1976.

248 *"to get people off," "concerned with"*   Henley in Tom Nolan, "California Dreamin' with the Eagles," *Phonograph Record*, June 1975.

248 *"If only for perfectly capturing"*   Young in Cameron Crowe, "The Eagles: Chips off the Old Buffalo," *Rolling Stone*, September 25, 1975.

249 *"We never glorified California"*   Henley in *Musician* interview, 1989, quoted in Karen O'Brien, *Shadows and Light*, p. 169.

249 *"We were in a solid gold shitter"*   J. D. Souther, author interview, October 13, 2004.

249 *"It's very romantic"*   Henley in Nolan, op. cit.

249 *"There was a certain intensity"*   Joe Smith, *Off the Record*, p. 353.

250 *"the half he owned"*   Marc Eliot, *To the Limit*, p. 137.

250 *"Irving Azoff went about"*   David Geffen, author interview, December 8, 2004.

250 *"There were always tremendous difficulties"*   Ibid.

251 *"Last time I saw Gene"*   Robert Marchese, author interview, October 22, 2003.

251 *"Gene was not in good shape"*   John York in Sid Griffin, "Dr. Byrd . . . and Mr. Hyde," *Mojo*, August 1998.

252 *"the Errol Flynns and Tyrone Powers"*   Nicks in Timothy White, *Rolling Stone*, September 3, 1981.

252 *"Don taught me"*   Nicks in "Blonde on Blonde," *Spin*, October 1997.

252 *"One of the things"*   Buckingham in Mat Snow, "Lindsey Buckingham: Your Money or Your Wife!," *Q*, September 1992.

253 *"It was party time"*   Fleetwood from Mat Snow, "Mick Fleetwood: The Ancient Tympanist," *Q*, May 1990.

253 *"That was the music business"*   Frey in Anthony DeCurtis, "Hotel California," *The Rolling Stone Book of the '70s*, p. 224.

253 *"I didn't feel coliseums"*   Linda Ronstadt, author interview, February 7, 1995.

253 *"There was a direction"*   Ibid.

253 *"L.A. is real comfortable"*   Ronstadt in Peter Herbst, "Rock's Venus Takes Control of Her Affairs: The *Rolling Stone* Interview," *Rolling Stone*, October 19, 1978.

254 *"Corporate rock became"*   Lenny Waronker, author interview, October 20, 2003.

254 *"She came in with massive attitude"*   Ibid.

254 *"Rickie in some ways"* Ron Stone, author interview, June 25, 1993.

255 "Small Change *was really"* Bones Howe, author interview, June 22, 1993.

256 *"The dream was unfulfilled"* Henley in DeCurtis, op. cit., p. 225.

256 *"He was really a tortured person"* Billy Payne, author interview, March 4, 1993.

256 *"There was a picture"* Ted Templeman, author interview, October 30, 2003.

256 *"He was pretty callous"* Martin Kibbee, author interview, March 1, 1994.

257 *"He came out to my house"* Billy Payne, author interview, March 4, 1994.

257 *"It was like everybody"* Souther, op. cit.

259 *"A lot of people"* Ibid.

259 *"With a cold eye"* Marcus, op. cit.

259 *"Jackson figured"* Waddy Wachtel, author interview, October 17, 2003.

259 *"Much of 1977"* Zevon in Paul Nelson, "The Crackup and Resurrection of Warren Zevon," *Rolling Stone*, March 19, 1981.

260 *"I went to the door"* Zevon in Tom Nolan, *Ross MacDonald: A Biography* (New York: Scribner, 1999).

260 *"I opened the door"* Wachtel, op. cit.

260 *"[There is] the unrealized shame," "This year"* Crosby in Steve Turner, *New Musical Express*, November 1, 1975.

261 *"How many times"* Nash in Ted Joseph, "Nasty Nash: Pre-Road Downers, Post-Album Dumping," *Crawdaddy*, September 1976.

261 *"I could see the control"* Wilde, op. cit.

261 *"I just left a trail"* Young in McDonough, *Shakey*, p. 500.

261 *"It's like when you look"* Joe Vitale, author interview, May 13, 1997.

262 *"I'm like a dinosaur"* Young in Richard Cook, "Neil Young: When Does a Dinosaur Cut Off Its Tail?" *New Musical Express*, October 9, 1982.

262 *"As soon as I heard"* Young in Cameron Crowe, "The Last American Hero," *Rolling Stone*, February 8, 1979.

263 *"The '80s are here"* Ibid.

263 *"Crosby, Stills, and Nash"* Geffen in Fredric Dannen, *Hit Men: Power Brokers and Fast Money inside the Music Business* (New York: Times Books, 1990), p. 134.

263 *"Do I think cocaine"* Young in Nick Kent, *The Dark Stuff*, p. 328.

263 "Hejira *was not understood"* Joni Mitchell, author interview, September 14, 1994.

264 *"from one solo pilot"* Mitchell in *Los Angeles Times* interview, December 8, 1996, quoted in Karen O'Brien, *Shadows and Light*, p. 180.

264 *"Somebody asked me"* Smith, op. cit.

264 *"I had had enough"* Geffen, op. cit.

265 *"By then I had"* Ibid.

265 *"At some point David"* Mel Posner, author interview, October 14, 2003.

265 *"David started feeling"* Roberts in McDonough, *Shakey*, op. cit., p. 555.

265 *"We stopped hanging out"* Ibid., p. 580.

266 *"If I didn't talk to her"* Geffen in Tom King, *David Geffen*, p. xiv.

Coda   Like a Setting Sun

267 *"The bartenders there"*   Robert Marchese, author interview, October 22, 2003.

268 *"The people who were successful"*   Stan Cornyn, author interview, October 20, 2003.

268 *"The real impetus"*   Mike Davis, *Ecology of Fear: Los Angeles and the Imagination of Disaster* (New York: Metropolitan Books, 1998).

268 *"Before we all had nice houses"*   Ronstadt in Jean Vallely, *Playboy*, 1980.

268 *"By then any notion"*   Ron Stone in Michael Walker, "Still Hazy after All These Years," *Los Angeles Times Magazine*, June 1, 2003.

269 *"I hate calling it magic"*   Mosher in Janelle Brown, "Pouring Music down the Canyon," *New York Times*, December 3, 2003.

269 *"If you look at* MTV Cribs"   Chris Darrow, author interview, October 4, 2003.

269 *"My sense is"*   Joel Bernstein, author interview, October 30, 2003.

269 *"I'm not in step"*   Souther in Debbie Kruger, debbiekruger.com, 1998.

269 *"There's no corporate room"*   David Anderle, author interview, October 9, 2003.

269 *"Everybody's a singer-songwriter"*   Mitchell in Dave DiMartino, *Mojo*, August 1998.

270 *"Lenny Waronker was"*   Randy Newman, author interview, July 26, 2003.

270 *"I think I heard"*   Ibid.

270 *"I remember having a conversation"*   Larry Waronker, author interview, October 20, 2003.

270 *"When I took over"*   Joe Smith, author interview, October 2, 2003.

271 *"You have to appreciate"*   Posner, author interview, October 14, 2003.

271 *"It was the greatest ride"*   Geffen, author interview, December 8, 2004.

271 *"There was this old hippie"*   Fred Goodman, author interview, February 11, 1997.

271 *"I don't think anyone"*   Souther, author interview, October 13, 2004.

272 *"Let's say hypothetically"*   Ned Doheny, author interview, February 23, 2004.

272 *"The understanding of history"*   Anderle, op. cit.

272 *"Maybe I should go"*   Ibid.

Suggested Reading

Anson, Robert Sam. *Gone Crazy and Back Again: The Rise and Fall of the Rolling Stone Generation*. New York: Doubleday, 1981.

Banham, Reyner. *Los Angeles: The Architecture of Four Ecologies*. Harmondsworth, England: Penguin, 1971.

Biskind, Peter. *Easy Riders, Raging Bulls: How the Sex, Drugs and Rock-and-Roll Generation Saved Hollywood*. New York: Simon & Schuster, 1998.

Brend, Mark. *American Troubadours: Groundbreaking Singer-Songwriters of the '60s*. San Francisco: Backbeat Books, 2001.

Bruck, Connie. *Master of the Game: Steve Ross and the Creation of Time Warner*. New York: Penguin, 1995.

Burns, Joan Simpson. *The Awkward Embrace: The Creative Artist and the Institution in America*. New York: Alfred A. Knopf, 1975.

Chapple, Steve, and Reebee Garofalo. *Rock 'n' Roll Is Here to Pay: The History and Politics of the Music Industry*. Chicago: Nelson-Hall, 1977.

Cohen, Ronald D. *Rainbow Quest: The Folk Music Revival and American Society, 1940–1970*. Amherst and Boston: University of Massachusetts Press, 2002.

Cornyn, Stan, with Paul Scanlon. *Exploding: The Highs, Hits, Hype, Heroes and Hustlers of the Warner Music Group*. New York: Rolling Stone Press/Harper Entertainment, 2002.

Crosby, David, with Carl Gottlieb. *Long Time Gone: The Autobiography of David Crosby*. New York: Doubleday, 1988.

Dannen, Fredric. *Hit Men: Power Brokers and Fast Money inside the Music Business*. New York: Times Books, 1990.

Davis, Clive, with James Willwerth. *Clive: Inside the Record Business*. New York: William Morrow, 1975.

Davis, Mike. *Ecology of Fear: Los Angeles and the Imagination of Disaster.* New York: Metropolitan Books, 1998.

Didion, Joan. *The White Album.* London: Flamingo, 1993.

DiMartino, Dave. *Singer-Songwriters: Pop Music's Performer-Composers, from A to Zevon.* New York: Billboard Books, 1994.

Doggett, Peter. *Are You Ready for the Country?* London: Viking, 2000.

Draper, Robert. *Rolling Stone Magazine: The Uncensored History.* New York: Doubleday, 1990.

Einarson, John. *Desperados: The Roots of Country Rock.* New York: Cooper Square Press, 2001.

———. *Mr. Tambourine Man: The Life and Legacy of the Byrds' Gene Clark.* San Francisco: Backbeat Books, 2005.

———. *Neil Young: Don't Be Denied.* London: Omnibus Press, 1993.

Einarson, John, with Richie Furay. *There's Something Happening Here: The Story of Buffalo Springfield—For What It's Worth.* London: Rogan House, 1997.

Eliot, Marc. *To the Limit: The Untold Story of the Eagles.* New York: Little, Brown, 1998.

Fawcett, Anthony, and Henry Diltz. *California Rock, California Sound: The Music of Los Angeles and Southern California.* Los Angeles: Reed Books, 1978.

Fein, Art. *The L.A. Musical History Tour.* London: Faber & Faber, 1990.

Flanagan, Bill. *Written in My Soul: Candid Interviews with Rock's Great Songwriters.* London: Omnibus, 1990.

Fong-Torres, Ben. *Hickory Wind: The Life and Times of Gram Parsons.* New York: Pocket Books, 1991.

———. *Not Fade Away: A Backstage Pass to 20 Years of Rock & Roll.* San Francisco: Backbeat Books, 1999.

Frame, Pete. *The Complete Family Trees.* London: Omnibus, 1993.

Goodman, Fred. *The Mansion on the Hill: Dylan, Young, Geffen, Springsteen and the Head-On Collision of Rock and Commerce.* New York: Times Books, 1997.

Holzman, Jac, and Gavan Daws. *Follow the Music: The Life and High Times of Elektra Records in the Great Years of American Pop Culture.* Santa Monica, Calif.: FirstMedia Books, 1998.

Hopkins, Jerry. *The Rock Story.* New York: Signet, 1970.

Hoskyns, Barney. *Ragged Glories: City Lights, Country Funk, American Music.* London: Pimlico, 2003.

———. *Waiting for the Sun: Strange Days, Weird Scenes, and the Sound of Los Angeles.* London: Viking, 1996; rev. ed. London: Bloomsbury, 2003.

Humphries, Patrick. *Small Change: A Life of Tom Waits.* London: Omnibus, 1989.

Jacobs, Jay S. *Wild Years: The Music and Myth of Tom Waits.* Toronto: ECW Press, 2000.

Kaiser, Charles. *1968 in America: Music, Politics, Chaos, Counterculture, and the Shaping of a Generation.* New York: Weidenfeld & Nicholson, 1988.

Kaufman, Phil, with Colin White. *Road Mangler Deluxe.* Glendale, Calif.: White-Boucke, 1993.

Kent, Nick. *The Dark Stuff: Selected Writings on Rock Music 1972–1993.* Harmondsworth, England: Penguin, 1994.

King, Tom. *David Geffen: A Biography of the New Hollywood*. London: Hutchinson, 2000.

Kort, Michele. *Soul Picnic: The Music and Passion of Laura Nyro*. New York: St. Martin's Press, Thomas Dunne Books, 2002.

Kurlansky, Mark. *1968: The Year That Rocked the World*. London: Jonathan Cape, 2004.

Luftig, Stacey (ed.). *The Joni Mitchell Companion: Four Decades of Commentary*. New York: Schirmer Books, 2000.

McDonough, Jimmy. *Shakey: Neil Young's Biography*. London: Jonathan Cape, 2002.

O'Brien, Karen. *Shadows and Light: Joni Mitchell*. London: Virgin Books, 2001.

Olsen, Eric, with Paul Verna and Carlo Wolff (eds.). *The Encyclopaedia of Record Producers*. New York: Billboard Books, 1999.

Orloff, Katherine. *Rock 'n' Roll Woman*. Los Angeles: Nash, 1974.

Phillips, John, with Jim Jerome. *Papa John*. Garden City: Dolphin Books, 1986.

Phillips, Michelle. *California Dreamin': The True Story of the Mamas and the Papas*. New York: Warner Books, 1986.

Pollock, Bruce. *In Their Own Words*. New York: Collier Books, 1975.

Priore, Domenic. *Riot on Sunset Strip: Rock and Roll's Last Stand in Hollywood, 1965–1966*. San Francisco: Chronicle Books, 2005.

Rensin, David. *The Mailroom: Hollywood History from the Bottom Up*. New York: Ballantine, 2003.

Rogan, Johnny. *The Byrds: Timeless Flight Revisited*. London: Rogan House, 1997.

———. *Crosby, Stills, Nash and Young: The Visual Documentary*. London: Omnibus, 1996.

———. *Neil Young: Zero to Sixty*. London: Calidore Books, 2000.

Rolling Stone, editors of. *Neil Young: The Rolling Stone Files*. London: Sidgwick & Jackson, 1994.

Sander, Ellen. *Trips: Rock Life in the Sixties*. New York: Charles Scribner's Sons, 1973.

Sanders, Ed. *The Family: The Manson Group and Its Aftermath*. rev. ed., Nemesis, 1993.

Scoppa, Bud. *The Byrds*. New York: Scholastic Book Services, 1971.

Shapiro, Mark. *The Long Run: The Story of the Eagles*. London: Omnibus, 1995.

Smith, Joe, with Mitchell Fink. *Off the Record: An Oral History of Popular Music*. London: Sidgwick & Jackson, 1989.

Unterberger, Richie. *Eight Miles High: Folk-Rock from Haight-Ashbury to Woodstock*. San Francisco: Backbeat Books, 2003.

Wade, Dorothy, and Justine Picardie. *Music Man: Ahmet Ertegun, Atlantic Records and the Triumph of Rock 'n' Roll*. New York: W. W. Norton, 1990.

Wexler, Jerry, with David Ritz. *Rhythm and the Blues: A Life in American Music*. New York: Alfred A. Knopf, 1993.

White, Timothy. *James Taylor: Long Ago and Far Away*. London: Omnibus Press, 2002.

Williams, Liza. *Up the City of Angels*. New York: G. P. Putnam's Sons, 1971.

Wiseman, Rich. *Jackson Browne: The Story of a Hold-Out*. New York: Doubleday, 1982.

Zimmer, Dave. *Crosby, Stills and Nash*. New York: Da Capo, 2000.

———. (ed.) *4 Way Street: The Crosby, Stills, Nash and Young Reader*. New York: Da Capo, 2004.

Hundreds of classic reviews and interviews with the artists featured in *Hotel California* can be found in the Rock's Backpages library at www.rocksback pages.com.

Credits

Song Lyrics

"Oh, California!" Words and music by David Ackles © 1970 (renewed) Warner-Tamerlane Publishing Corp. USA. Reproduced by permission of International Music Publications Ltd. All rights reserved.

Photo Credits

Page 159 top: Courtesy of Billy James; pages 159 bottom, 162 bottom right, 163, 164 top, 165, 166, 168, 169 bottom, 172 top, 173, 175, 176, 177, 178, 179 top, 180, 181, 183, 184, 185, 186: © Henry Diltz; pages 160 top, 161, 162 bottom left, 164 bottom: ©Nurit Wilde; page 160 bottom: Courtesy of Chris Darrow; pages 162 top, 171 top: photograph by Barney Hoskyns; page 167: Courtesy of Mo Ostin Archive; page 169 top: © Jim McCrary; pages 170, 174, 179 bottom, 182: © Michael Ochs Archives; page 171 bottom: © Joel Bernstein; page 172 bottom: Courtesy of Stan Cornyn.

Index

Albums are set in *italic* type. Song titles are set within quotation marks. Film titles set in *italic* type are qualified. Page numbers in *italic* type refer to illustrations.